The Masculine Woman in Weimar Germany

Monographs in German History

THE MASCULINE WOMAN
IN WEIMAR GERMANY

Katie Sutton

berghahn
NEW YORK • OXFORD
www.berghahnbooks.com

Published in 2011 by
Berghahn Books
www.berghahnbooks.com

©2011, 2013 Katie Sutton
First paperback edition published in 2013

Library of Congress Cataloging-in-Publication Data

Sutton, Katie.
The masculine woman in Weimar Germany / Katie Sutton.
p. cm. — (Monographs in German history ; v. 32)
Includes bibliographical references and index.
ISBN 978-0-85745-120-0 (hardback) — ISBN: 978-1-78238-105-1 (paperback) —
ISBN: 978-1-78238-106-8 (retail ebook)
1. Sex role—Germany—History—20th century. 2. Women—Germany—History—20th
century. 3. Lesbians—Germany—History—20th century. 4. Gender identity—Germany—
History—20th century. 5. Germany—History—1918–1933. I. Title.
HQ1075.5.G3S88 2011
305.40943'0904—dc22

2011000413

British Library Cataloguing in Publication Data

A catalogue record for this book is available from the British Library

Printed in the United States on acid-free paper

ISBN: 978-1-78238-105-1 paperback
ISBN: 978-1-78238-106-8 retail ebook

CONTENTS

FIGURES

Acknowledgments

Research for this book was enabled by funding from the German Academic Exchange Service (DAAD) and the Australian government. Institutional support was provided by the University of Melbourne, and by the following German institutions, whose archivists, librarians, and curators I would like to thank for assisting me in my research and granting permission to reprint images from their collections: the Staatsbibliothek zu Berlin together with the BPK Bildagentur für Kunst, Kultur und Geschichte, the libraries of the Humboldt-Universität and Freie Universität, the Berlin Kunstbibliothek (SMB), the Deutsche Kinemathek, the Deutsche Nationalbibliothek in Leipzig, and the Lesbenarchiv Spinnboden (Berlin). I am extremely grateful to a number of individuals who read and commented on various versions of the manuscript. My deepest thanks go to Alison Lewis for her encouraging and thought-provoking feedback throughout the life of this project. Many thanks also to Heather Benbow, Birgit Lang, Leo Kretzenbacher, Sara Lennox, Kerstin Barndt, the anonymous readers for Berghahn Books, and several members of Women in German for their helpful comments. In addition, I would like to thank Erhard Schütz for advice on source materials, Brangwen Stone for her marvelous proofreading, and the careful copyeditors at Berghahn. My family has been very supportive and I thank them here, as well as Helen and Tassilo Bonzel, Maria Schmillenkamp, Udo Tober, and Omama, who shared with me the story of how she snuck off to Cologne to get her first *Bubikopf.* Finally, my wholehearted thanks go to Katharina Bonzel, who supported this project from start to finish in so many ways.

Earlier versions of several sections of this study have previously appeared in *German Politics and Society,* the *Edinburgh German Yearbook, From Weimar to Christiania: German and Scandinavian Studies in Context* (ed. Florence Feiereisen and Kyle Frackman, 2006) and *Quer durch die Geisteswissenschaften: Perspektiven der Queer Theory* (ed. Elahe Haschemi Yekani and Beatrice Michaelis, 2005).

"THE MASCULINIZATION OF WOMAN"

✻

The de-womanization of woman—her emergence from the realm of the four big "Ks"—children, kitchen, cellar, church [*Kinder, Küche, Keller, Kirche*]—is a worldwide phenomenon. … [T]his is the New Woman, who on both sides of the Atlantic has ordered herself to appear hiplessly thin and lithe, and who, with her short hair and long strides, in both the Old World and the New, seeks to resemble a boy.

Rudolph Stratz, *Die Woche,* 7 February 1925

The masculinization of woman displaces masculinity, and the weak strong sex stands baffled in the face of this ambush.

Anita Daniel, *Berliner Illustrirte Zeitung,* 31 August 1924

*T*he "masculinization of woman" (*Vermännlichung der Frau*) was central to representations of the changing female ideal in post–World War I Germany. Indeed, so often were variations on this phrase cited in the 1920s popular media that it is safe to assume that it was a cliché that had burned itself well into the national psyche. A cartoon published in the satirical journal *Simplicissimus* in 1925, at a point when anxieties about gender merging and female masculinization were reaching a climax, exemplifies this phenomenon. Entitled "Lotte at the Crossroads," it depicts a slender, short-haired woman in masculine jacket and tie, one hand holding a cigarette and the other in her pocket, as she ponders whether to enter the toilet door designated "For Ladies" or "For Gentlemen" (see Figure I.1). By inviting readers to ridicule Lotte's masculine attire, her emulation of

---

Notes for this section begin on page 21.

Figure I.1. "Lotte at the Crossroads." *Simplicissimus,* 4 May 1925, 79.
Source: BPK Bildagentur für Kunst, Kultur und Geschichte

masculine gestures and habits, and her inability to pass this most fundamental of gender "tests," this image points effectively to the perceived cultural threat posed by the masculine "New Woman" of interwar Germany.

While some commentators used the symbolic power of this figure in her short skirt and pageboy haircut to enthuse about women's entrance into nontraditional, "masculine" fields of work, leisure, or consumption, by more conservative commentators she was held up as a threat to, and a warning against deviating too far away from, traditional ideas about men's and women's roles. Such conflicting accounts fed into wider debates concerning the state of Western civilization and the health and fertility of the German "race" following the rupture and trauma of the war, with commentators delighting in contrasting the traditional, maternal or virginal woman of the Wilhelmine era with the masculinized, selfish, sexually liberated, and overtly nonreproductive woman of the present. Precisely because of the flexibility and currency of gender as a signifier of social arrangements and hierarchies, the masculinization of women provided 1920s German audiences with a means not only of charting social change, but of reimposing traditional societal norms.

The New Woman and the anxieties she came to symbolize were hardly unique to Germany in the 1920s. A host of studies published in recent decades confirms that this interwar female "type" could be found everywhere from Europe to North America, and from Australia to Japan. Yet despite a relative unity of appearance—the short *Bubikopf* haircut favored by 1920s German women was said, for example, to have originated in Paris, while fashions such as straight-waisted dresses and tuxedo jackets were popular on both sides of the Atlantic—nationally specific factors and experiences led to vastly different interpretations of this figure in different cultural contexts. Thus Mary Louise Roberts emphasizes the devastation of World War I in her study of women in 1920s France, Liz Conor thematizes colonialist interactions with indigenous populations in her study of the Modern Girl in the Australian media, and the late nineteenth-century feminist movement is central to both Carroll Smith-Rosenberg's and Laura Behling's studies of the new or "masculine" woman in North America.[1]

This volume contributes to this growing body of research with a close examination of the German context, and differs from existing analyses of the New Woman and gender relations in Weimar Germany in two major ways. Firstly, it is the only study to engage in a sustained way with discourses of the "masculinization" of the modern woman, which cultural histories of this period frequently mention but rarely examine in detail. This focus is informed by Judith Halberstam's study of "female masculinity," in which she articulates the analytical advantages of examining masculinity separate from its supposedly "natural" location, the male body.[2] Secondly, this study redresses the marginalization of nonheterosexual women and genders within research on interwar Germany, where "queer" genders and sexualities have all too often been relegated to separate—albeit pioneering—studies focusing exclusively on homosexual subcultures or texts. By contrasting mainstream representations of gender circulating in 1920s German popular culture with depictions of bodies and relationships that did not conform to societal norms of binary gender or heterosexuality, this book sheds light on the breadth and complexity of female masculinities circulating within Weimar society.

Germany in 1925 was a nation slowly and bitterly coming to terms with its defeat in World War I and the humiliating terms of the Treaty of Versailles, a society experimenting with its first attempt at political democracy, plagued by ongoing economic and political insecurities, including the revolutionary unrest of 1918/19 and the hyperinflation of 1923, and facing unprecedented levels of social, cultural, and demographic transformation. Conservative forces saw the newly formed republic and its constitution as symptomatic of national decline, and although anxieties about national weakness and sterility also resonated in other national contexts at this period, in Germany this crisis of masculinity acquired particular intensity following the war defeat. With millions of men dead and millions more wounded or suffering from mental illness, "(e)ven where men's bodies remained intact—and the injuries inflicted by the new technology were appalling—male gender identity was in tatters."[3] With so many men unfit to carry out their patriarchal duties as fathers and husbands, concerns about Germany's emasculated manhood and uncertain reproductive future were compounded by women's increasing movement into social and political life.

After the war, young women and men began to swarm from the provinces to the cities in search of work, many of them joining the expanding ranks of white-collar clerical and service sector workers theorized by Siegfried Kracauer in his 1929 study *Die Angestellten* (The Salaried Masses).[4] This demographic shift formed part of Germany's much larger transformation into an industrialized, rationalized, technologized, and consumer-based economy, rapidly replacing the pre-capitalist, agricultural structures of the prewar era. Enjoying an increase in leisure time within this newly rationalized economy, many Germans turned to new forms of recreational activity that would enable them to forget the horrors of war and celebrate their newfound consumer freedoms. Jazz dances, the cinema, five o'clock teas, radio, popular magazines, and mass sporting events came to characterize the "Golden Twenties," as did the stern, modernist lines of the Bauhaus design school, the pragmatic, unsentimental tones of the New Objectivity movement in literature, theater, and film, or the paintings of Otto Dix and George Grosz of a decadent and sexualized Berlin metropolis. Even though many of these cultural products remained out of reach for large sections of the population, who struggled on a daily basis with unemployment, poverty, and domestic responsibilities, such images continue to dominate cultural histories of the Weimar period. And no other figure has been seen to more closely embody the spirit and adventurousness of this new era than the sexually and financially independent New Woman in her tailored suits and *Bubikopf* crop. From images of Marlene Dietrich in top hat and tails to the Taylorized synchronicity of mass female dance troupes such as the Tiller Girls, from female aviators flying solo around the world to the masses of young women workers streaming along the streets of the metropolis, this new female "type" occupies a crucial place in popular imaginings of pre-Nazi Germany.

Yet it is important to ask just who this "New" woman was, and to what extent she reflected the reality of German women's lives at this time. Certainly, women were participating in unprecedented numbers in the new, rationalized economies of work and leisure as employees, consumers, social commentators, authors, actors, and artists. Historians of Weimar women's work have shown, however, that despite widespread concerns that women (and especially married women) were taking men's jobs, the rationalization of the workplace did not greatly increase their *overall* presence in the paid labor force, which remained at just over a third of the female population, and that women's involvement in wartime industries was followed by attempts to restore prewar gender roles. Despite formal political advancements, therefore, many women's experiences continued to be defined primarily by domestic responsibilities and constrained by assumptions based on class, race, marital status, and age. Perceptions of changing gender roles in society, then, may well have had more to do with the increasing *visibility* of women in the workplace than a marked increase in participation: in the reorganized labor market of the post–World War I era, women's jobs became a more distinct and socially visible category as many women moved from domestic and agricultural work in the provinces to industrial and white-collar jobs in the cities.[5]

Employment conditions were not the only factors prompting a review of women's role in interwar German society. Other hotly discussed issues included the "surplus" of women of marriageable age as a result of the high numbers of male war casualties, which increased the necessity of self-subsistence even among women who might have otherwise chosen traditional family forms; the declining birth rate and high number of abortions, both of which were frequently interpreted in the Weimar media as evidence of women's rejection of marriage and family; the entrance of small numbers of women into the universities and professions such as law and medicine; and an increasingly visible homosexual presence and subculture, particularly in the Berlin metropolis, the center of the world's first organized homosexual emancipation movement. Formal political gains also played an important role, with female suffrage and women's equality with men enshrined in the Constitution of 1919. This extension of democratic citizenship rights to women, which prompted unprecedented female political involvement and identification, particularly in the early years following the war, helps to mark the birth of the Weimar Republic as "a rupture in the history of both German civil society and German gender relations."[6]

In the wake of such achievements, the bourgeois feminist movement of the late nineteenth century had become a relatively weak political force by the 1920s, its "bluestocking" members generally portrayed in the contemporary press as dowdy, elitist, man-hating spinsters who had been all but replaced by the mass phenomenon of the cosmopolitan postwar "New" woman.[7] Yet older feminist discourses, as well as stereotypes of female emancipists, continued to feed into 1920s representations of women in important ways. In particular, Weimar-era discussions of women's "masculinization" often drew on older associations between feminism and sex-gender "inversion," or the sexological idea of a "third sex," discussed below. Furthermore, certain aspects of the women's rights cause were taken up by other groups at this period with new vigor. The Sex Reform movement, for example, was active in the publication of "enlightenment literature" (*Aufklärungsliteratur*) promoting contraception and sexual satisfaction for young married couples. Meanwhile, socialist feminists championed issues that were seen to particularly oppress working-class women, including access to safe and legal abortion as well as relationship forms such as "companionate marriage" that resisted patriarchal and capitalist hierarchies and soon enjoyed considerable popularity among the youth of the new republic.[8]

Typologies of the Weimar New Woman

Even though the masculine woman dominated much Weimar commentary on women and gender roles, she was not always synonymous with the "New" woman, who was rarely understood as a single or homogenous "type." In fact, scholars agree that the New Woman was a remarkably diverse signifier who could be positioned as anything from rationalized worker to housewife, "new" mother to consumer, Olympic athlete to female *flâneur:* "This New Woman was not merely a media myth or a demographer's paranoid fantasy, but a social reality. … She existed in office and factory, bedroom and kitchen, just as surely as in café, cabaret and film."[9] The factor unifying the multiple and often contradictory accounts of this cultural phenomenon is her role as a symbol of transformation and rupture: she represented a "crisis" in gender roles that was, in turn, a response to the "shock of modernity."[10]

The 1920s German media reflects a population seeking ways to reinstate a sense of order in their rapidly changing and often apparently incoherent society, and Lynne Frame has shown that detailed systems of categorization played an important role in this process. In particular, she demonstrates how the appearance and lifestyle of the New Woman constituted a favorite subject of this taxonomizing impulse, serving "as a barometer of modern society, its progress and its discontents."[11] Accordingly, a newspaper article published in 1927 delineated three key female types: the Germanic "Gretchen" with her long, virginal braid, the youthful and Americanized "Girl," whose carefree, athletic typecasting made her the German equivalent of the sporty Anglo-American flapper, and the cosmopolitan, boyish, and sharply dressed "Garçonne." Although media reports suggest that the Girl was the most numerous social type, her popularity linked to that of dancing troupes such as the Tiller Girls, it was the Garçonne who was seen to represent the most masculine and historically advanced form of female development, with a sexual and intellectual potency that "often gives rise to conflict. … Uniting a sporting, comradely male entrepreneurial sense with heroic, feminine devotion, this synthesis—if successful—often makes her so superior to the man she loves that she becomes troublesome."[12] Other prominent female types in the German media of this period include the tragic proletarian mother of communist publications, the athletic "Sportsgirl," the upper-class "English girl," and the sexually dangerous and vehemently nonreproductive "vamp" or *femme fatale,* exemplified in contemporary film roles such as Louise Brooks's Lulu in *Die Büchse der Pandora* (Pandora's Box, dir. G. W. Pabst, 1929), or Marlene Dietrich's man-eating Lola Lola in Josef von Sternberg's *Der blaue Engel* (The Blue Angel, 1930).

Throughout this study, it will be essential to distinguish between the symbolic role of such gendered types and their mediated relationship to real bodies and people, as I examine how discourses surrounding the "masculinization" of women were employed by Weimar commentators as both metaphor for and mirror of social change. Thus the first chapter on women's fashions shows that toward the end of the Weimar era the sexually naïve Gretchen type was increasingly pitted against the cosmopolitan Garçonne in debates about "ideal" womanhood. Whereas the Gretchen stereotype came to symbolize all-German, anti-industrialist, and anti-republic sentiments, the masculinized Garçonne, named after a 1922 novel by French author Victor Margueritte, represented the epitome of not only modern womanhood but modern, industrialized society—a product of the social and gender role changes set in train by the war. As one commentator observed: "(I)t was the war that brought about, unnoticed at first, the birth of the Garçonne type. The woman on the battlefield, who put on a uniform and cut off her hair, was the first to want to share not only the fate, but also the appearance of men."[13] In the early to mid 1920s, the Garçonne featured in the Weimar media as a modern, fashionable version of masculinized womanhood, whose erotic appeal lay not least in her intellectual qualities and cool approach to men and sexuality: "She never falls in love, enjoys a good time every once in a while, and constantly compromises herself. ... But when she is alone, she can do without man and makeup very well."[14] Her edginess contrasted favorably with what many were beginning to describe as the mass uniformity and superficiality of the Girl. Yet more than with any other female type, the concerted modernity and independence of the Garçonne also led critics to associate her with negative discourses of gender "inversion" and sexual "perversion," arguing that the New Woman was taking her newfound freedoms too far.

In light of this independent, cosmopolitan, gender-bending image, it is hardly surprising that the Garçonne aesthetic proved particularly appealing to members of the female homosexual subculture that began to flourish during the Weimar era. From 1930 to 1932 she lent her name to a popular homosexual women's magazine, and from 1931 onward to a Berlin women's club in the Kalckreuthstraße. She was not, however, the only female "type" popular in subcultural circles at this period; these ranged from the feminine homosexual vamp to the masculine "Gentleman" or "Gigolo."[15] This rapid increase in specifically lesbian aesthetic models formed part of a larger boom in what might today be termed "queer" cultural and political activity, particularly in the metropolis of Berlin. Despite the ongoing legal prohibition on male homosexuality under Paragraph 175 of the Criminal Code—a target of homosexual rights activism in Germany since the turn of the century—the 1920s saw the development of a multifaceted homosexual rights movement centered in Berlin, as well as a veritable explosion of bars, clubs, and organizations catering to homosexuals and transvestites. Berlin's female homosexual scene boasted up to fifty clubs during this period, the diversity of which was chronicled in the paintings of Jeanne Mammen and in Ruth Roellig's 1928 study *Berlins lesbische Frauen* (Berlin's Lesbian Women).[16] Meanwhile, lesbian artists such as cabaret singer Claire Waldoff and erotic dancer

Anita Berber enjoyed high cultural currency, and stars such as Marlene Dietrich flirted heavily with bisexuality on both stage and screen. At a more grassroots level, during this period an impressive range of homosexual publications were founded, often affiliated with political advocacy organizations such as the League of Human Rights (Bund für Menschenrechte, BfM) or the German Friendship Association (Deutscher Freundschaftsverband, DFV). The representation of "masculine" women within such subcultural periodicals is a central focus of this study.

Positioned at the juncture between fascination and rejection, tradition and modernity, heterosexual erotic appeal and the threat of sexual perversion, the masculine woman of Weimar Germany was at the center of popular discourses about gender and social change. Whether in the form of the sophisticated Garçonne, the muscular female athlete, or the "virile" homosexual woman, all of whom will be examined in subsequent chapters, the masculine woman functioned alternately as ideological template, role model, interpretive lens, and scapegoat for German audiences. Clearly, such discussions about the masculinization of women were as much about men and male cultural anxieties as about women or their changing appearances, for as Katharina von Ankum has emphasized, "the cultural construction of woman embodies the projections of male hopes and anxieties."[17] Throughout this study, I argue that images such as "Lotte at the Crossroads" provided readers of both sexes with a vent for cultural anxieties about female emancipation, women's work, or changing gender roles within the family.

The understanding that a focus on women necessarily holds ramifications for our broader understanding of gender and social structures has prompted some Weimar scholars to focus as much on men and masculinities as on women and femininities in their analyses; Richard McCormick's study is exemplary in this regard. Such approaches are laudable, and they inform my comparison of the masculine woman with less prominent discourses of the "feminine man" in chapter 1. However, I have chosen not to focus in equal measure on these simultaneous cultural phenomena for two reasons. Firstly, to do so would limit my analysis of a still decidedly underresearched historical gender formation—indeed, given the extent of 1920s German media discourse surrounding women's masculinization, it is hard to explain the overwhelming neglect of this topic within cultural histories of the period, a neglect only partially rectified by recent studies of women's fashions, sport, popular fiction, and the homosexual subculture, which are discussed in the following chapters. Certainly, Patrice Petro makes a convincing argument about the increasing conservatism of gendered media imagery toward the end of the Weimar era, observing that although images of the masculinized New Woman were often accompanied by representations of feminized men, it was generally only female gender identity that was questioned, reinforcing the idea of female sexuality as "other." Yet this and many other studies of the Weimar New Woman brush too lightly over the "queer" associations of this figure, which constitute a major focus here.[18] Secondly, to focus equally on the masculinized woman and the feminized man would be to ignore the marked imbalance of Weimar media coverage toward the former: for the most part, it was abundantly clear that Weimar commentators were discussing *masculine* characteristics and visual styles in relation to *female* bodies; and only sometimes were men and male "feminization" implicated in this process of gender transformation.

Sources

The popular media played an important role in shaping and refracting the ways in which women and men formed their views of themselves, each other, and their society at this critical juncture in German history. With a particular focus on the print media, this book examines what made the masculine woman's challenge to traditional gender roles simultaneously threatening and fascinating to German audiences, and why ideas about women's masculinization became increasingly associated with negative discourses of degeneracy, perversion, and failure toward the end of the Weimar era. The time frame covered by my research generally follows the conventional historical periodization of the Weimar Republic, from the signing of the Constitution in 1919 to the Nazi seizure of power on 30 January 1933, but where possible I also refer to periodicals from the early Nazi years that were not subject to immediate bans in order to consider continuities into the post-Weimar period. Although a focus on media and other cultural products entails the study of perceptions and anxieties rather than more "concrete" historical facts, such popular discourses are, as Roberts insists, "cultural realities in themselves and warrant our closest attention."[19] The Weimar period provides a particularly fruitful basis for a study of the masculine woman because of the extraordinary quantity and depth of public commentary on changing gender relations in an ever expanding range of media outlets.

The rapid industrialization and urbanization of German society in the early twentieth century led to growing demand for new media genres to suit the ever faster tempo of metropolitan life and the increasingly fragmented and democratized public sphere, characterized by the emergence of the new urban white-collar classes, the breakdown of traditional class boundaries, and the rise of a mass consumer culture. By the mid 1920s over four thousand newspapers, tabloids, magazines, weeklies, and illustrated papers were published in Germany. Berlin, which had no fewer than fifty daily morning papers, dominated this interwar publishing scene, producing over 30 percent of all German periodicals by the late 1920s. Many of these enjoyed a nationwide circulation, their metropolitan origin only adding to their cosmopolitan appeal.[20] Within this astonishingly active publishing scene, the masculinization of woman was debated in a wide range of popular journals, women's and fashion magazines, satirical periodicals, and illustrated daily newspapers. Reflecting a broad spectrum of audience demographics whose views were shaped by factors including political convictions, workplace conditions, socioeconomic background, education, location, and gender, these publications depicted the masculine woman through radically different images, from a figure of identification and fascination to a symbol of national degeneracy and despair.

Yet even within individual periodicals the masculine woman was represented in conflicting ways that changed over time, and that could be shaped as much by the opinions of individual reporters—who often wrote for numerous publications—as by the larger political positioning of the periodical or publishing house in question. Popular novelist Vicki Baum, for example, wrote at various points for three different publications produced by the liberal Ullstein house, *Die Dame* (The Lady), *Uhu* (Owl), and the *Berliner Illustrirte Zeitung* (Berlin Illustrated Newspaper), in addition to publishing her best selling novels. Although adjusting her writing style for each publication, she consistently produced groundbreaking representations of self-assured modern women facing real problems ranging from workplace discrimination to abortion, and in doing so appealed to readers of various classes and situations. In contrast, journalist Anita Daniel's contributions to the same publications tended to be much more conservative in their gender politics and included some of the sharpest critiques of the masculine woman.

At one end of the media spectrum, I examine upmarket fashion and women's magazines such as *Die Dame* and *Sport im Bild* (Sport in Pictures), the latter published by the nationalist-conservative Scherl-Verlag. These publications, *Die Dame* in particular, were major trendsetters in a field that also included the likes of German *Vogue*, *Elegante Welt* (Elegant World), and *die neue mode* (the new fashion). Alongside opinionated fashion articles, they featured pieces on a wide range of cultural and artistic topics in genres ranging from travel reports to short stories. These magazines targeted elegant women of means and leisure who could afford to follow the latest whims of fashion, although they were also responsible for setting broader trends in women's clothing, which working girls could emulate using cheap fabrics and sewing machines. They emphasized the cosmopolitan appeal of the masculine Garçonne, whilst subtly restricting her gender transgressions in ways that could be reconciled with the traditional feminine roles of wife and mother.

Illustrated periodicals such as the *Berliner Illustrirte Zeitung* (hereafter *BIZ*) and the more conservative *Die Woche* (The Week) aimed for a much greater mass and unisex appeal, largely via photographic commentaries on topical themes. Situated between the traditional genres of newspaper and magazine, these publications benefited from recent technical developments that enabled the mass reproduction of good-quality photographs and performed a function not unlike that of the early cinematic newsreels, although with a more white-collar than working-class audience. The *BIZ* was the most widely read magazine of its kind in Weimar Germany, with a nationwide circulation figure of almost two million by 1930 (its Munich counterpart, the *Münchener Illustrierte Zeitung*, was in second place with a circulation of 700,000 by this date), and claimed to be the largest in Europe.[21] The illustrated newspapers approached gender issues in a more reactionary manner than did the fashion magazines, providing some of the most sensationalist contemporary commentary on the masculine woman.

From 1924 on these publications were joined on the nation's newspaper stands by a range of trendy new monthly magazines such as *Uhu* and *Das Magazin* (The Magazine), targeting a young, educated, socially liberal mixed-sex readership. These magazines enjoyed reasonably strong circulation figures, and by 1928 *Das Magazin* was selling 180,000 copies a month.[22] Such periodicals were not averse to the odd longer article or social commentary, and published some of the most extensive and progressive commentaries on the masculinization of women, but their primary focus was on leisure and entertainment. Meanwhile, satirical journals such as *Simplicissimus* (which had its publication base in Munich) and *Ulk* likewise offered more discerning intellectual commentaries on current affairs in the form of critical cartoons, verses, and texts; however, their conservative stance toward questions of gender politics often had more in common with that of the illustrated newspapers than the new magazines.

An important counterpoint to these mainstream media outlets—which, despite their significant differences, shared a predominantly heteronormative outlook on gender relations and social structures—are a number of publications targeting homosexual women. At least six such publications were produced during the mid to late 1920s, the most prominent of which were *Die Freundin* (The Girlfriend, also a frequent term of self-description among homosexual women at this period), published from 1924 to 1933 with censorship-related interruptions, and *Frauenliebe* (Womanly Love), published from 1926 to 1930, after which it underwent a makeover to become *Garçonne* (1930–1932) (for ease of distinction the latter name will henceforth be used to refer to the entire run of this magazine). Their niche audiences, limited advertising possibilities, and regular run-ins with the *Schund- und Schmutz* censorship authorities resulted in circulation figures that were considerably lower than for the periodicals cited above—in 1928 the *Frauenliebe* reported a distribution of ten thousand copies per issue—however, they represent a valuable and still underresearched resource within Weimar cultural history.[23]

Produced for a primarily lower- to middle-class female homosexual audience, the content of these magazines reflects the ambitions but also the restrictions experienced by this subcommunity of New Women, struggling for daily survival on the low white-collar salaries of shop assistants and stenographers and torn, as recent scholarship has shown, between a yearning for public respectability on the one hand, and exploration of the new possibilities for same-sex eroticism offered within the Berlin metropolis on the other.[24] They tell us little about the upper-class and society women whose financial independence and social standing offered greater freedom to experiment with "masculine" styles or alternative sexual relationships, or the working-class homosexual women who left few traces of their sexual lives. Yet as some of the first mass-produced periodicals for female homosexuals not only in Germany, but throughout the world, these "subcultural" sources—a term that more accurately represents their coverage of homosexual, bisexual, and transgender content than narrower descriptors such as "lesbian" or "female homosexual"—constitute a source of unique importance for the history of sexuality in the early twentieth century.

This primary focus on media sources is complemented in the final two chapters by a look at a range of fictional and nonfictional texts and films, incorporating methodological approaches from cinema and literary studies. These texts, which include novels by "mainstream" authors such as Erich Kästner, Irmgard Keun, and Vicki Baum, "lesbian" novels and short fiction, and films including Leontine Sagan's groundbreaking *Mädchen in Uniform* (Girls in Uniform, 1931), address female masculinities within Weimar German society with greater freedom and transgressive potential than was possible in media reports, and in doing so highlight the complexity and multiplicity of this cultural phenomenon. Furthermore, most enjoyed both popular and critical success upon their release, thus negotiating the split between "high" and "low" culture in a way that McCormick describes as conducive to the new aesthetic movement of New Objectivity, with its focus on mass culture and the unsentimental depiction of the realities of life in the modern industrialized metropolis.[25]

The question of "popular" versus "high" culture becomes particularly important when examining representations of gender for, as Vibeke Petersen observes, the relative lack of research into Weimar women's role in cultural production and consumption can be at least partly explained by the conventional gendering of "high" culture as masculine and "low" culture as feminine. Patrice Petro and Kerstin Barndt's respective studies of melodramatic cinema and of New Woman fiction have been particularly influential in readdressing women's role as participants in Weimar cultural processes, demonstrating their active involvement as writers, readers, and spectators in constructing, interpreting, and challenging gendered media images. They show that the popular media represented a particularly accessible cultural site for women in this period, providing a discursive space that challenged the public/private divide and directly sought to engage female audiences. In her study of contemporary women's magazines, Joke Hermes reminds us that a postmodern feminist position demands that we understand female readers as "producers of meaning rather than the cultural dupes of the media institutions."[26] In reading 1920s German sources, this also involves refraining from assumptions about male- or female-authored arguments, and considering the intersections of other contributing factors including socioeconomic status, locality, sexuality, and race.

Yet in many of the sources examined here, issues of class and race are either marginalized or exoticized as "other" to the unarticulated norm of white, middle-class Germanness. As has been observed in the US context, the desire for a "mass" appeal can have the effect of negating discussion of issues that fall outside of the mainstream, "since mass is often associated with race, the white race, and with class, the middle class."[27] Popular Weimar periodicals tended to relegate explicit discussions of class to party-political newspapers, focusing instead on seemingly more "modern" social questions such as the generation gap or the battle of the sexes. These questions reflected, in turn, changing social demographics and the loosening of the traditional German class system during the interwar era, illustrated by the entrance of middle-class daughters into the workforce. Ideas about racial or religious alterity likewise informed discourses of female masculinization in subtle rather than overt ways. Thus it was not the popular African American dancer Josephine Baker with her erotic dances and banana skirts whom critics of the modern woman targeted, but rather white, middle-class, "German" women, who were perceived as losing sight of their duties to marry and reproduce. On the other hand, anti-Semitic stereotypes did creep into some of the more negative representations of the sexually perverse masculine woman, and the increasing cultural conservatism of the late Weimar period cannot be understood in separation from the growing support for German nationalism that would help usher in the National Socialists.[28]

Female Masculinities

In recent decades, historians of sexuality have responded to the traditional neglect of individuals and communities who did not conform to society's heterosexual and gendered norms, tracing the emergence and decline of categories such as "the homosexual," criticizing essentialist relationships between sex/gender categories and actual bodies and experiences, and suggesting numerous, often conflicting strategies for achieving more accurate and inclusive histories of gender and sexuality.[29] A particular focus has been on the problems involved in imposing current categories of sex, gender, and sexuality onto individuals who lived in the past, and the need to strike a balance between historically appropriate terminology on the one hand and comprehensibility and relevance for current audiences on the other. Such issues have clear implications for the present study, which foregrounds questions of gender, sexuality, representation, and identity. In particular, my emphasis on the masculine woman of Weimar Germany necessitates an engagement with recent theoretical discussions of "female masculinity."

Judith Halberstam argues that masculinity becomes legible only "where and when it leaves the white male middle-class body," and insists that female masculinity must be seen not as derivative of male-embodied masculinities, but as a legitimate gender formation in its own right; a position from which to successfully challenge hegemonic models of gender conformity and generate social change. Stressing the historical and cultural diversity of this phenomenon, Halberstam articulates a "queer methodology" for researching female masculinities in past societies, which prioritizes historical specificity whilst also drawing on present-day theoretical insights in order to better make sense of the complexities of other eras: "it attempts to remain supple enough to respond to the various locations of information on female masculinity and betrays a certain disloyalty to conventional disciplinary methods." One of the consequences of this approach is that Halberstam refrains from (mis-)reading past representations of female masculinity simply as evidence of lesbianism, an academic approach that, as she observes, "covers over the multiple differences between earlier forms of same-sex desire."

While I return to this problem of interpretation in chapter 3, here I want to emphasize one of Halberstam's central arguments, namely, that equating past female masculinities with lesbian subjectivity runs the risk of artificially separating this widespread gender phenomenon from "the making of modern masculinity itself."[30] This insistence that female masculinities have played a crucial role in the construction of dominant understandings of gender guides my examination of the masculine woman in Weimar Germany. Thus in addition to examining a range of "queer" female masculinities—which, as Halberstam shows, have generally been perceived as more socially threatening and "excessively" masculine than heterosexual versions of the masculine woman—this book also focuses extensively on *heterosexual* female masculinities, and in particular, on how the "masculinization" of German women was seen to impact upon relations between women and men. At the same time, I am particularly interested in liminal representations, where the threat of "queer" female sexuality—whether conceptualized in terms of sex-gender "inversion," "homosexuality," or simply as independence from men—haunts mainstream discourses of the masculinized New Woman, and lends force to critiques of this figure.

Critics of Halberstam's terminology have variously suggested that it is too homogenous, that it embraces an overly essentialized understanding of sexed bodies and social genders, and that it marginalizes feminine-identified women. Claudia Breger, for example, argues that Halberstam's phrase confirms the very binarism it purports to deconstruct, and proposes the interchangeable alternatives "feminine masculinities" and "masculine femininities" to describe the complex matrices of feminine and masculine gender identities in the past. Yet this approach risks being too relativist to be of sustained historical use; as Breger herself acknowledges, "it is nonetheless important that the articulation of 'male' and 'female' third sex identities is not altogether symmetrical in the historical texts."[31] Because there were, and continue to be, real differences between the social, political, and cultural experiences and representation of men perceived as "feminine" and women perceived as "masculine," Halberstam's articulation of female masculinity retains its theoretical edge over Breger's more relativist position. In order to emphasize the multiplicity and heterogeneity of forms of female-bodied masculine gender "performance," though this study generally employs the plural phrase "female masculinities."

The "invisibility of the femme" also deserves attention in light of my sustained focus on female masculinities, for as Biddy Martin observes, it is the more mannish women that were the most prominent type of "third sex" or female homosexual in early twentieth-century Germany.[32] The danger here is that women who desire other women, but who are better able to "pass" as heterosexual because of their feminine identification, disappear within academic research, not unlike the way such women were marginalized within turn-of-the-century sexology as "pseudohomosexuals" in contrast to the "congenital" masculine female invert, as I discuss below. A study such as this must therefore tread a delicate line. It is certainly important to affirm the legitimacy and agency of the homosexual femme, and within Weimar studies important work has begun in this area.[33] Furthermore, the Weimar homosexual periodicals demonstrate that not only did many homosexual women understand themselves via the categories of either "feminine" or "masculine/virile," but that they also engaged critically with these categories and carefully debated relationship models based around such eroticized gender difference, as I discuss in chapter 3. Yet there are pertinent justifications for a specific focus on the *masculine* woman of 1920s Germany, for more than any other social or cultural type it was she who was viewed by contemporaries as a symbol of social disruption and change, whereas the feminine heterosexual woman largely retained her status as the age-old ideal of womanhood. Furthermore, it was the masculine or "virile" homosexual woman who bore the brunt of media homophobia and criticism, as her alleged perversion was used to demonize even heterosexual women who dared to adopt "masculine" clothes, jobs, or political privileges. By highlighting nonheteronormative gender formations, this study seeks to contribute to the wider political project of affirming and legitimating a range of embodied experiences in the present as well as in the past, thus forming part of a larger critical history of sexuality.

In accordance with this goal, I employ terms and ideas that have been extensively theorized and problematized within feminist, gender, and queer studies, including Judith Butler's frequently cited notion that gender is "performative" rather than a "natural" expression of sexed bodies, and that "sex"—which has traditionally been understood as a biological given—is no less constructed than "gender," which in turn has conventionally referred to the social and cultural attributes seen to adhere to "naturally" sexed bodies.[34] Such theoretical foundations are crucial, for they grant "queer" gender performances a legitimacy and authenticity equal to that of more normative gender constellations that would restrict masculinity to male bodies and femininity to female bodies. At the same time, my frequent use of inverted commas, particularly when employing more recent terms such as "queer," "transgender," "cross-dressing," and "passing," is intended to highlight the nonessentialist and contested nature of these signifiers, particularly in the context of historical research. I persist in using these terms, however, because they often enable more nuanced insights than a strict adherence to historically specific German terms, many of which arose out of late-nineteenth century sexological discourse, including "invert" (*Invertierte*) or "third sex" (*drittes Geschlecht*). My analytical focus on female masculinities and masculine women likewise involves a degree of anachronism and essentializing. I consider this justified not only for the sake of brevity, but also in order to better understand how self-identified masculine or virile women in Weimar Germany conceptualized their own gender and sexuality, as well as the limits and freedoms that such identity categories imposed on their lives.

So far I have pointed toward the prevalence of the masculine woman in Weimar popular culture, situated this figure in relation to wider discourses of the 1920s New Woman, and highlighted the theoretical relevance to this study of recent research into female masculinities. The following section surveys a further important discursive context for 1920s representations of the masculine woman, namely, sexological and medical discourses of sex-gender "inversion."

Sexological Theories of the Masculine Woman

Conflicting representations of female gender and sexuality in the Weimar media reflect contemporary disagreements within the scientific and medical professions about the nature of sex-gender "inversion." As George Chauncey has convincingly argued in an essay that builds on Foucauldian frameworks, what is now understood as "female homosexuality," a concept that privileges same-sex desire as the central marker of identity, is in fact a creation of the early twentieth century. Chauncey traces a gradual shift in scientific focus in the decades following 1900 from sexual behavior to sexual object choice, resulting in a change in terminology from "sexual invert," which covered a range of cross-gender behavior, to "homosexual." While this chronology has been rightly criticized for failing to account for the simultaneous development of ideas about transsexuality, it provides a useful framework for summarizing turn-of-the-century sexological discourses on the masculine woman.[35]

The first detailed study of female sexual inversion was undertaken by Austrian sexologist Richard von Krafft-Ebing as part of his major work, *Psychopathia Sexualis* (1886). Krafft-Ebing identified four levels of female "contrary sexual instinct," ranging from milder, reversible forms of same-sex attraction through to more extreme forms of sex-gender inversion, the latter characterized by a strong preference for men's clothing, evidence of "masculine" emotions, intellect, and behavior, an active role in sexual relations, and even "masculine" physical characteristics such as small breasts. Within this typology, Krafft-Ebing distinguished between two major categories of inverts: masculine women (*Mannweiber*) whose condition was inborn and who were susceptible to mental and physical degeneration; and feminine women or "pseudohomosexuals," whose sexuality was acquired and to whom he attributed moral inadequacy. He describes an "unforgettable" meeting with a woman he considers typical of the former category, with her "hard features, sinewy, muscular build, small hips, and masculine gait, wearing closely shorn hair, a man's hat, pince-nez, gentleman's overcoat, and boots with heels." Closer inspection revealed the woman to be a talented painter with a penchant for drink, cigarettes, and "masculine" sport, who enjoyed great popularity in the "company of ladies." In this study Krafft-Ebing emphasized that although female inversion had been subject to less scientific and legal scrutiny than its male equivalent, it was by no means less common; on the contrary, he suggested, one need only look at the women of the metropolis to find many examples of women whose short hair and masculinely tailored clothing points to "uranism" (homosexuality).[36]

British sexologist Havelock Ellis subsequently simplified Krafft-Ebing's categorical schema in *Sexual Inversion* (1897), rejecting the latter's "minute classification of sexual inverts," and distinguishing between only two categories of female inversion. The first covered "feminine" women whose homosexuality, "while fairly distinct, is only slightly marked." While such women are highly attractive to the "actively inverted woman," Ellis suggests that they are less attractive to men: "One may perhaps say that they are the pick of the women whom the average man would pass by." The second class of women are the "true" or "congenital" sexual inverts, characterized by "a more or less distinct trace of masculinity" and indifference toward men. Although Ellis notes that not all female inverts choose to emphasize their masculinity—thereby moving more closely toward a model that emphasized homosexual desire over gender identity—he does observe "a very pronounced tendency among sexually inverted women to adopt male attire," and describes the female invert's masculine body language and manner as follows:

> The brusque, energetic movements, the attitude of the arms, the direct speech, the inflexions of the voice, the masculine straightforwardness and sense of honour, and especially the attitude towards men, free from any suggestion either of shyness or audacity, will often suggest the underlying psychic abnormality to a keen observer.[37]

Ellis is more reluctant than Krafft-Ebing to assign masculine physical attributes to the female invert, but nonetheless notes the frequent presence of a "firm musculature," a "decidedly masculine type of larynx," a pronounced taste for smoking, dislike for domestic occupations, and athletic capacity. Using this taxonomy, he conceived of sexual relationships between women in heteronormative terms, requiring a masculine/active and a feminine/passive partner. In this insistence on binary systems of gender difference as the basis for homosexual attraction, and more specifically, on the necessity of a masculine partner within lesbian relationships, Ellis echoed the opinion of many of his sexological peers.[38]

Although not a sexologist, Viennese philosophy student Otto Weininger's theories on gender difference and sexuality, articulated in his single major work *Geschlecht und Charakter* (Sex and Character, 1903), also enjoyed widespread popularity in Germany in the first decades of the twentieth century. Weininger argued that each individual is biologically "bisexual," consisting of unique proportions of "male" (M) and "female" (W) components. Depending upon the balance of "M" and "W," they can be placed along a hierarchical continuum that descends from the "ideal" (manly) man, to the "ideal" (feminine) woman, although he notes that these "pure" extremes exist only in theory. Hermaphrodites, homosexual (feminine) men, and (masculine) women were located near the center of this continuum, consisting of approximately equal parts of "M" and "W." Weininger also explained the laws of sexual attraction according to this theory, arguing that the most masculine men will be attracted to the most feminine women, whereas effeminate men will be attracted to masculine women. Notorious for the anti-Semitic and misogynist arguments that dominate the second half of his work, Weininger made the women's emancipation movement one of his main targets, claiming that it is excessive proportions of "M" that lead certain women to strive for emancipation.[39] In making this argument Weininger echoed Krafft-Ebing and Ellis, who had likewise associated female emancipation with inversion, the latter arguing that "a tendency develops for women to carry this independence still further and to find love where they find work." The turn-of-the-century "invert," as Breger clarifies, "designated women who, according to misogynist discourse, were 'masculinised' by their entry into previously male realms of research and professional life."[40] In 1920s Germany, such scientific legitimation of the links between female emancipation and inversion provided welcome fodder to critics of women's political advancement and increasing social mobility.

Ideas about sex-gender inversion continued to inform the work of one of the most prominent Weimar-era sexologists and homosexual rights activists, Magnus Hirschfeld, founder of the Institute for Sexual Science (Institut für Sexualwissenschaften) in Berlin in 1919. In his earlier work Hirschfeld had popularized the idea of sex-gender inverts as a naturally occurring—and thus politically defensible—"third sex," coined the term "transvestite" (thus distinguishing it from notions of homosexuality), and developed a widely cited theory of "sexual intermediaries." In 1918 he undertook an extensive examination of female inversion in the second volume of his major work, *Sexualpathologie* (Sexual Pathology), dividing his "sexual intermediary" concept into five subcategories that could be applied to both "male" and "female" inverts: hermaphroditism (genital sexual ambiguity); androgyny (nongenital sexual ambiguity, including behavioral characteristics); transvestism; homosexuality; and "metatropism" (which covered a range of fetishes as well as sadomasochism and erotic role reversals).[41]

The "masculine woman" (*männliches Weib*) features in several of these subcategories. Those classified as "androgynous" are attributed a masculinity that is marked on the body, including a tall, muscular figure, small breasts, a masculine larynx, and "masculine" behaviors such as gestures, movements, and even the style of urinating. When dealing with the category of the homosexual, meanwhile, Hirschfeld rejected the psychoanalytic interpretations that were gaining increasing currency at this period, including Freud's Oedipal theory, to reiterate his longstanding biological and hormonal arguments about sexual intermediaries. Like earlier sexologists, Hirschfeld argued that homosexual women are either masculine or feminine, and most likely to be attracted to members of the opposite type. Yet his theory of homosexuality also shows signs of the shift toward sexual object choice, as he argues that even though there is a marked tendency for feminine and masculine to attract, this is not always the case.[42] He thus moved a small distance away from earlier, more essentialist theories that equated "true" female homosexuality exclusively with masculinity and desire for the feminine.

As Hirschfeld's rejection of the Oedipal theory indicates, by the 1920s sexologists were increasingly finding it necessary to contend with newer, psychoanalytic models of female inversion, the most prominent of which was Freud's 1920 essay "The Psychogenesis of a Case of Homosexuality in a Woman." Chauncey observes that such theories challenged the hegemony of congenital interpretations of homosexuality to such an extent that older theorists such as Ellis spent much of their later work refuting them, while others sought to combine psychological and biological theories.[43] Yet it was the sexological theories that provided the more frequent reference point for cultural commentators of the Weimar period, and with which German audiences were assumed to be reasonably familiar, as I demonstrate in chapter 3. From an analytical perspective, too, I agree with Halberstam that the sexological texts generally provide a more productive way into the study of female masculinities at this period than do psychoanalytic models, which were not only less well-known at the time, but also more restrictive in conceptualizing female sexual and gender behavior as derivative of male identity.[44]

Although sexological analyses of the masculine woman provided an important "scientific" point of reference for 1920s commentators, historians have emphasized that the sexologists' narrow, clear-cut taxonomies often did not equip them to deal with the nuances of the individuals that walked into their consulting rooms, and upon whose personal narratives they based their research. In a growing body of work that focuses on individual case studies rather than the sexological interpretations thereof, these scholars emphasize the ways in which individuals resisted hegemonic interpretations of their identities and lives.[45] Inspired by such research, this study not only interrogates the influence of sexological research on mainstream perceptions of gender and sexuality in 1920s Germany, but highlights instances where sexological models were rejected or modified by the individuals they sought to describe.

In order to do justice to the remarkable breadth of female masculinities within the realm of Weimar mass culture, this book is organized thematically. Chapter 1 examines representations of women's "masculinized" fashions and hairstyles, arguing that these provided German readers with a means of negotiating larger, less tangible changes in gender and social roles. At the same time, I investigate the particular meanings that masculine visual styles held within the homosexual subculture at this period. Chapter 2 focuses on the figure of the female athlete, examining how media discussions of women's masculinization incorporated discussions of physical culture and the female body. These first two chapters interrogate the changing limits of acceptable representation of the masculine woman over the course of the Weimar period and beyond, and identify a range of media strategies aimed at defusing her threatening potential.

"Queer" female masculinities constitute the focus of chapter 3, which examines popular media stereotypes of the masculine homosexual woman, the influence of sexological discourses on discussions of women's masculinization, and finally, the ways in which members of the homosexual subculture debated and distinguished between different forms of masculine female embodiment, from "virile" homosexual women, to "female transvestites," to biological females who lived their lives "passing" as men. In chapter 4, the focus shifts to questions of performance, cross-dressing, and masquerade in the context of the theatrical and cinematic trouser role (*Hosenrolle*), a centuries-old European tradition whereby women dressed as men and played male roles on stage. Drawing on theories of transgression and the carnivalesque, I argue that media representations of the trouser role responded to the need of German audiences to engage on a non-threatening level with women's masculinization. Cinematic texts, on the other hand, opened up powerful new means of representing cross-gender identifications and same-sex desires. Finally, chapter 5 moves even further away from the Berlin mass media, not only in its focus on literary representations of the masculine woman, but via a thematic interrogation of questions of place. Contrasting the works of well-known German authors with short stories from the subcultural magazines and Anna Elisabet Weirauch's popular lesbian-themed trilogy *Der Skorpion* (The Scorpion), I examine how Weimar authors positioned the masculine woman in relation to the cultural divide between the Berlin metropolis and the provinces, and used their medium to reflect on questions of gender and identity in more detailed and complex ways than was possible for journalists in the mainstream press.

Notes

1. Mary Louise Roberts, *Civilization without Sexes: Reconstructing Gender in Postwar France, 1917–1927* (Chicago: University of Chicago Press, 1994); Liz Conor, *The Spectacular Modern Woman: Feminine Visibility in the 1920s* (Bloomington: Indiana University Press, 2004); Carroll Smith-Rosenberg, "The New Woman as Androgyne: Social Disorder and Gender Crisis, 1870–1936," in Carroll Smith-Rosenberg, *Disorderly Conduct: Visions of Gender in Victorian America* (New York: Oxford University Press, 1985), 245–96; Laura L. Behling, *The Masculine Woman in America, 1890–1935* (Urbana: University of Illinois Press, 2001).
2. Judith Halberstam, *Female Masculinity* (Durham, NC: Duke University Press, 1998).
3. Ingrid Sharp, "Riding the Tiger: Ambivalent Images of the New Woman in the Popular Press of the Weimar Republic," in *New Woman Hybridities*, ed. Ann Heilmann and Margaret Beetham (New York: Routledge, 2004), 120. For an excellent discussion of male crisis in relation to Weimar cultural production see also Richard W. McCormick, *Gender and Sexuality in Weimar Modernity: Film, Literature, and 'New Objectivity'* (New York: Palgrave, 2001), 59–98.
4. Siegfried Kracauer, *Die Angestellten. Aus dem neuesten Deutschland* [1929] (Frankfurt/Main: Suhrkamp, 1971).
5. For analyses of women's workplace participation and visibility in Weimar Germany see e.g. Renate Bridenthal and Claudia Koonz, "Beyond *Kinder, Küche, Kirche*: Weimar Women in Politics and Work," in *When Biology Became Destiny: Women in Weimar and Nazi Germany*, ed. Renate Bridenthal, Atina Grossmann, and Marion Kaplan (New York: Monthly Review Press, 1984), 33–65; Atina Grossmann, "*Girlkultur* or Thoroughly Rationalized Female: A New Woman in Weimar Germany?" in *Women in Culture and Politics: A Century of Change*, ed. Judith Friedlander, Blanche Wiesen Cook, Alice Kessler-Harris, and Carroll Smith-Rosenberg (Bloomington: Indiana University Press, 1986), 62–80; Tim Mason, "Women in Germany, 1925–1940: Family, Welfare and Work. Part I," *History Workshop* 1 (1976): 74–113.
6. For a reevaluation of the role of female citizenship within Weimar historiography see Kathleen Canning, "Claiming Citizenship: Suffrage and Subjectivity in Germany after the First World War," in Kathleen Canning, *Gender History in Practice: Historical Perspectives on Bodies, Class & Citizenship* (Ithaca: Cornell University Press, 2006), 212–37, 219 cited here.
7. On the decline of the bourgeois feminist movement see Richard Evans, *The Feminist Movement in Germany, 1894–1933* (London: Sage, 1976), 235–75; Elizabeth Harvey, "The Failure of Feminism? Young Women and the Bourgeois Feminist Movement in Weimar Germany 1918–1933," *Central European History* 28, no. 1 (1995): 1–28.
8. On the Sex Reform movement and socialist feminism see Atina Grossmann, *Reforming Sex: The German Movement for Birth Control and Abortion Reform, 1920–1950* (New York: Oxford University Press, 1995); Cornelie Usborne, *The Politics of the Body in Weimar Germany: Women's Reproductive Rights and Duties* (Basingstoke: Macmillan, 1992); on companionate marriage see e.g. Jost Hermand and Frank Trommler, *Die Kultur der Weimarer Republik* (Frankfurt/Main: Fischer, 1988), 80–89.
9. Grossmann, "*Girlkultur*," 64; see also Katharina von Ankum, ed., *Women in the Metropolis: Gender and Modernity in Weimar Culture* (Berkeley: University of California Press, 1997); Kerstin Barndt, *Sentiment und Sachlichkeit: Der Roman der Neuen Frau in der Weimarer Republik* (Cologne: Böhlau, 2003); Petra Bock, "Zwischen den Zeiten: Neue Frauen und die Weimarer Republik," in *Neue Frauen zwischen den Zeiten*, ed. Petra Bock and Katja Koblitz (Berlin: Edition Heinrich, 1995), 21–25; Anke Gleber, *The Art of Taking a Walk: Flanerie, Literature, and Film in Weimar Culture* (Princeton: Princeton University Press, 1999); Atina Grossmann, "The New Woman and the Rationalization of Sexuality in Weimar Germany," in *Powers of Desire: The Politics of Sexuality*, ed. Ann Snitow, Christine Stansell, and Sharon Thompson (New York:

Monthly Review Press, 1983); Patrice Petro, *Joyless Streets: Women and Melodramatic Represen-tation in Weimar Germany* (Princeton: Princeton University Press, 1989).

10. On modernity and gender (crisis) see Rita Felski, *The Gender of Modernity* (Cambridge, MA: Harvard University Press, 1995); McCormick, *Gender and Sexuality.*

11. Lynne Frame, "Gretchen, Girl, Garçonne? Weimar Science and Popular Culture in Search of the Ideal New Woman," in Ankum, *Women in the Metropolis,* 13.

12. M. G., "Drei Frauen stehen heute vor uns. Die drei Typen: Gretchen, Girl, Garçonne," *8-Uhr-Abendblatt,* 4 June 1927, cited in and translated by Frame, ibid., 12. A more extensive contemporary exploration of the "Girl" phenomenon can be found in Fritz Giese, *Girlkultur: Vergleiche zwischen amerikanischem und europäischem Rhythmus und Lebensgefühl* (Munich: Delphin-Verlag, 1925). Because *Garçonne* was also the name of a homosexual women's maga-zine, I use capitals to designate female "types" and italics to designate publications.

13. K., "Vom Puppengesicht zum Charakterkopf: Wandlungen des Frauenideals," *Die Dame,* no. 16, 1st May Issue 1927, 3.

14. Ursula von Zedlitz, "Teestunden," *Die Dame,* no. 13, 2nd March Issue 1926, 39.

15. On female homosexual "types" at this period see Heike Schader, *Virile, Vamps und wilde Veilchen: Sexualität, Begehren und Erotik in den Zeitschriften homosexueller Frauen im Berlin der 1920er Jahre* (Königstein/Taunus: Ulrike Helmer, 2004), 107–21.

16. Roellig's study was republished in the 1980s with additional secondary material as Adele Meyer, ed., *Lila Nächte: Die Damenklubs im Berlin der zwanziger Jahre* (Berlin: Edition Lit. Europe, 1994). For an analyis of works by Mammen and other female artists of the Weimar era in relation to the figure of the Garçonne see Marsha Meskimmon, *We Weren't Modern Enough: Women Artists and the Limits of German Modernism* (Berkeley: University of California Press, 1999), 199ff.

17. Katharina von Ankum, "Introduction," in Ankum, *Women in the Metropolis,* 6.

18. Petro, *Joyless Streets,* 107, 119. Alice Kuzniar also notes this omission in Petro's study in *The Queer German Cinema* (Stanford: Stanford University Press, 2000), 273n4. Marti M. Lybeck's recent dissertation on female homosexuality in late nineteenth and early twentieth-century Germany represents an important exception here, and is discussed further in chapter 3: "Gen-der, Sexuality, and Belonging: Female Homosexuality in Germany 1890–1933" (PhD diss., University of Michigan, 2007).

19. Roberts, *Civilization without Sexes,* 6.

20. On the Weimar publishing scene see Anton Kaes, Martin Jay, and Edward Dimendberg, *The Weimar Republic Sourcebook* (Berkeley: University of California Press, 1994), 641; Wilhelm Marckwardt, *Die Illustrierten der Weimarer Zeit: Publizistische Funktion, ökonomische Entwick-lung und inhaltliche Tendenzen (unter Einschluß einer Bibliographie dieses Pressetyps 1918–1932)* (Munich: Minerva, 1982), 14f., 34.

21. *Berliner Illustrirte Zeitung,* no. 43, 26 October 1930, 1928f. Marckwardt cites a figure of 1,844,000 in 1929, decreasing to 1,469,000 by 1932; for more on the illustrated periodicals see his *Illustrierten,* v, 12, 70, 95ff.

22. This and other circulation figures cited below are from *Sperlings Zeitschriften- u. Zeitungs-Adreßbuch: Handbuch der deutschen Presse,* vol. 54 (Leipzig: Verlag des Börsenvereins der Deut-schen Buchhändler, 1928).

23. Other magazines for female homosexuals at this period included *Ledige Frauen* (Single Women), *Frauen Liebe und Leben* (Women's Love and Life), and *Blätter Idealer Frauenfreundschaft* (Pages of Ideal Women's Friendship). However, there were high degrees of organizational crossover between certain publications: *Ledige Frauen* replaced *Die Freundin* during its 1928 ban from public display on newsstands, and *Frauen Liebe und Leben* replaced *Frauenliebe* when it was also banned during 1928. For a detailed profile of these magazines, including information on editors, major contributors, and censorship, see Schader, *Virile,* 42–82.

24. An excellent assessment of the class profile of the homosexual magazines and the influence of bourgeois ideas about female sexuality and respectability on content can be found in Lybeck, "Female Homosexuality," chaps. 6 and 7; see also Schader, *Virile*, 62.

25. McCormick, *Gender and Sexuality*, 13.

26. Vibeke Rützou Petersen, *Women and Modernity in Weimar Germany: Reality and Representation in Popular Fiction* (New York: Berghahn Books, 2001), 5; Petro, *Joyless Streets*, xxiii; Barndt, *Sentiment und Sachlichkeit*; Joke Hermes, *Reading Women's Magazines: An Analysis of Everyday Media Use* (Cambridge: Polity Press, 1995), 5.

27. Jennifer Scanlon, *Inarticulate Longings: The Ladies' Home Journal, Gender, and the Promises of Consumer Culture* (New York: Routledge, 1995), 5.

28. The connection between anti–New Woman sentiment and anti-Semitism was first made in an essay by Atina Grossmann, and is examined further in chapter 5: "The New Woman," 167.

29. While this field of scholarship is too extensive to reference here, Michel Foucault's *History of Sexuality* remains a central text, in particular vol. 1: The Will to Knowledge (London: Penguin, 1998).

30. Halberstam, *Female Masculinity*, 10 and 46, see also 12f., 59.

31. Claudia Breger, "Feminine Masculinities: Scientific and Literary Representations of 'Female Inversion' at the Turn of the Twentieth Century," *Journal of the History of Sexuality* 14, no. 1/2 (2005): 81ff., 83 cited here; see also Jean Bobby Noble, *Masculinities without Men? Female Masculinity in Twentieth-Century Fictions* (Vancouver: UBC Press, 2004), introduction; Rachel Adams, "Masculinity without Men," *GLQ: A Journal of Lesbian and Gay Studies* 6, no. 3 (2000): 472ff.

32. Biddy Martin, *Femininity Played Straight: The Significance of Being Lesbian* (New York: Routledge, 1996), 64, 93. Although disavowal of the feminine has featured in several critiques of Halberstam's study, Halberstam does not ignore the femme in her study, not least in her analysis of butch-femme models: *Female Masculinity*, 122ff.

33. See e.g. Lybeck, "Female Homosexuality"; Nancy Nenno, "*Bildung* and Desire: Anna Elisabet Weirauch's *Der Skorpion*," in *Queering the Canon*, ed. Christoph Lorey and John Plews (Columbia: Camden House, 1998); Schader, *Virile*.

34. Judith Butler, *Gender Trouble: Feminism and the Subversion of Identity* (New York: Routledge, 1999).

35. George Chauncey Jr., "From Sexual Inversion to Homosexuality: The Changing Medical Conceptualization of Female 'Deviance,'" in *Passion and Power: Sexuality in History*, ed. Kathy Peiss, Christina Simmons, and Robert A. Padgug (Philadelphia: Temple University Press, 1989), 88; cf. criticisms in Halberstam, *Female Masculinity*, 86.

36. R. von Krafft-Ebing, *Psychopathia sexualis: Mit besonderer Berücksichtigung der konträren Sexualempfindung. Eine medizinisch-gerichtliche Studie für Ärzte und Juristen*, 15th ed. (Stuttgart: F. Enke, 1918), 281–86, 284 cited here.

37. Havelock Ellis and John Addington Symonds, *Sexual Inversion* [1897] (New York: Arno, 1975), 31, 78f., 87, 95ff., and passim; an earlier version of this text had appeared in German in 1896.

38. For critiques of the heteronormative imperative of the early sexologists see Chauncey, "Sexual Inversion," 89f., 94; Halberstam, *Female Masculinity*, 76ff.

39. Otto Weininger, *Geschlecht und Charakter: Eine prinzipielle Untersuchung* [1903] (Munich: Matthes & Seitz, 1997), 34f., 80, 84. For critical perspectives on Weininger see e.g. Nancy A. Harrowitz and Barbara Hyams, eds., *Jews & Gender: Responses to Otto Weininger* (Philadelphia: Temple University Press, 1995).

40. Ellis and Symonds, *Sexual Inversion*, 82ff., 100; Breger, "Feminine Masculinities," 80; see also Smith-Rosenberg, "The New Woman."

41. Magnus Hirschfeld, *Sexuelle Zwischenstufen: Das männliche Weib und der weibliche Mann*, 2nd ed., vol. 2, *Sexualpathologie: Ein Lehrbuch für Ärzte und Studierende* (Bonn: A. Marcus &

E. Webers, 1922), passim, but see esp. 96–120. Other key early works include *Berlins drittes Geschlecht* [1904] (Berlin: Rosa Winkel, 1991), and *Die Transvestiten: Eine Untersuchung über den erotischen Verkleidungstrieb* (Berlin: Med. Verlag Alfred Pulvermacher, 1910).

42. Hirschfeld, *Sexuelle Zwischenstufen*, 180, 210, 212.

43. Sigmund Freud, "The Psychogenesis of a Case of Homosexuality in a Woman," in *Sexuality and the Psychology of Love* (New York: Collier, 1963), 133–59; Chauncey, "Sexual Inversion," 109.

44. Halberstam, *Female Masculinity*, 77ff., 285n4.

45. See e.g. Lucy Bland and Laura Doan, *Sexology Uncensored: The Documents of Sexual Science* (Cambridge: Polity Press, 1998), 3; Chauncey, "Sexual Inversion," 87f., 109; Halberstam, *Female Masculinity*, 47, 79ff; Darryl Hill, "Sexuality and Gender in Hirschfeld's *Die Transvestiten*: A Case of the 'Elusive Evidence of the Ordinary,'" *Journal of the History of Sexuality* 14, no. 3 (2005): 316–32.

Chapter 1

"WHICH ONE IS THE MAN?"

The Masculinization of Women's Fashions

The "masculinization" of women's fashions is currently one of the most popular topics in all of the illustrated papers.

Elsa Herzog, *Sport im Bild,* December 1924

We have only a business-oriented hairdresser to thank for the popular topic of woman's masculinization.

Izabela Lesser, *Die Dame,* September 1926

*O*ne of the most pervasive images from post–World War I Europe is that of the slender but muscular, short-haired, cigarette-sporting flapper in a low-waisted, curve-denying dress and simple cloche hat. The cultural, social, and political history of this decade is intricately bound up with what was being played out on the surface of women's and men's bodies—with the clothes they wore, how they cut their hair, and the accessories they chose. It was no accident that the unprecedented level of political and social mobility attained by German women by the early 1920s found its most visual representation in fashion, nor that fashion, as one of the most obvious forms of social gender differentiation, became the focus of some of the most biting social criticism about changing relationships between German women and men. Drawing on a range of print media, and particularly fashion and illustrated periodicals such as *Die Dame, Sport im Bild,* and the *BIZ,* this chapter traces how the "masculinization of woman" became a cliché of German fashion reporting by the mid 1920s—as shown by the two examples cited

---

Notes for this section begin on page 62.

above—before being gradually replaced during the final years of the republic with more traditionally "feminine" images. However, this chronology does not tell the whole story, for not only were there important lines of continuity between 1920s "masculine" women's fashions and the visual styles that replaced them, but within the emerging female homosexual subculture masculine fashions took on meanings that resisted mainstream encodings and trends.

Just as fashion theorists warn against reading trends in visual styles as a mirror of social or cultural facts, my focus here is not on the intricacies of Weimar fashion developments per se, but rather on how commentators interpreted the social *meanings* of women's hair and clothing.[1] When 1920s journalists discussed "masculine" women's clothing, they were not referring to women donning men's clothes; rather, their interest lay in the erotic effects and social implications of applying men's tailoring styles and accessories to clothing designed expressly for women. This chapter examines a series of discrete but largely simultaneous 1920s fashion phenomena that were at the center of discussions of women's external masculinization, including the hugely popular *Bubikopf*, a short haircut for women, the tuxedo, trousers, and the monocle. An analysis of these styles enables the establishment of a broad chronology for the rise and fall of masculine women's fashions in Weimar Germany, and offers valuable insights into contemporary "queer" appropriations of these looks. Other sartorial symbols associated with the cosmopolitan aesthetic of Garçonne fashions (*Garçonne-Mode*) included felt hats, long coats, low-waisted "Jumper" dresses, and even short skirts, which by displaying the legs helped to emphasize a previously male-oriented area of fashion. This chapter also briefly charts developments in men's fashions at this period, for as fashion scholars insist, the history of dress and gender can only be understood in terms of the interrelationship *between* categories of male and female.[2]

An important precursor to the simplified lines of 1920s women's fashions was the late nineteenth-century dress reform movement in Europe and North America, which sought sensible, rational, and more natural alternatives to the perceived frivolity and eroticism of hoops and corsets. Historians differ in their assessments of this movement: some argue that it reflected women's increasing social mobility, particularly following the cycling craze of the 1890s, while others insist that it had limited influence on later developments, with the middle classes continuing to value a women's luxurious wardrobe as a symbol of economic prosperity. Yet some degree of long-term influence is undeniable, for by the early twentieth century women's clothes had become less centered on breasts and hips, and aimed instead for a more low-key "visual unity of bodily form."[3] World War I accelerated this trend, as clothing for women and men alike was characterized by severe lines and military references, economic rationing restricted the use of more flamboyant designs and fabrics, and women required suitable uniforms for their entry into previously "masculine" occupations such as factory work. By the early 1920s, with growing numbers of women moving to the cities and entering the workforce, demand was steadily increasing for practical but fashionable clothing. Technical developments enabling the production of affordable ready-to-wear clothing and the rise of a mass consumer culture contributed to a widespread democratization of women's fashions at this period.

My analysis of masculine women's fashions in 1920s Germany builds upon research by scholars such as Gesa Kessemeier, Sabine Hake, and Julia Bertschik. Kessemeier's research is groundbreaking in terms of the detail with which she chronicles Weimar fashions, including a chapter on "masculine" styles, but her timeframe of 1920 to 1929—after which, she argues, the New Woman was replaced by a new, more feminine version of womanhood—restricts her ability to examine why this change occurred at this particular historical moment, or how masculine visual styles continued to influence women's fashions beyond this period. In contrast, I argue that some of the most interesting discussions of women's masculinization took place in the years immediately preceding the National Socialist takeover in 1933, after which most of the magazines examined here were forced to either cease publication or underwent a thorough Nazification. Bertschik's survey of several centuries of German fashion and literary history is more informative about continuities across the Weimar and Nazi periods. However, neither of these studies engages with the question of what might be termed "queer" visual styles, despite the widespread presence within the Weimar media of the stereotypical masculine lesbian in suit, tie, and monocle. Hake discusses this aspect only briefly when she suggests that public anxieties about liberated female sexuality "found a convenient stereotype in the lesbian 'butch' and the rituals of a homosexual subculture where, so it seemed, gender was reduced to a choice of costumes."[4] This chapter combines new research on the female homosexual magazines with a fresh reading of mainstream fashion publications to shed new light on the role of masculine visual styles for women in Weimar German culture and society.

"The Story of the Braid that Was Chopped Off and Then Grew Back"

The mass advent of the *Bubikopf,* an umbrella term for women's short haircuts that could range in style from a chin-length pageboy bob to a tightly cropped "Eton," was without doubt the most controversial fashion phenomenon in interwar Germany. With a name that evoked a boyish version of masculinity, the *Bubikopf* was, as one commentator enthusiastically declared at the peak of its popularity, "an epoch-making, astonishing twentieth-century cultural phenomenon, which is quite deservedly moving the entire (ladies') world."[5] Embraced by millions of German women from all class backgrounds as a sign of their modernity and fashion sense, and widely touted for its practicality, the *Bubikopf* was the subject of countless articles, cartoons, poems, and images in the contemporary media. More than any other style, it cut to the heart of social and cultural anxieties concerning the masculinization of woman, providing commentators and readers alike with a discursive space in which to negotiate changing relations between women and men.

It is difficult to pinpoint the exact beginnings of the *Bubikopf* phenomenon, which contemporary journalists correctly identified as part of an international trend that reached at least as far as the US, France, and England. In 1925 the Ullstein publications the *BIZ* and *Die Dame* each credited a Parisian stylist named "Antoine" with its invention, although Hake has argued that it first appeared in the US during the war.[6] As early as January 1921 the trendsetting *Sport im Bild* hailed the *Bubikopf* as "the latest fashion," although journalist Elsa Herzog remained cautious, noting that not every woman would be ready to sacrifice "her most beautiful decoration."[7] By 1924, the beginning of a period of increased economic stability following the currency reform of the previous year, short crops had begun to prevail not only in the fashion spreads but also on the streets of the metropolis. The popular illustrated weekly *BIZ* ran photos with provocative captions such as: "The *Bubikopf* epidemic: Should all women adopt this style?" The fashion bible *Die Dame* declared that "everyone" was wearing one, and the trendy *Uhu* and *Das Magazin* featured countless models and celebrities sporting this new style.[8] Widely viewed as attractive, practical, youthful, and flattering, the *Bubikopf* also proved remarkably resistant to persistent predictions of its demise. As *Die Dame* observed in 1925, any protestations against this unstoppable force were in vain: "One criticizes, one praises, one forbids, one allows ... the end result is the scissor cut [*Scherenschnitt*]."[9]

Yet as time passed, the print media devoted increasing space to criticisms of the *Bubikopf* and began to position it as a threatening visual symbol of the masculinization of Germany's womanhood. Growing discomfort at the thought of hordes of German women racing off to the salon to remove their girlish braid, the so-called *Gretchenzopf*, is evident in the responses of female film stars interviewed on this topic in 1925 by *Das Magazin*. Although praising the practicality of the *Bubikopf* and even sporting their own smart crops, actors Xena Desni, Erna Morena, and Asta Nielsen warn readers that many women who adopt this style risk appearing "unfeminine." Nielsen, in particular, was obliged to note her own role in pioneering this style through her numerous trouser roles. Long-haired colleague Lily Dagover took such concerns a step further, pouring scorn on women who insist upon masquerading "like a man in dress and behavior and hairstyle." Describing the ongoing masculinization of women and feminization of men in terms of cultural drama [*Kulturdrama*], Dagover cautions women against giving up their strongest weapon—their feminine charms: "What good does it do a woman to cut off her hair and run around dressed like a man! In spite of all efforts she will only ever manage to be a weak and poor copy." From such forceful insistence on gender difference as the cornerstone of heterosexual attraction, it was only a short leap to fellow actor Lotte Neumann's positioning of female masculinization as degenerate and perverse: "as soon as she starts to dress like a man, it is a degeneration and to be condemned. *Bubikopf* and pageboy styles can be charming, but everything beyond that is an evil."[10]

Such criticisms highlight both the central problem and main attraction of the *Bubikopf*—its associations with gender ambiguity and transgression. Women's appearances provided a familiar and comprehensible forum around which much larger anxieties about social, cultural, and demographic changes coalesced, and commentators used their criticisms of this style as a means of restoring a sense of control and stability in at least one area of their rapidly changing society. Journalists from across the media spectrum explicitly linked women's visual masculinization to the industrialization and modernization of German society, part and parcel of which was a shift toward increasing gender equality, as the *BIZ* declared in 1925: "The ideal of beauty changes with the style of the time, which has turned us into independent women who can look after ourselves; our lives are increasingly similar to men's; the *Bubikopf* is no whim of fashion, but rather a manifestation of a new cultural era."[11] Some even employed the biblical analogy of Samson and Delilah to argue that women's increasing influence in society was inversely related to the length of their hair: "in contrast to Samson—woman's masculine sense of power seems to be rooted precisely in her shorn-off hair."[12] Observing a similar pattern in 1920s France, Roberts points out that this was in fact a double inversion of the Samson myth: "first, because less, not more, hair granted power, and second, because women themselves became virilized Samsons—rather than shearing Delilahs!"[13] In such ways, the "masculinization" of women's appearances became a powerful and tangible symbol of the "masculinization" of women's lives in the workplace, in politics, and in sexual relationships.

Correspondingly, attempts to recuperate the femininity of women who had succumbed to this trend were always about more than just hair. One of the more nuanced methods, favored by women's fashion magazines such as *Die Dame*, involved highlighting the historical and geographical contingency of gendered signifiers such as hair. Thus some journalists insisted that just as men have not always been required to wear their hair short, the coding of certain hair and clothing styles as masculine is a reflection of society's current needs rather than an eternal truth: "Each era forms its own ideas about masculine and feminine appearances, and tends to confuse these ideas with masculinity and femininity."[14] A less subtle strategy favored by the illustrated periodicals involved undermining the cultural threat of the masculine woman through ridicule and caricature. Cartoons of young, virginal daughters and bourgeois wives taking themselves off to the local hairdresser to rid themselves of their braids addressed anxieties about women's growing independence and movement away from the patriarchal restrictions of family and husband, at a time when many young and especially middle-class women were heading into the cities and the workforce and becoming wage earners for the first time.

Other caricatures thematized a visual merging of male and female genders, particularly among the younger generation, although it was nearly always the gender transgression of the masculinized woman that formed the primary target of such satire, as opposed to that of the feminized man. In 1925, for example, the *BIZ* published a photograph of five short-haired, athletic women in skimpy tricots engaged in an archery contest with the provocative reader competition question: "How many men are present?" Not surprisingly, the answer informs us that all are in fact women. Another cartoon in the same paper showed a scene at the hairdressing salon, in which a closely shaven woman and a middle-aged man with a fresh pageboy cut gawk into the mirrors after the barber has mixed up their haircuts—presumably confused by his short-haired female client. Meanwhile, the trendy *Uhu* featured a cartoon of an embarrassed older woman at the swimming pool surrounded by fashionable young bubikopfed women declaring: "Heavens, I've wandered into the gentleman's baths—" (Figure 1.1); and as late as 1933 published a photograph of a decidedly androgynous heterosexual couple with the caption "Lovers: which one is the man?"[15] As Halberstam observes, such cases of mistaken identity are not really about women appearing as men (there is no real reason for the reader to doubt that these are women), but rather about failing to pass the "female" gender test, according to which one must be "readable at a glance."[16] At their most positive, illustrations of gender merging could be used to comment in reasonably noncondemnatory ways on notions of heterosexual camaraderie and equality, such as a 1926 *BIZ* cartoon and verse entitled "Modern Couple" featuring two identically dressed young people on a motorcycle, in which the only indications of gender differentiation are a somewhat larger torso on the one and a slight curve of breasts on the other (Figure 1.2).[17] Yet while short hairstyles and masculine fashions helped to extend the limits of what was readable as feminine by the German public at this period, the prevalence of articles mocking the masculine woman demonstrates that such styles also inspired a fiercer, more defensive policing of gender boundaries.

Some of the most extreme responses to the masculine threat of the *Bubikopf* went so far as to suggest that adverse physical consequences could follow for women who transgressed gender boundaries by adopting this style: specifically, that cutting off the hair on one's head would result in inappropriate growth on other parts of the body. In a typical example from 1924, the *BIZ* published a photograph of a young, bobbed woman wearing an oversized bow tie and neat mustache, accompanied by the "horrific news" from a North American fashion guru that "[w]hen one does not permit hair to flourish on the head, it will grow on the face and body. The ladies will grow mustaches."[18] Hair, in its role as both an extension of the body but also a secondary sex characteristic, provided critics with a handy means of reaffirming the biological limits of gender, as such "horrific" images were used to set "natural" boundaries to the masculinization of

Figure 1.1. "The Mixed-up Sex." *Uhu,* July 1926, 103.
Source: BPK Bildagentur für Kunst, Kultur und Geschichte

zeuge, Feld-, Förder- und Stallbahnen be-
wegen Dünger, Brennstoffe, Ernte, Futter;
motorisch betriebene Höhen- und Seitenförde-
rer bringen das Heu und Getreide auf Boden
und Schober; die pneumatische Förderung
schafft Korn, Häcksel und Spreu von der Dresch-

...e der landwirtschaftlichen Betriebe, vor
allem der Bauernwirtschaften, zu erprobter
moderner Wirtschaftsführung zu bringen, wie
sie hier nur kurz angedeutet werden konnte. Aufgaben von ge-
waltiger volkswirtschaftlicher Bedeutung harren hier der Lösung.

Zeichnung von
Max Zschoch.

Modernes Paar.
Motorrad, Soziussitz,   Körper sind gleichgeschweift,
Bubikopf gleichen Schnitt's, Pullovers gleichgestreift —
Hornbraune Brille.   Frühlingsidylle.   Anita.

Figure 1.2. "Modern Couple." *Berliner Illustrirte Zeitung,* 9 May 1926, 608.
Source: BPK Bildagentur für Kunst, Kultur und Geschichte

women. Other commentators took a somewhat different approach, proclaiming the increasing popularity of male facial hair as an explicit reaction to women's gender transgressions, and expressing delight that here, at last, was a facet of masculinity that could not be mimicked by women: "It seems that men will start wearing beards—as a protest against the masculinization of woman."[19] At a time when conceptions of gender were becoming ever less reliant on notions of differ-ence, German commentators recognized the power of appealing to an apparently unassailable biological characteristic, as facial hair came to represent a last, rather desperate attempt to reclaim masculinity for men.

Whereas commentators across the mainstream media increasingly viewed the *Bubikopf* as a threatening symbol of women's masculinization, magazines target-ing homosexual women offered alternative interpretations of this style. For many homosexual women at this period, the *Bubikopf* became an important element of a masculinized, or "virile" erotic aesthetic—the term favored in subcultural publications of this period for what might now be described as "butch" styles, and which also included tuxedos, monocles, male nicknames, and masculine-connoted habits such as smoking. Publications such as *Die Freundin* and *Gar-çonne* regularly featured cover models in dark suits with short, slicked-back hair (see Figure 1.3), published short stories in which a cropped haircut could signify anything from boyish erotic playfulness to dark mystery and sexual intrigue, and

Figure 1.3. Cover image, *Garçonne,* February 1931.
Source: Deutsche Nationalbibliothek, Leipzig

ran advertisements for *Bubikopf* stylists catering to a specifically homosexual audience with "discreet service" and "gentlemen's cuts." A number of scholars have discussed the importance of masculine "codes" as signifiers of female homosexual

visibility and identification in Germany at this period, showing how these functioned to constitute as well as stabilize the emerging female homosexual subculture.[20] While I return to this argument in chapter 3, here I want to highlight the
importance of the *Bubikopf*—particularly in its tightly cropped Eton and Titus
variants—as a powerful code of visual recognition and identification among German homosexual women that remained popular within the subculture until at
least the early 1930s, after which the magazines examined here ceased to exist and
many homosexual women were forced to live a more covert sexual existence.[21]
Consequently, contributors to these magazines warned of the potentially tragic
consequences of parents disapproving of this style in their daughters, for whom
the *Bubikopf* might be not just a "whim of fashion" but a symptom of their inner homosexual leanings, and even compared the need of homosexual women
to wear short hair and masculine clothing to the compulsion of male-to-female
transvestites to wear women's clothing.[22]

Yet the *Bubikopf*'s role as an expression of masculine or "virile" sex-gender
identity also created divisions within the contemporary subculture, with some
commentators rejecting the assumption that homosexual women would naturally be in favor of this new style. Thus "Paulowna" declared in the *Freundin* that
not only was the *Bubikopf* entirely unsuitable for German women, but: "I believe
I can safely claim that in the dreams of the homosexual woman it is the girl or
woman with long hair, with braids, who plays a role."[23] Although she thus seeks
to extend her own conservative and nationalistic definitions of female beauty to
all homosexual women, Paulowna's perspective is significant for its attempt to
claim a role for long hair and femininity within the contemporary female homosexual aesthetic—a reversal of mainstream attempts to broaden heterosexual
ideals of female aesthetics to include short hair.

After several years at the height of fashion, the *Bubikopf* was gradually replaced
in the late 1920s and early 1930s with longer, wavier, more overtly feminine
styles, exemplified by photographs of Miss Germany winners between 1928 and
1931 (see Figure 1.4), and by August 1927 *Das Magazin* was able to declare
with some confidence that the now "banal" *Bubikopf* had been "dethroned."[24] Although this move away from closely shorn styles was part of a larger, international
trend and was dismissed by some contemporaries as simply part of the natural
fashion cycle, in the context of late Weimar Germany it was also subject to specific and nationalistic encodings, which are explored in the final section of this
chapter. That said, it is important to note that relatively short styles remained *de
rigeur*—undoubtedly a concession to the practicality of the *Bubikopf*, as well as to
the years it would take women to grow back their locks. As *Die Dame* observed in
1930, women had become less tolerant of "impractical" styles in the wake of the
Bubikopf, and this was reflected in the continued popularity of short hairstyles in
media images even into the 1930s.[25]

„MISS GERMANY" 1932?

Ihre Vorgängerinnen:

1928

1929

1930

Photos: Binder — Schneider —

1931

— Sonderhoff — Heinz Ritter

Die alljährlich wieder-kehrende Wahl der „Miß Germany" findet in diesem Jahre nicht wie bisher im Januar statt, sondern erst zu einem Zeitpunkt, in dem die Weltwirtschaftslage die Vornahme einer zwar hin nicht notwendigen Sitte gestattet. Das Pariser Komitee hat die Parole ausgegeben, daß sämtliche in Frage kommenden vierundzwanzig europäischen Staaten, die sich bisher mit der Wahl ihrer offiziellen Schön-

Figure 1.4. "'Miss Germany' 1932?" *Das Magazin,* January 1932, 6806.
Source: BPK Bildagentur für Kunst, Kultur und Geschichte

"The Characteristic of the Modern Garçonne": Tuxedos and Suits

Beneath a photograph of a woman in a dark jacket, matching short skirt, crisp white shirt with waistcoat and bowtie, and sternly bobbed dark hair, a caption in *Das Magazin* in 1926 declared the tuxedo "the latest acquisition of the masculine woman." Carefully placed accessories include a pair of white gloves tucked into a jacket pocket and a monocle dangling at her hip (Figure 1.5). Next to the *Bubikopf,* the tuxedo or formal dinner suit—known in German as the *Smoking* and one of the most obvious borrowings from men's tailoring—was among the most prominent visual signs of the "masculinization of woman" in Weimar me-

Die letzte „Errungenschaft" der männlichen
Frau — der Smoking

Eine englische Amazone beim
Concours hippique

Figure 1.5. "The Latest Acquisition of the Masculine Woman—the Tuxedo."
Das Magazin, August 1926, 761.

Source: BPK Bildagentur für Kunst, Kultur und Geschichte

dia coverage, and was central to the wardrobe of the cosmopolitan Garçonne. It appeared almost simultaneously with the first *Bubikopf* styles—in 1921 fashion stalwart *Sport im Bild* featured a female model wearing a "dress and jacket combination with tuxedo finish in gentlemen's style"[26]—and by 1925/26 such garments had come to dominate women's evening and daywear alike.

Weimar fashion gurus emphasized the gender-bending potential of the tuxedo by advising women who wore this garment to also adopt masculine forms of etiquette. "Ladies wearing this suit, like gentleman, remove their hats at tea," observed *Die Dame* in 1926, beside an illustration of a woman whose body language—one hand on her hips, the other holding a cigarette, her gaze cool and piercing—followed clearly masculine codes.[27] Such fashion tips point to a growing cultural awareness that women could carry off convincing performances of masculinity, as the tuxedo and its daywear cousin, the tailored suit—both of which were most commonly worn with a simple, straight skirt—became even more important symbols of female masculinization in 1920s Germany than trousers.

Accordingly, the tuxedo featured in some of the most reactionary accounts of the masculine woman. In 1925 a *BIZ* article entitled "Now that's Enough! Against the Masculinization of Woman" featured numerous images of short-haired women in severely masculine suits and ties, declaring that what had begun as a "capricious game of women's fashions" and a "delightful joke" had reached unacceptable, indeed even disgusting levels (see Figure 1.6).[28] Two years later, a front-page competition in the same paper, "What Do You Say about Fräulein Mia?" (Figure 1.7) encouraged readers to contribute witty responses to an image of a woman with shortly cropped and sternly parted hair in a dark suit, tie, and monocle, who was pictured striding purposefully across the office alongside a rather effeminate male colleague to the amusement of their more conventionally gendered fellow workers. While Mia's femininity is seemingly displaced onto her male companion, it is, as Petro has observed, only *her* gender identity that is under attack.[29] As seen already with "Lotte at the Crossroads" (Figure I.1), women dressed in suits and ties and trying to enter women's public bathrooms, only to fail this most everyday of gender tests, were another frequent target of satire.[30] By inviting readers to ridicule such exaggerated performances of masculinity, the mainstream media offered a vent for anxieties about women's masculine gender performances in other areas of life, such as the workplace, politics, and marriage.

Yet the cultural threat of the masculine woman to male social hegemony and heteronormative social structures was also countered using more subtle means. Particularly popular within the upmarket fashion magazines were what I term "narratives of transformation": the idea that women could be different things—and different genders—at different times of day simply by changing their clothes. Thus fashion journalists argued that one could be masculine in the morning as one went about one's business and recreational activities, before adopting a more feminine, decorative look for the afternoon and evening. This allocation

Figure 1.6. "Now That's Enough! Against the Masculinization of Woman." *Berliner Illustrirte Zeitung*, 29 March 1925, 389.

Source: BPK Bildagentur für Kunst, Kultur und Geschichte

Figure 1.7. "What Do You Say about Fräulein Mia?" *Berliner Illustrirte Zeitung,*
13 November 1927.

Source: BPK Bildagentur für Kunst, Kultur und Geschichte

of gendered fashions to particular times of day is evident in captions such as "Gentlemanlike in the Morning, Ladylike in the Afternoon" (a play on the adjective *herrlich,* which could also mean "heavenly"), and in photographic series that depict the transformation of "the elegant woman of today" from masculine Garçonne in the morning to elegant lady in the evening via the adornment of a dress, jewelry, and a white wig (figures 1.8 and 1.9).[31]

Although such narratives of transformation posited gender play as a liberating experience that offered women the opportunity to achieve spectacular aesthetic and erotic contrasts, they could also function as a conservative coercive force. By providing a normative feminine counterpoint to masculine fashions through the promotion of an overtly feminized aesthetic for evening wear, such narratives constituted an effective means of containing the threat of excessive masculinization to certain times of day or activities: "To be a boy in the morning and a lady in the evening is the current ideal of the lady of fashion."[32] Marjorie Garber has argued that "cross-dressing can be 'fun' or 'functional' so long as it occupies liminal space and a temporary time period; after this carnivalization, however, … the cross-dresser is expected to resume life as he or she was." According to

Die elegante Frau von heute: Am Vormittag und —   dieselbe (mit weißer Perücke) am Abend —!   Phot. Man Ray

Figures 1.8 and 1.9. "The Elegant Woman of Today: In the Morning and— the Same Woman (with White Wig) in the Evening—!" *Das Magazin,* October 1925, 74–75.

Source: BPK Bildagentur für Kunst, Kultur und Geschichte

the dictates of Weimar fashion, women could experiment with gender trans-gression for a brief period each day, but with the tacit understanding that this would be followed by a more feminine gender performance in the afternoon and evening—not coincidentally those times of day in which mixed-gender activi-ties were more common. Such performances of femininity were not only about returning women to their traditional roles as wives and mothers, but also about reining in the threat of sexual alterity: in a climate of destabilized gender norms, as Hake observes, typically feminine clothes became a defense not only against accusations of masculinization, but also against associations with feminism and lesbianism.[33]

On the other hand, for at least some members of the female homosexual sub-culture it was precisely the masculine associations of the tuxedo that constituted its appeal. The subcultural magazines depict masculine evening wear such as tux-edos and monocles as an important means of identifying masculine homosexual women, and even as the preferred attire of intellectual or artistic members of the "third sex." In one story in *Die Freundin,* the mere presence of women in tuxedos is enough to signify to the protagonist that she is in a homosexual club and con-vey a sense of belonging: "This is your home, this is where you belong." Similarly, a *Garçonne* author used the tuxedo to stake an erotic claim in describing how her protagonist's "upright, aristocratic appearance" was shown to its best advantage in her black tuxedo suit, "giving her at the same time a light masculine touch, which was only emphasized by the whip resting in her right hand."[34] Gertrud Lehnert observes that the stark elegance of such styles became the "trademark" of the emancipated, chic, woman-oriented women of the 1920s.[35] Conversely, main-stream media representations of tuxedoed women were never entirely innocent of homosexual associations. Rather, the impact of images such as "Fräulein Mia" relied at least partly on audience familiarity with sexological theories that linked masculine gender performance with female sexual inversion.

In Germany, suits and tuxedos had been associated with stereotypes of fe-male inversion since at least the beginning of the Weimar period, as is demon-strated by a cartoon published in 1921 in the satirical *Simplicissimus.* Entitled "Hirschfeldiana," it features a corpulent Magnus Hirschfeld, presumably at his Berlin Institute for Sexual Science, resting his hand in a fatherly gesture on the shoulder of his young female secretary, whose short hair and angular features are complemented by a sharp suit and bowtie (Figure 1.10). Her refusal to comply with conventional gender expectations is underlined by the reference to "Diana," goddess of hunting, and her sexual alterity is confirmed as she types out a dicta-tion relating to Paragraph 175, the section of the German Criminal Code that criminalized male homosexual acts. In short, there is no question that she is a member of the "third sex" on which Hirschfeld had published widely since the early years of the twentieth century.

Hirſchfeldiana

(Zeichnung von E. Thöny)

„Bitte, ſchreiben Sie, Fräulein: Beim Wiederaufbau unſres darniederliegenden Wirtſchaftslebens erfordert das Gebot der Stunde den ſofortigen Abbau des § 175."

Figure 1.10. E. Thöny, "Hirschfeldiana." *Simplicissimus,* 1 April 1921, 11.
Source: BPK Bildagentur für Kunst, Kultur und Geschichte

The threat of female perversion encapsulated in such images was increasingly employed as a weapon for warding off the specter of women's masculinization in the late Weimar period, although in a less sudden way than that described by Laura Doan in reaction to the Hall trial in Britain. Doan insists that it was not until the late 1920s in Britain that the scandal surrounding Radclyffe Hall's novel *The Well of Loneliness* gave the masculine woman a lesbian face, arguing that the obscenity trial for *The Well* in 1928 had a similar social impact for homosexual women as the earlier Wilde trial had for homosexual men. She thus directly links the demise of masculine fashions in late 1920s Britain to their increasing association with lesbianism, whilst also arguing that many queer women came to adopt the masculine fashions popular in the mid 1920s as a visual signifier of their nonnormative sex-gender identities, thereby contributing to the rise of a distinct female homosexual subculture in Britain.[36] While this latter argument can be usefully extended to Weimar Germany, as I have already begun to argue in relation to the *Bubikopf,* the Hall trial—which received only limited media coverage in Germany—did not affect fashion developments in that country. More importantly, nor was there any similar critical moment in the late Weimar period signposting this transition from trendy to perverse; rather, it is more accurate to speak of a gradual increase in media anxiety surrounding the nonmaternal masculine modern woman. At the same time, however, we must acknowledge the "queer" erotic fascination that continued to surround this figure in both heterosexual and homosexual contexts even into the final years of the republic, and which at times—one need only think of images of Marlene Dietrich in top hat and tails in Josef von Sternberg's *Morocco*—undoubtedly heightened the cosmopolitan appeal of gender-ambiguous visual styles for women.

Like the *Bubikopf*'s replacement with longer, wavier styles, the decline of the tuxedo in favor of more feminine attire in the late Weimar period is typical of the general trajectory of masculine women's fashions in late 1920s Germany. After reaching the height of popularity in 1925/26 in the form of dark, cleanly tailored replicas of the male tuxedo, this garment was increasingly subject to feminizing variations, as designers incorporated more frivolous, decorative fabrics and styles, a highlight of which was the tuxedo in silver or gold lamé. By the end of the decade the tuxedo had largely faded from mainstream fashion discourse, to the extent that retrospective articles framed it as a somewhat ridiculous example of masculine excess. But as with the *Bubikopf,* this chronology does not tell the whole story, for related garments such as women's tailored suits remained popular well beyond the mid 1920s and managed to achieve a more permanent place on the female fashion scene during the Nazi era. In 1931 fashion journalist Johanna Thal contemplated the ongoing success of such garments, which she does not hesitate to link to women's "masculinized" activities during the war and newfound political significance in German society. She is careful, however, to distinguish the suit from the tuxedo: thus, while the former had "never really gone completely out of fashion" and remained symbolic of the active and assertive woman, the tuxedo, it seems, had by this stage come to represent an excessive masculinity "which today we are no longer fond of remembering. For over the years we have become much more feminine."[37] Thal's article demonstrates how the tailored suit, once masculinely connoted, had by the late Weimar period been incorporated into a new, more functionally oriented female clothing norm—in contrast to the tuxedo, which was unable to continue bearing the weight of its masculine associations.

Fashion historians have linked the growing tolerance of women's suits at this period to larger structural changes in fashion in the early twentieth century, whereby male and female bodies began to be addressed as comparable entities and ideas about what constituted femininity were reappraised. Kessemeier, for example, argues that by 1927 the normalization of style elements and body shapes once considered masculine had been so successful that the "feminization" of female fashion could take place only on the margins, for example through fabrics or accessories.[38] Within this context, accusations of female masculinization gradually became defunct, as clothing, physical characteristics, and behavior formerly coded masculine became incorporated into a new, mainstream feminine aesthetic. In 1930 the *Sport im Bild* summarized this new feminine ideal as "a tall, but not too tall woman with the gait of a queen, the hips of a boy, the bosom of a young girl, the shoulders of a student who has trained for rowing regattas, and the delicately colored face of an old painting—that is she, the woman of today!"[39] Not only did women's fashions thus come to incorporate some of the more functional and attractive aspects of the "masculine" styles of the mid 1920s, but by the early 1930s there were hints that fashion trends were coming full circle, as reporters began to remark on the reemergence of a masculine or "gentlemanlike" line:

> Contrasts in fashion are perhaps the characteristic feature of the new season. Dress and jacket combinations in very severe cuts that are almost a return to the masculine, and suits in dainty, soft, fanciful forms with such sweet blouses that the effect is thoroughly feminine.[40]

Such examples complicate any straightforward assumptions about the conservative gendering of fashion in the late Weimar and early Nazi periods, demonstrating that the stern, masculine lines of the mid 1920s were never completely eradicated, a finding I return to in the final section of this chapter.

"The Woman in Trousers"

Although numerous fashion spreads bore this title, the "woman in trousers" was a less controversial symbol of women's masculinization in the Weimar era than either the tuxedo or the *Bubikopf*. A 1924 article on Garçonne fashions featured a trousered woman in only one of seven photographs, and fashion journals of this period depicted trousers most prominently either as attire for sporting activities such as skiing, hiking, or hunting, for certain occupations, in feminized variations such as the pajama, or on female actors engaged in trouser roles (see chapter 4).[41] Yet Weimar commentators were nonetheless well aware of this garment's symbolic and historical associations with masculinity; consequently, women's trousers provided a further focus for discussions about the visual masculinization of women.

Despite the fact that 1920s fashion journalists occasionally questioned the aesthetic appeal of wearing breeches for sport, the fiercest debates surrounding women's athletic attire had already taken place in the late nineteenth century. The development of split skirts for women cyclists and breeches for female equestrians riding "in the gentleman's saddle" had helped to pioneer women's trouser-wearing in other spheres: "It is not so long ago that the female cyclist in trousers caused a general sensation," observed women's magazine *Frau und Gegenwart* (Woman and the Present) in 1927. By the 1920s wearing pants for such activities barely raised eyebrows, such that "today it is the done thing in Berlin to make up ladies' riding costumes with breeches."[42] It certainly helped that trouser-wearing for such sports was compartmentalized as a suitable morning activity for wealthy women who would spend the rest of the day engaged in more feminine pursuits—a variation on the transformation narratives discussed above. Thus, although the female equestrian represented one of the more extreme visual embodiments of masculine styles for women with her stern suit, hat, and riding crop—leading her to frequently attract the label "Amazon"—she remained within the boundaries of acceptable gender appearance and was not a major target of critics of masculinization.

In contrast, the mid-decade introduction of the pajama—which could function as both glamorous leisure suit and sleepwear—provided commentators with a more controversial version of women's trousers. Although the pajama initially made its way into the fashion stakes behind an exoticized façade, even early accounts of this fashion demonstrate a need to downplay its masculine associations: "It is not the masculine touch in fashions that so favors the pajama, for these trousers are oriental and decidedly feminine."[43] The gender-bending aspect of pajama-wearing, with its nod to the theatrical trouser role, was central to its charm as an erotically titillating but harmless offshoot of masculine women's fashions—an "amusing fantasy" that was seen to in fact strengthen heteronormative structures by stimulating desire within the domestic boundaries of the home. That said, not all examples of pajama wearing were directed toward the male heterosexual gaze. As with the tuxedo and the *Bubikopf*, numerous references in the homosexual magazines—including advertisements for pajama balls, at which every woman in trousers was promised a prize, or short stories featuring virile protagonists in short hair and silken pajamas—demonstrate that this garment not only crossed over into the subcultural realm, but carried particular meanings within this context as a signifier of same-sex desire.

As was the case with other "masculine" styles, mainstream journalists soon shifted their attention from the erotic appeal of pajamas to their role as a symbol of gender transgression. Jesting that women wear pants in order to compensate for the fact that they cannot physically *become* men, Trude John argued that although this is a fashion designed to titillate male partners, once women are actually wearing the trousers they are liable to also adopt masculine ways of thinking and behaving: "When they wear them, they talk about love in the same tone in which they would discuss changing a car tire!"[44] Here John draws on a number of stereotypes about the modern woman, including her unromantic, "objective" attitude toward heterosexual relationships and her familiarity with new technologies such as the automobile. Others were quick to echo her concerns, warning that women would not readily relinquish the power they had symbolically gained by donning trousers. Taking such arguments to an extreme, the *BIZ* explicitly situated the pajama as a sign of the ongoing and unacceptable masculinization of Germany's womanhood:

> No longer did women want to appear asexual like the angels; instead, fashion became increasingly determined to masculinize the feminine appearance. The female habit of donning men's sleepwear became increasingly widespread, and even extended to wearing these garments as morning dress.[45]

Published in 1925, the use of the past tense in this excerpt is more an example of wishful thinking than an accurate indication that this was a fashion already on the way out. More important is the way the masculinized woman is situated here as an overtly sexual being—indeed, it is the very process of masculinization that is seen to have led to her sexualization. Whereas other commentators sought to diminish the modern woman's sexual potential by situating her discursively in terms of an immature, boyish adolescence (a strategy discussed further in relation to the trouser role in chapter 4), these two examples point to a clear break with Wilhelmine bourgeois ideals of women as the asexual "angel of the house," and toward growing anxieties surrounding the nonmaternal and fiercely independent woman of the present.

As they had done for the masculine styles described above, commentators reacted to the threat of such a sexualized, masculinized modern womanhood by devising ways to restore the femininity of the trouser-wearing woman. Some chose to emphasize the pajama's luxurious and decorative femininity, and likewise that of garments such as the divided skirt (*Hosenrock*) and the beach pajama (*Strandpyjama*) that became popular in the late 1920s: "The pajama of 1926, which is only somewhat related to trousers, is feminine in effect, luxurious, and of a refined nature," wrote journalist Lily von Nagy. This process of feminization could also involve adding ornamentations such as embroidery or lace, as fashion journalists sought to distance women's trousers from any associations with feminist political goals or gender-transgressive "Amazon behavior" (*Mannweibgehaben*). In this vein, fashion writer Ruth Goetz insisted that women's trousers pose no threat to normal gender relations: "Trousers as female attire are a question of fashion, certainly born of the rhythm of the times, but not influenced by the normal relationship between the sexes, which in spite of women's work and sport continues to be based on difference and complementariness."[46] Nonetheless, a number of commentators felt compelled to set strict spatial and temporal boundaries for trouser-wearing, advising women to indulge in this fashion only in the garden, at the beach, in the bedroom, or for travel; a few warned against wearing them for anything except sport. Within these narrowly defined spheres, however, trousers gradually underwent a process of normalization and incorporation into mainstream women's wear, particularly as an element of the upper-class lady of leisure's wardrobe. As Claire Goll declared in *Sport im Bild* in 1931: "If things continue as they are, one day our grandchildren will laugh out loud when they see a photograph showing us in a skirt."[47]

The Monocle: Resisting the Male Gaze?

Anita Berber sported one while dressed as an "Eton Boy" in 1924, while a 1926 article looked back on the "Lady of 1925" gazing coolly through her eyeglass while smoking a cigarette (see Figure 1.11): for women with the requisite panache, the flamboyant monocle was the ideal complement to the tuxedo, and the finishing touch to the boyish Garçonne look.[48] The monocle's appeal can be at least partly attributed to its links to elite bohemian and intellectual subcultures of a Wildean hue—the upper-class European dandy of the late nineteenth century is barely imaginable without one. Like the cigarette, as Garber has argued, the monocle has a tradition as a "powerful—and powerfully ambivalent" signifier of erotic style within both heterosexual and homosexual contexts.[49] From an analytical perspective, it is also interesting for the way it inverts the traditional spectator position of the "male gaze," transforming the wearer from observed to observer and drawing attention to her own agency and desires.[50] I argue that the monocle functioned as a further important signifier of women's masculinization in 1920s Germany, and like the *Bubikopf*, tuxedos, and trousers, served as an important signifier of queer female desire.

Weimar contemporaries were well aware of the monocle's sexually ambiguous associations, and consequently it was almost impossible to discuss the monocle as a female accessory without also confronting larger discourses of

Figure 1.11. "The Lady of 1925." *Das Magazin,* January 1926, 54.

Source: BPK Bildagentur für Kunst, Kultur und Geschichte

masculinization and sexual alterity. An unusual attempt to counter the threat of masculinization appeared in *Die Dame* in 1927, where one M. M. Sman frames such gender performances as a psychological maneuver aimed at disguising women's underlying vulnerability and neediness:

> The appearance of the lady with a monocle can only become contentious as the culmination of that modern female type which a misunderstanding has labeled masculinized, whereas the gallant psychologist should know that under the mask of the boyish street urchin a woman's need for love and affection is doubly present, precisely because it is being so bravely denied![51]

Sman's discursive strategy neatly contains the monocle-wearing woman within a heterosexual matrix of male domination and female passivity, and reverses the arguments made two years later by Frenchwoman Joan Riviere in her famous psychoanalytic essay "Womanliness as a Masquerade." In that essay Riviere argued that women, and particularly intellectuals, use the "masquerade" of womanliness—which can be manifested in coquettish heterosexual flirtation and clothing alike—to hide their anxieties about behavior or careers considered by the wider society to be "masculine": "Womanliness therefore could be assumed and worn as a mask, both to hide the possession of masculinity and to avert the reprisals expected if she was found to possess it."[52] By taking the opposite approach, positing masculinity as the masquerade and women as secretly passive, Sman seeks to defuse the threat of gender and sexual transgression associated with the monocle-wearing woman, offering a far more conservative account of modern femininity than Riviere.

Commentators within the female homosexual subculture were, not surprisingly, less reticent about the cultural associations between the monocle, female masculinity, and sexual "inversion." During the late 1920s and early 1930s *Die Freundin* and *Garçonne* published numerous advertisements for balls and fashion parades celebrating subcultural visual styles, showcasing "our most elegant masculine women" or awarding prizes for "the most beautiful feminine woman"; some of these were specifically "monocle balls" at which patrons were offered free eyeglasses. A popular Berlin women's club bore the name "Monokel-Diele," and numerous short stories in the homosexual magazines feature monocle-clad women. In her 1928 survey of Berlin's female homosexual clubs, scene observer Ruth Roellig even describes the monocle as a compulsory addition to the masculine evening wear favored by Berlin's virile female homosexuals:

> Generally these slender, often very elegant figures dress in a suit of black cloth, consisting of a narrow, smooth skirt, and gentlemanly jacket, under which they wear a silk shirt with collar, cuffs and tie, which has lately been joined by the obligatory monocle, a small extravagance which has established itself even in distinguished bourgeois society. The smooth Eton cut is the preferred hairstyle, and one can certainly say that the sight of this somewhat

masculinized, sophisticated woman is not disagreeable, especially when combined with a young, intelligent face.[53]

Scholars of other national contexts have likewise noted the prominence of the monocle as a marker of lesbian subcultural belonging at this period. Drawing on Shari Benstock's research, for example, Garber argues that alongside the tuxedo and the cropped haircut, the monocle and the cigar/ette "are the most recognizable and readable signs of the lesbian culture of Paris" in the 1920s. In contrast, Doan's British study insists on the multiple symbolic possibilities of such signifiers, and argues that Garber's approach "forecloses interpretive possibilities and rigidly conjoins accessory and identity."[54] I would like to suggest a middle line in relation to the German sources, for although the monocle, like other "masculine" fashions at this period, *did* carry different meanings depending on context, and did not *necessarily* connote female homosexuality, it nonetheless played an important role as a signifier of virile female identities within the Weimar subculture.

Furthermore, I question the relevance to the German context of Garber's assertion that the wealthy lesbians of the early twentieth century who wore monocles and tuxedos and behaved like men "ironically reinscribed the 'male' (or the pseudo-male) as the position of power." Drawing on Lacanian psychoanalysis, Garber argues that the upward displacement of the phallus symbolized by the monocle takes on particular meanings with a female wearer: "Simultaneously a signifier of castration … and of empowerment, the monocle when worn by a *woman* emphasizes, indeed parodies, the contingent nature of the power conferred by this instrumental 'affectation.'"[55] With regard to the German sources there are two problems with this argument. Firstly, it assumes that all homosexual women who wore monocles were wealthy. Yet despite this accessory's upper-class traditions, and although it was undoubtedly easier for wealthier homosexual women to adopt masculine visual styles in their daily lives, numerous references to the monocle within Weimar homosexual magazines—which were primarily oriented toward women from lower- and middle-class socioeconomic backgrounds—show that this masculine erotic signifier belonged to an emerging female homosexual aesthetic that cut across class lines. Secondly, Garber's argument assumes a reasonably straightforward—albeit ironic—connection between female masculinity and "masculine" power, even within queer subcultures. As I discuss in chapter 3, however, questions of power and masculine privilege were fiercely contested and rarely taken for granted within the subcultural magazines, even as ironic reinscriptions. Consequently, while the erotics of the monocle in Weimar Germany drew on codes of gendered, sexual, and class alterity, often all at once, we must be cautious of associating this accessory only with lives shaped by social, cultural, or gendered privilege.

The monocle's associations with female homosexuality also lent it a certain titillating appeal within mainstream contexts. The accessory featured regularly in advertisements for Berlin clubs such as the "Eldorado," which tempted voyeuristic heterosexual patrons with the spectacle of "inverted" couples dancing within its walls, while a short story in the inaugural issue of *Das Magazin* used the monocle to help signify an urban queer underworld: "Both women ... belong to the demi-monde. One sees this in their unnaturally garish lipstick, the monocle of the one, the décolleté of the other."[56] In more brutal fashion, the satirical *Simplicissimus* linked the monocle to all manner of negative stereotypes, ranging from sexual perversion to the modern woman's rejection of maternal duties. In one image two flat-chested, high-heeled women stride across the beach in modern bathing costumes, one of them, sneering through her monocle at a well-endowed woman sitting peacefully with her child, commenting: "How bourgeois—the broad's wearing a bosom" (Figure 1.12). Unlike the overtly feminine, childbear-

Was es alles gibt!

"Wie bürgerlich — das Weib trägt Busen!"

Figure 1.12. E. Thöny, "How Bourgeois—the Broad's Wearing a Bosom," *Simplicissimus,* 18 May 1925.

Source: BPK Bildagentur für Kunst, Kultur und Geschichte

ing, and thus firmly heterosexual "broad" (*Weib*) in the foreground, these women embody female masculinization both physically and socially: they have steeled their bodies to rid themselves of breasts and curves, abandoned traditional markers of femininity such as long hair, and prefer to spend their leisure time in each other's—nonreproductive—company than in that of a man or children.

In other examples from *Simplicissimus,* the monocle serves to underline the narcissism and perversion of the modern woman, possibly referencing a 1917 lecture by Freud on "The Libido Theory and Narcissism," which addressed these same themes.[57] A 1928 cover depicts a monocled, felt-hatted woman in a skirted tuxedo studiously applying her makeup in a mirror while oblivious to the rippling manhood of the disgruntled Greek statue upon which she sits (Figure 1.13). Similarly, a two-part cartoon from the same issue entitled "Tragedy of

Figure 1.13. Karl Arnold, "This Issue Belongs to the Lady." *Simplicissimus,* 13 February 1928.

Source: BPK Bildagentur für Kunst, Kultur und Geschichte

Creation" shows, firstly, a satisfied God placing the finishing touches on a naked, long-haired Eve as Adam slumbers to one side, only to be approached in the second image by a woman wearing a suit and monocle and sporting a cigarette, evincing the disgusted cry: "I'm not spared a thing!"[58] It is not necessary for the cartoonist to explicitly link this woman's gender transgression to her sexuality—her masculine dress, accessories, and body language, combined with the absence of Adam, are enough to signal to contemporary audiences that this was yet another example of the nonreproductive plague of "inversion" threatening Germany's womanhood.

Given that cartoonists in mainstream periodicals assumed audience familiarity with stereotypes of female sex-gender inversion, it is quite possible that the monocle's explicit masculine and homosexual associations accelerated its demise. Supporting this argument is a further cartoon from late 1932, which features three women in a room sharply decorated and furnished in the style of New Objectivity (Figure 1.14). Sitting primly to the left in a long, unadorned dress and nervously petting her dog is the virginal "Hilde." To her right are two somewhat older women: the first, overweight and over-accessorized, briefly looks up from her magazine to extend her pointy nails toward Hilde in a mildly threatening gesture of comfort; the second, a slender, curveless woman suggestive of Garçonne stereotypes, stands behind the first—their proximity pointing to a sexual relationship—balancing a cigarette between her fingers as she squints condescendingly at Hilde through her monocle. The caption highlights the growing intolerance toward such "perverse" displays of female gender and sexuality in the late Weimar period, and the increasing cultural hegemony of the "normal," overtly feminine, and heterosexual woman: "You see, Hilde, you no longer need to be dismayed about not being perverse. Normal is quite in fashion again this winter."[59]

For a brief period in the mid 1920s it had been acceptable for women to challenge traditional ideas about who should be looked at, and who should do the looking, by donning the type of eyewear long associated with male stereotypes of the dandy and "masculine" intellectual pursuits. Yet by the early 1930s, increasing cultural conservatism was beginning to dictate that women again become objects rather than subjects of the gaze. As journalist Anita Daniel remarked in 1931: "Women with a decidedly clear gaze are sometimes a little uninviting to men."[60] Although the monocle retained its appeal within the female homosexual subculture as a signifier of "virile" gender identity, the aura of perversion that increasingly surrounded it in the later Weimar years helped to confirm its demise as a mainstream fashion accessory. The monocle might have suited the masculine tuxedo of 1925, but it did not complement the long evening dress of 1930, nor could it compete with the feminine vulnerability of "unprotected shortsightedness."[61]

Berlin W

(E. Schilling)

„Sieh mal, Hilde, du brauchst nicht mehr betrübt zu sein, weil du nicht pervers bist. Das Normale ist diesen Winter direkt wieder Mode."

Figure 1.14. E. Schilling, "Berlin W." *Simplicissimus,* 27 November 1932, 417.
Source: BPK Bildagentur für Kunst, Kultur und Geschichte

Dandies and Cavemen: The "Feminization" of Men's Fashions

If the women become more masculine, the young men must become more feminine.[62]

Concerns about the feminization of male fashions formed an important counterpart to the widely publicized masculinization of women's visual styles in Weimar Germany. And just as the latter formed an important discursive space in which to negotiate women's changing place in postwar society, coverage of men's clothing developments was often less about aesthetics and more about providing an opportunity for contemporaries to reflect on the current state of German manhood. I noted earlier that men's gender performances were generally viewed as more stable than women's at this period; as *Die Dame* remarked in 1925, "for every one female impersonator there are thousands of male impersonators."[63] Nonetheless, men's fashions experienced a minor crisis during the mid Weimar period, as effeminate, "dandy" styles clashed with more traditional, "rakish" visions of masculinity.

Just as the popularity of the monocle as a female accessory harked back to nineteenth-century stereotypes of the elegant, narcissistic, and gender-ambiguous dandy, Weimar men's fashions saw a revival of this aesthetic model. At least some commentators saw the unashamedly fashion-conscious dandy as a positive, trendsetting figure: "the social ideal of his epoch."[64] Interwar Germany was considered particularly conducive to such feminized models of masculinity: as *Sport im Bild* remarked, "some periods are decidedly dandesque." Above all, it was the generation of men who had come of age during the 1920s, and thus avoided the masculine initiation ground of warfare, who were considered most likely to be afflicted by such fashion-consciousness: "Particularly the young men: they are the real fashion slaves, they consider it unworthy of discussion that one could deviate from fashion."[65]

That reports of an increasingly feminized, fashion-conscious German manhood should focus on the younger generation is hardly surprising, for studies have shown that it was the nation's youth who most strongly embodied the new gender order of equality, companionate marriage, and a sober, pragmatic approach to issues of love and sex.[66] The dandy, many thought, was a fitting model for the "soft" masculinity that characterized this younger generation, and at a larger level, the defeated nation itself. He was, furthermore, an appropriate aesthetic counterpart to the masculine woman, with both cultural types situated outside of traditional gender roles and heteronormative structures. Accordingly, middlebrow fiction author Wolfgang von Lengerke insisted on the homosocial interests of the male dandy in an article for *Sport im Bild* when he wrote that: "d'Orsay was not a dandy because he conquered the women. A dandy is only interested in conquering his own type."[67]

With the threat of male homosexuality perceptible just beneath the surface of discussions of the effeminate dandy, a number of commentators drew on stereotypes of male sexual perversion in ways that again highlight the German public's increasing familiarity with sexological ideas. In 1930 the satirical *Ulk* published a cartoon, "Separation of the Sexes," showing two clubs for female and male homosexuals, respectively. While the women stride around or embrace one another on the dance floor in their sharp suits, monocles, and short-cropped hair, their male counterparts lounge foppishly against each other near the bar, their tight-waisted suits, womanly curves, and androgynous features all reaffirming popular associations between homosexuality and gender inversion. This and many similar images point to a growing discomfort with effeminate depictions of masculinity by the latter half of the 1920s, a trend McCormick likewise observes when he notes that the "crisis of male subjectivity," said by some critics to have thoroughly pervaded Weimar cultural output, encompassed not only male trauma and concerns about impotence and infertility in the wake of the war, but also fears about latent homosexuality.[68] Increasingly, conservative commentators were contrasting the allegedly weak, infertile young men of the present with the soldiers of their father's generation, viewing them as symptomatic of a larger national decline.

The feminization of men's fashions provoked a backlash similar to that evident in women's visual styles, although on a much smaller scale and from an earlier date: from the mid 1920s we can already see a renewed focus on more masculine, "rakish" (*salopp*) looks. Leading fashion journalist Elsa Herzog described this development in terms of a "crisis" in men's visual styles, torn between the feminine slenderness of the dandy and a more solid, cumbersome look that emphasized comfort, simplicity, and a return to the manly fashions and facial hair of the 1880s (as noted earlier, an emphasis on male hair was also a response to the *Bubikopf* style). This aesthetic conflict was given visual expression in 1924 by *Dame* fashion illustrator Ernst Dryden, who juxtaposed a row of slender, dandesque men waving cigarettes and twiddling walking canes with four solidly built, cigar-smoking figures with mustaches, hands in pockets, and hats pulled firmly around their ears.[69] As early as 1925, Hubert Miketta in *Das Magazin* declared that the turn toward "Anglo-Saxon" simplicity had won out over more decorative male fashion principles, describing a transformation from the "excessive militaristic slenderness" of the war years toward a more solid build and civilian informality in the present. By the late 1920s and early 1930s a clear move toward overtly masculine styles for men was evident, characterized by dark fabrics and bulky, virile male models.[70]

The most obvious sign of a backlash against the feminized male in the late-Weimar media was a wave of images featuring exaggeratedly masculine, hairy-chested "children of nature" (*Naturburschen*) and "cavemen" (see Figure 1.15). By the early 1930s variations on the caveman stereotype were popular among

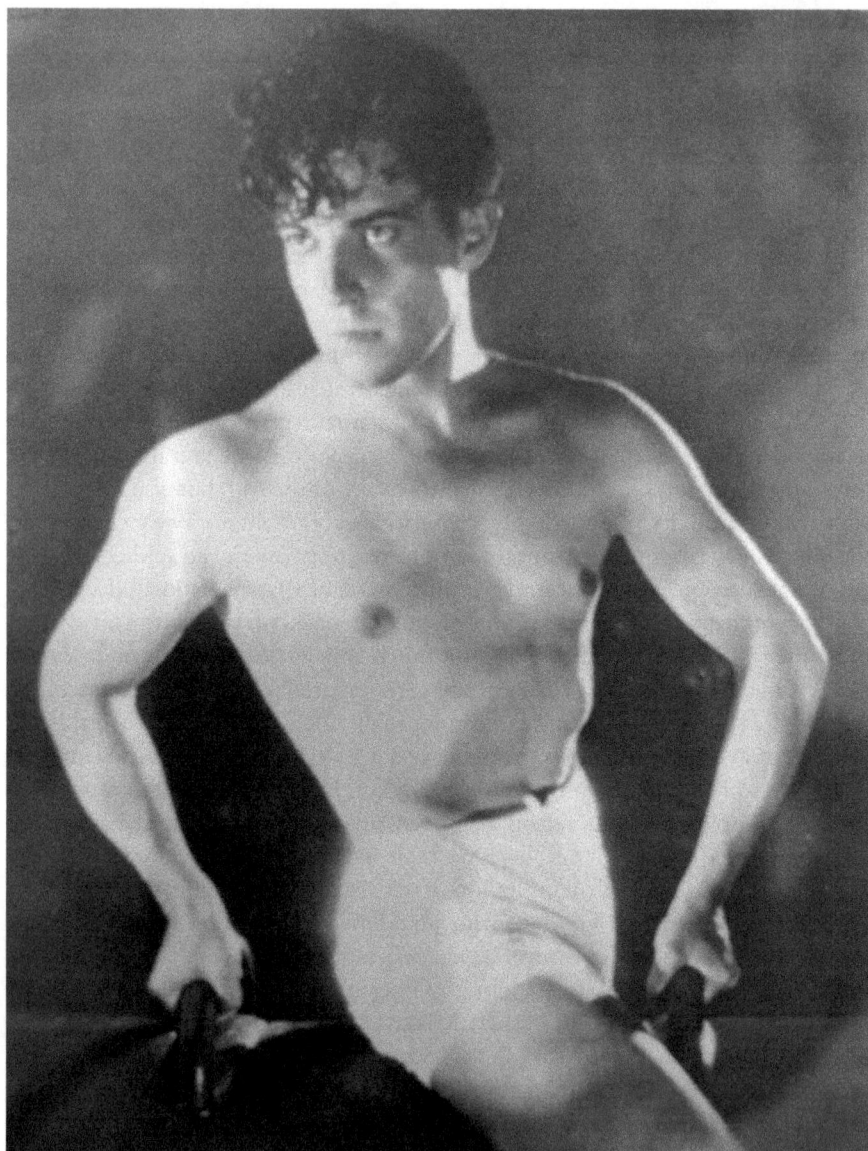

Figure 1.15. "*Naturburschen* wanted…" *Uhu,* August 1931, 25.
Source: BPK Bildagentur für Kunst, Kultur und Geschichte

fashion movers and shakers on both sides of the Atlantic and reportedly were striking a chord with young women. Describing how exotic film actor Ramon Novarro had successfully transformed himself into such a *Naturbursche* in his recent films, *Uhu* detailed the demise of the Germanic dandy in no uncertain terms—symbolized here by the sentimental protagonist of Goethe's classic novel, *The Sorrows of Young Werther:*

> So Werther's time is up. Stepping into the place of the delightful dreamer in blue coattails … is the caveman of our cocktail parties dressed in severe black and white, whose trained heart never beats any faster, neither during sporting activity nor even in the closest proximity to female creatures.

Clearly, by 1931 the feminine man was no longer "in," while his "rakish" and "caveman" successors were demanding more passive feminine mates: "Girls are once again dreaming of strong male arms."[71]

Yet just as elements of women's masculine visual styles continued to influence women's fashions even into the 1930s, the feminine man did not disappear entirely. In late 1930 *Uhu* not only continued to advocate the "tuxedo pajama" for women, but suggested that gentleman attend to the "feminine touch" via close-fitting silk morning robes.[72] As late as February 1933, several weeks after the National Socialist seizure of power, the same magazine published an article describing the decidedly camp young man of the modern metropolis. Representing his generation, "Georg" has moved from the countryside to the industrialized metropolis and is shaped by the "feminizing" influences of his new environment: he not only cooks, cleans, and darns his own socks; he also views women as equals and colleagues; prefers to date those who pay their own way; and, having grown up with the legacies of female emancipation and male war destruction, is determined to forge a different path from the militaristic, patriarchal men of his father's generation. This sensitive figure is portrayed as an ideal partner for the modern woman and a pioneer of a new male type, who manages to adopt certain positive feminine characteristics "without thereby forfeiting the best of his own sex." As the author optimistically suggests, while such men may not have experienced the same degree of visual transformation as women during the past decade, they have nonetheless changed in more subtle ways: "in their habits, their taste, their way of thought, they have changed just as much as women have."[73] Thus despite widespread calls for more traditionally gendered attire in the late Weimar period, this "return" to prewar gender ideals and appearances remained incomplete, as I explore in the final section of this chapter.

From New Objectivity to a "New Morality": Women's Fashions in the Late Weimar Period

> Things are probably … not as bad as they look. After all, this disintegration of bourgeois tradition has so far only seized the city dwellers. Even the *Bubikopf* is a rare and conspicuous phenomenon fifty kilometers outside of Berlin. In Rathenow and Angermünde, in Küstrin and in Kottbus there are still braids and there are still Gretchen.[74]

This 1932 observation on the differences between rural and urban attitudes toward "modern" fashions such as the *Bubikopf* points to the most pervasive trend within late-Weimar fashion discourse: the return to clearly polarized, traditional gender ideals for men and women. Just as this author situates the *Bubikopf* in the cities and looks to the provinces for comforting images of preindustrial, middle-class Germanic womanhood, it is no accident that the return of the Gretchen in late-Weimar fashion discourse coincided with the National Socialist seizure of power and increasing censorship of the German media, presaging the anti-Semitic takeover of the Jewish fashion houses of the metropolis.[75] Although the trend toward more feminine styles for women and more masculine styles for men was echoed on an international scale, it took on particular meanings within the German context under the increasing influence of Nazi ideals of a preindustrial, patriarchal society in which women's place was defined by the dictum "children, kitchen, church" (*Kinder, Küche, Kirche*). Describing this increasingly conservative and racialized feminine aesthetic, Susanne Meyer-Büser observes that the transformation from "New Woman" to "New *German* Woman" is symbolic of a broader transformation in societal values at the end of the Weimar Republic.[76] After a decade of experimentation, there was a widespread desire to return to a more ordered, "normal," maternal vision of femininity, which in turn became coded as more German and stood for a larger desire for stability and clarity in public life.

Fashion commentators expressed relief at the long dresses and grown-out *Bubikopf* haircuts that symbolized the conservative turn in women's fashions. This soon came to be known as "the new fashion," and it was closely associated with ideas about a so-called *neue Sittlichkeit,* or "new morality." Exhaustion with masculine women's fashions had come to be considered as symptomatic of a more general exhaustion with modern urbanized life, and in particular with the sober, rational aesthetic of New Objectivity seen to most definitively characterize Weimar modernity: "But too much tomboyishness gets on one's nerves in the long run. Wherever one looked, wherever one listened: 'objectivity.' … Tired of too much 'masculinity,' women once again want to be pretty, they once again want to be real women."[77]

Just weeks after the National Socialists had taken control of the German parliament in 1933, another *Uhu* article used photographs to help tell the "story of the braid that was chopped off and then grew back" (Figure 1.16). The first image shows the masculine woman of 1925 with a tight Eton crop, "a style from the years when the highest ideal was to be confused with a man." The second shows the same woman in 1933 with a wavy, feminine cut, long earrings, and makeup, while the third photograph incorporates German nationalist stereotypes, featuring a woman with her hair parted down the middle and a long braid wound around her head, with the caption: "The new—good old—Gretchen style: the latest in hair fashion." The accompanying commentary describes how "a woman

Die Geschichte vom abgeschnittenen und wieder langgewachsenen Haar:

Eine Dame aus dem Jahre 1925 mit Eaton-Schnitt . . . Dieselbe Dame acht Jahre später: 1933

Frisur aus den Jahren, da es das höchste Ideal war, mit dem Mann verwechselt zu werden.

Acht Jahre später der auf Fraulichkeit frisierte Kopf derselben Frau.

Die neue — gute alte — Gretchenfrisur

Das Neueste auf dem Gebiet der Haarmode.

78

Figure 1.16. "The Story of the Braid that was Chopped Off and then Grew Back." *Uhu*, March 1933, 78.

Source: BPK Bildagentur für Kunst, Kultur und Geschichte

has firstly and above all to be a woman, a charming, desirable woman. And with great skill they are transforming their severe, austere look into one that is more womanly."[78] Whereas the *Bubikopf* had once symbolized women's independence, the return of the Aryan Gretchen stereotype was widely viewed as indicative of German women's welcome realization that female emancipation was always an impossible goal.

Widespread anxiety and hardship following the economic crisis of 1929 and the increasing social and cultural influence of the National Socialists must both be seen as contributing to this late-Weimar push toward traditionally gendered and Germanic female stereotypes. Yet despite the efforts of some commentators, the end of the republic did not signal the end of masculine fashions for women in any straightforward way. As I have demonstrated, the extensive experimentation with alternative ways of wearing one's gender that had characterized 1920s women's fashions continued to influence clothing styles into the 1930s. Furthermore, it is too simplistic to explain the demise of masculine women's fashions in late Weimar Germany purely in terms of social conservatism and xenophobia, for as many Weimar-era commentators themselves acknowledged, this development had many different causes, of which the incessant push for innovation in fashion was but one. The move away from overtly "masculine" styles had begun as early as 1926, in the middle of a period of relative economic and political stability that lasted from 1924 to the onset of the Depression in 1929, and long before the National Socialists had gained a definitive stronghold over German culture and society. Accordingly, any explanation that relies too heavily on a straightforward appropriation of National Socialist ideology remains inadequate.

Moreover, notions such as "fashion" and "modernity" by no means became defunct under National Socialism, as two recent studies have demonstrated. Dismissing the historical narrative of "*Bubikopf* to Gretchen" as an "unexamined stereotype," Bertschik demonstrates that Nazi fashion discourse was in fact "exceedingly diverse," not least because of its desire to remain viable at an international level. Similarly, Irene Guenther has shown that Nazi fashions consisted of a unique blend of modern aesthetics and innovation and of anti-modern tradition and assimilation, resulting in the development of several female fashion types that went far beyond the Nazi propaganda of clean-scrubbed women in dirndls. Both scholars observe that it was in the interests of National Socialist propaganda to cultivate a specifically German *Hochmode* or high fashion (a Germanized form of haute couture), whether as a means of glamorizing the new Nazi elite or of appealing to wealthier and more educated women. Furthermore, Bertschik demonstrates how particular masculine styles for women reemerged in the Third Reich in the uniforms of the League of German Girls (Bund Deutscher Mädel, BDM) and the work clothes of female munitions workers, as part of a larger "uniformization" and "masculinization" of German society at this period.[79] Thus, rather than falling victim to a simple return to traditional ideas about femininity and masculinity in the late Weimar period, some of the more successful, practical, and stylish aspects of the mid 1920s boom in gender-bending fashions became incorporated into new aesthetic norms.

Furthermore, although traditional feminine ideals came to dominate late-Weimar fashion coverage, some commentators protested against this trend, seeing it as symbolic of a reversal of the political and social gains made by women during the past decade. Popular novelist and journalist Vicki Baum called for a "strike" on this issue, while fashion journalist Stephanie Kaul lamented an aesthetic development that aimed to turn "athletically trained, comrade-oriented women" back into poor, slavish creatures. Attacking the increasing conservatism of the "new morality," commentators in mainstream and subcultural periodicals alike complained at length about the excessive decorativeness and impracticality of the "new fashion," and even the fashion bible *Die Dame* published a cartoon satirizing the "new inobjectivity" of fashion, featuring a woman in a flouncy dress standing in a room furnished in stark Bauhaus style.[80]

In a newly democratic society confronted with regular economic and political crises, and negotiating unprecedented freedoms within the cultural arena, the desire for stability in at least one realm—that of gender relations—can be seen as a central factor behind the late 1920s push toward familiar, unambiguously feminine styles. The mid-1920s emergence of masculine fashions for women provided a visual forum in which German men and women could confront, explore, and attack the specter of the New Woman, who had not only come to symbolize the rapid transformations in post–World War I gender relations, but was also inextricably linked to less tangible developments affecting German life. This chapter has argued that concerns about women's encroachment into "male" spheres of action were given voice within fashion discourse through critiques of masculine visual styles and recommendations that women reintroduce more feminine styles into their wardrobes—a development that took place in reverse in men's fashion. Yet even though by 1933 the masculine woman had been largely replaced in fashion spreads by more feminine, conservative ideals, the semantic associations of descriptors such as "feminine" had changed for good and no longer encompassed the corsets, frills, and waist-length hair of the prewar era. In an analysis of women's citizenship at this period, Kathleen Canning argues that we must probe the ways in which efforts to restore familiar gender structures and ideologies remained incomplete, "to challenge this sense of closure, and to explore the persistence of gender crisis into the later years of the Republic."[81] Fashion developments had to cater to the more slender, practical, and athletic image, lifestyle, and demands of the modern woman even following the onset of the Nazi era, as the sartorial experimentations of the 1920s continued to influence and inform German fashions, as well as ideas about German womanhood, beyond the Weimar period.

The push to recuperate femininity for women in late-Weimar fashion existed alongside other, less normative interpretations of women's visual styles, particularly among the emerging female homosexual subculture. Masculine sartorial signifiers continued to hold particular significance within this context well beyond the mid 1920s, an argument I develop in subsequent chapters. Whereas Doan pinpoints the 1928 Hall trial as the moment at which a distinct lesbian subculture emerged in Britain, arguing that the ensuing public awareness of lesbianism led to the quick demise of masculine fashions, I have demonstrated that this was not the case in Germany, where the reading public had been familiar with stereotypes of the masculine female homosexual since at least the beginning of the Weimar era. Associations with sexual inversion certainly did not prevent the rise to prominence of masculine women's fashions in mid-1920s Germany—on the contrary, they may even have briefly contributed to their erotic and cosmopolitan appeal. However, the late-Weimar media's increasing attention to the threat of sexual inversion and perversion may well have contributed to the subsequent demise of such styles, as the weight of nonconformity became too much for most women to bear.

The next chapter continues this exploration of the masculine woman in the Weimar media in relation to the figure of the female athlete. Although there are numerous parallels in the way the media negotiated female masculinities in the contexts of fashion and sport, the explicit thematization of the female body in athletic discourse lent additional urgency to comparisons between men and women in modern German society, and to concerns about women's strength, independence, and refusal to restrict themselves to the role of wife and mother.

Notes

1. See e.g. Anne Hollander, *Sex and Suits* (New York: Alfred A. Knopf, 1994); Barbara Vinken, *Mode nach der Mode: Kleid und Geist am Ende des 20. Jahrhunderts* (Frankfurt/Main: Fischer, 1993).
2. See e.g. Ruth Barnes and Joanne B. Eicher, eds., *Dress and Gender: Making and Meaning in Cultural Contexts* (Providence: Berg, 1992); on the masculine connotations of short skirts see Gesa Kessemeier, *Sportlich, sachlich, männlich: Das Bild der 'Neuen Frau' in den Zwanziger Jahren: Zur Konstruktion geschlechtsspezifischer Körperbilder in der Mode der Jahre 1920 bis 1929* (Dortmund: Ed. Ebersbach, 2000), 98.
3. Hollander, *Sex and Suits*, 127; see also Julia Bertschik, *Mode und Moderne: Kleidung als Spiegel des Zeitgeistes in der deutschsprachigen Literatur (1770–1945)* (Cologne: Böhlau, 2005), 91–111; Gundula Wolter, *Hosen, weiblich* (Marburg: Jonas, 1994), 82–102.
4. Kessemeier, *Sportlich, sachlich, männlich*; Bertschik, *Mode;* Sabine Hake, "In the Mirror of Fashion," in Ankum, *Women in the Metropolis*, 196.
5. "Etwas vom Bubikopfe," *Das Magazin,* no. 14, October 1925, 100.
6. Hake, "In the Mirror," 187.
7. E. H[erzog], "Frisuren," *Sport im Bild,* no. 2, 21 January 1921, 100.
8. "Die Bubenkopf-Epidemie," *Berliner Illustrirte Zeitung,* no. 23, 8 June 1924, 639; "Die Mode: Alle tragen die Bubenkopf-Frisur!" *Die Dame,* no. 17, Late May 1924, 2.
9. "Simsons Rache [sic]," *Die Dame,* no. 11, 2nd February Issue 1925, 9.

10. Thea Malten, "Hie Zopf, hie Bubenkopf," *Das Magazin*, no. 10, June 1925, 78–85. While Dagover rails heavily against the *Bubikopf* here, by December of the same year she was pictured newly shorn in the *BIZ*: "Der Bubenkopf: Die Alten gegen die Jungen," *Berliner Illustrirte Zeitung*, no. 49, 6 December 1925, 1648.

11. "Bubenkopf oder nicht?" *Berliner Illustrirte Zeitung*, no. 26, 28 June 1925, 832.

12. Anita [Daniel], "Die Vermännlichung der Frau," *Berliner Illustrirte Zeitung*, no. 35, 31 August 1924, 997; see also Trude John, "Die männliche Frau," *Das Magazin*, no. 24, August 1926, 760; "Simsons Rache," 9f. A more extensive contemporary discussion of the symbolic relationship between hair length, masculinization, and female emancipation can be found in H. Handke, *Der Bubikopf von Agamemnon bis Stresemann* (Berlin: Verlag für Kulturpolitik, 1926), 93ff.

13. Roberts, *Civilization without Sexes*, 87.

14. "Variationen über den Smoking: Die Wirkung einer Zeitungsnachricht," *Die Dame*, no. 13, 2nd March Issue 1926, 8; see also "Bleibt der Bubenkopf?" *Die Dame*, no. 1, 1st October Issue 1925, 2f; "Alles ist schon dagewesen!" *Das Magazin*, no. 26, October 1926, 152.

15. "Wieviel Männer sind hier dabei?" *Berliner Illustrirte Zeitung*, no. 30, 26 July 1925, 933; "Humor/Irrtum beim Frisör," *Berliner Illustrirte Zeitung*, no. 24, 13 June 1926, 763; "Das verkannte Geschlecht," *Uhu*, no. 10, July 1926, 103; "Das Liebespaar," *Uhu*, no. 5, February 1933, 5.

16. Halberstam, *Female Masculinity*, 23.

17. A short ironic verse emphasized this merging: "Motorbike, pillion seat/Bubikopf in identical cut/tortoiseshell glasses. / Bodies curved flowingly/sweaters striped similarly/Spring idyll." Anita [Daniel], "Modernes Paar," *Berliner Illustrirte Zeitung*, no. 19, 9 May 1926, 608.

18. "Eine Schreckensnachricht," *Berliner Illustrirte Zeitung*, no. 41, 12 October 1924, 1216.

19. "Der Mann im Barte," *Berliner Illustrirte Zeitung*, no. 49, 7 December 1924, 1472.

20. See Hanna Hacker, *Frauen und Freundinnen: Studien zur "weiblichen Homosexualität" am Beispiel Österreich 1870–1938* (Weinheim and Basel: Beltz Verlag, 1987); Schader, *Virile*.

21. The undercover lives of lesbians under National Socialism are explored in Claudia Schoppmann, *Days of Masquerade: Life Stories of Lesbians during the Third Reich* (New York: Columbia University Press, 1996).

22. See e.g. Käte-Karl in "Eine Bubikopftragödie," *Die Freundin*, no. 8, 15 April 1925, 2; Charlotte Paul, "Meinungsaustausch über Tagesfragen: Für oder gegen den Bubikopf," *Die Freundin*, no. 6, 19 March 1928, 7.

23. Paulowna, "Meinungsaustausch über Tagesfragen: Für oder gegen den Bubikopf," *Die Freundin*, no. 7, 2 April 1928, 6.

24. Trude John, "Der entthronte Bubikopf," *Das Magazin*, no. 36, August 1927, 1258.

25. St. K[aul], "Pariser Frisuren für die verschiedenen Frauentypen," *Die Dame*, no. 1, 1st October Issue 1930, 46.

26. Johanna Marbach, "Was trägt die elegante Frau?" *Sport im Bild*, no. 16, 22 April 1921, 549.

27. J. Th[al], "Die Sommermode," *Die Dame*, no. 16, 3rd April Issue 1926, 18.

28. "Nun aber genug! Gegen die Vermännlichung der Frau," *Berliner Illustrirte Zeitung*, no. 13, 29 March 1925, 389.

29. "Was sagen Sie bloß zu Fräulein Mia?" *Berliner Illustrirte Zeitung*, no. 46, 13 November 1927, 1841 (cover); Petro, *Joyless Streets*, 107. Responses to this competition are discussed in chapter 3.

30. For theoretical discussions of the "bathroom problem" see Kath Browne, "Genderism and the Bathroom Problem: (Re)materialising Sexed Sites, (Re)creating Sexed Bodies," *Gender, Place and Culture* 11, no. 3 (2004): 338; Halberstam, *Female Masculinity*, 23.

31. "Herrlich am Vormittag/Fraulich am Nachmittag," *Die Dame*, no. 18, 2nd May Issue 1925, 22; "Die elegante Frau von heute: Am Vormittag und—dieselbe (mit weißer Perücke) am

Abend—!" *Das Magazin,* no. 14, October 1925, 74f. Kessemeier also discusses how fashion magazines divided a woman's day into "masculine" and "feminine" periods in *Sportlich, sachlich, männlich,* 100ff., 204–6.

32. Julie Elias, "Was man auf Reisen trägt," *Sport im Bild,* no. 12, 11 June 1926, 531.

33. Marjorie Garber, *Vested Interests: Cross-dressing and Cultural Anxiety* (London: Routledge, 1992), 70; Hake, "In the Mirror," 199.

34. L. M., "Freundinnenliebe," *Die Freundin,* no. 15, 9 October 1929, 2; Käthe Seegebarth-Wundram, "Wiedergefunden," *Garçonne,* no. 12, 10 June 1931, 3. Although dates were not always printed on issues of *Garçonne,* where these could be established with reasonable certainty they are cited together with the issue number for greater clarity.

35. Gertrud Lehnert, *Wenn Frauen Männerkleider tragen: Geschlecht und Maskerade in Literatur und Geschichte* (Munich: dtv, 1997), 158.

36. Laura Doan, *Fashioning Sapphism: The Origins of a Modern English Lesbian Culture* (New York: Columbia University Press, 2001), xii, 122ff., and passim.

37. J. Th[al], [Fashion pages] *Die Dame,* no. 2, 2nd October Issue 1931, 18.

38. Kessemeier, *Sportlich, sachlich, männlich,* 111, 116; see also Hollander, *Sex and Suits,* 97f., 127.

39. Dinah Nelken, "Die Auferstehung der Frau," *Sport im Bild,* no. 4, 15 February 1930, 223.

40. St. K., "Die neue Mode," *Die Dame,* no. 13, 2nd March Issue 1933, 10.

41. "Garçonne-Moden," *Das Magazin,* no. 2, October 1924, 204–6.

42. Käte Hertz, "~~Der Rock~~ Die HOSE SIEGT in der Sportmode," *Frau und Gegenwart,* no. 37, 13 September 1927, 13; "Die Frau in Hosen," *Das Magazin,* no. 5, January 1925, 85. On the history of pants in relation to women's cycling see Bertschik, *Mode,* 111–17; Ellen Gruber Garvey, "Reframing the Bicycle: Advertising-Supported Magazines and Scorching Women," *American Quarterly* 47, no. 1 (1995): 66–101; Wolter, *Hosen, weiblich,* 153–69; and on women's riding attire see Hollander, *Sex and Suits,* 73ff.

43. "Pyjamas," *Die Dame,* no. 5, 2nd November Issue 1924, 19.

44. Trude John, "Hosenparade: Eine Sammlung amüsanter Hosenrollen," *Das Magazin,* no. 72, August 1930, 5031ff.

45. "Nun aber genug," 389.

46. Lily von Nagy, "Die Frau im Pyjama," *Uhu,* no. 3, December 1925, 48, 50; Ruth Goetz, "Die Frau in Hosen," *Das Magazin,* no. 31, March 1927, 683ff. On the "feminization" of women's trousers see also Kessemeier, *Sportlich, sachlich, männlich,* 220f.

47. Claire Goll, "Maskerade von morgens bis Mitternacht," *Sport im Bild,* no. 6, 24 March 1931, 340.

48. "Garçonne-Moden," 204; Hubert Miketta, "Der Typ der Dame von gestern und von übermorgen," *Das Magazin,* no. 17, January 1926, 54.

49. Garber, *Vested Interests,* 152. On the sexual ambiguity of the dandy see also Rhonda K. Garelick, *Rising Star: Dandyism, Gender, and Performance in the fin de siècle* (Princeton: Princeton University Press, 1998), 3–14; Vinken, *Mode nach der Mode,* 25–31.

50. I am drawing here on analyses of the "male gaze" and female spectatorship by feminist film theorists, as well as Anke Gleber's arguments on the female *flâneur,* whom she argues offered "a resistant gaze … and a subject position that stands in opposition to women's traditional status as an image on the screens and in the streets": *Art of Taking a Walk,* 188; see also Laura Mulvey, "Visual Pleasure and Narrative Cinema," in *Film Theory and Criticism: Introductory Readings,* ed. Gerald Mast, Marshall Cohen, and Leo Braudy (New York: Oxford University Press, 1999), 746–57; Mary Ann Doane, "Film and the Masquerade," in Mast et al., *Film Theory and Criticism: Introductory Readings,* 758–72.

51. M. M. Sman, "Die Dame und das Monokel," *Die Dame,* no. 9, 2nd January Issue 1927, 45.

52. Riviere, "Womanliness as a Masquerade," reprinted in Anna Tripp, ed., *Gender* (Houndmills, Basingstoke: Palgrave, 2000), 133. On the relationship between 1920s women's fashions and

theories of masquerade, see also Jane Gaines and Charlotte Herzog, *Fabrications: Costume and the Female Body* (New York: Routledge, 1990), 1–27; Petro, *Joyless Streets,* 114ff.

53. Roellig, reprinted in Meyer, ed., *Lila Nächte,* 17.
54. Garber, *Vested Interests,* 153; Doan, *Fashioning Sapphism,* 108.
55. Garber, *Vested Interests,* 154f.
56. F. Wolfgang, "Cocain," *Das Magazin,* no. 1, October 1924, 52.
57. Sigmund Freud, "The Libido Theory and Narcissism," in *Introductory Lectures on Psychoanalysis,* ed. James Strachey and Angela Richards (London: Penguin, 1973), 461–81.
58. O. Gulbransson, "Schöpfungstragödie," *Simplicissimus,* no. 46, 13 February 1928, 620.
59. E. Schilling, "Berlin W," *Simplicissimus,* no. 35, 27 November 1932, 417.
60. Anita [Daniel], "Die Dame mit Brille," *Die Dame,* no. 24, 2nd August Issue 1931, 3.
61. Ibid., 4.
62. "Juanita Tanner ist verliebt in die jungen Männer der Großstädte," *Uhu,* no. 5, February 1933, 57.
63. "Der Damen-Imitator," *Die Dame,* no. 24, 2nd August Issue 1925, 15.
64. Wolfgang von Lengerke, "Das Mysterium des Dandy," *Sport im Bild,* no. 1, 9 January 1930, 25.
65. B. E. Lüthge, "Dandies," *Sport im Bild,* no. 48, 3 December 1920, 1349; "Der Bubenkopf: Eine alltägliche Geschichte," *Berliner Illustrirte Zeitung,* no. 24, 14 June 1925, 742.
66. Hermand and Trommler, *Kultur der Weimarer Republik,* 80–92; Detlev Peukert, *The Weimar Republic: The Crisis of Classical Modernity,* trans. Richard Deveson (London: Penguin, 1991), 86–104.
67. Lengerke, "Das Mysterium des Dandy," 25.
68. "Trennung der Geschlechter," *Ulk,* no. 14, 4 April 1930, 106; McCormick refers here particularly to post–World War II critics such as Peter Gay and Theodor Adorno: *Gender and Sexuality,* 56, 98.
69. Elsa Herzog, "Der neue saloppe Stil des Herrn," *Sport im Bild,* no. 17, 5 September 1924, 990; Dryden, "Elegantiasis: Ein Kapitel von der Herrenmode. Text und Zeichnungen von Dryden-Wien," *Berliner Illustrirte Zeitung,* no. 28, 13 July 1924, 800.
70. Hubert Miketta, "Der tägliche Anzug des Herrn: Eine modische Plauderei von Hubert Miketta," *Das Magazin,* no. 11, July 1925, 66. On this development see also Petro, *Joyless Streets,* 124; Bertschik, *Mode,* 223f. and 301f.; Kessemeier, *Sportlich, sachlich, männlich,* 223f.
71. Mary Lucy, "Naturburschen gesucht," *Uhu,* no. 11, August 1931, 27, 30.
72. "Laßt Fotos sprechen! Fotografien als Zeitkritik," *Uhu,* no. 2, December 1930, 32.
73. "Juanita Tanner," 57f. This article was presumably intended as a commentary on a contemporary book by Willson Whitman, published in the US under the pseudonym "Juanita Tanner": *The Intelligent Man's Guide to Marriage and Celibacy* (Bobbs-Merrill Co., 1929).
74. Julius Bab, "Gretchen: Die schönste deutsche Frauengestalt," *Uhu,* no. 6, March 1932, 49.
75. On the fate of Jewish fashion houses see Irene Guenther, *Nazi chic? Fashioning Women in the Third Reich* (Oxford: Berg, 2004), chap. 5.
76. Susanne Meyer-Büser, ed., *Bubikopf und Gretchenzopf: die Frau der zwanziger Jahre* (Heidelberg: Edition Braus, 1995), 8.
77. Stephanie Kaul, "Wer ist eigentlich an dem langen Kleid schuld?" *Uhu,* no. 1, October 1930, 36, see also 34ff.
78. "Die Geschichte vom abgeschnittenem und wieder angewachsenen Zopf," *Uhu,* no. 6, March 1933, 78f.
79. Bertschik, *Mode,* 274, 276, 284, 288–311; Guenther, *Nazi chic,* 91f. and passim.
80. Baum cited in Bertschik, *Mode,* 196; Kaul, "Wer ist eigentlich an dem langen Kleid schuld," 32–26; Trier, "Zeitgegensätze: Neue Sachlichkeit in der Wohnung—neue Unsachlichkeit in der Mode," *Die Dame,* no. 3, 1st November Issue 1929, 18.
81. Canning, "Claiming Citizenship," 223.

Chapter 2

"IN THE BEGINNING THERE WAS SPORT"
The Masculinized Female Athlete

Certainly, much has been written and said about this "masculine woman." That there is something masculine about her appearance, her clothing, her behavior is indisputable, and the reason for this lies in our age of sport. ... For it is impossible to characterize a sex as "weak" when a steadily increasing number of its representatives swings half hundred-weights around in the air like cherries, jumps two meters high, ... can compete with the fish in swimming and the birds in flying, a sex that drives, cycles, rides horses, dances, plays tennis, polo, golf; that hunts, rows, boxes, climbs mountains and up onto the pillion of a motorcycle!

Trude John, *Das Magazin,* August 1926

*I*n this 1926 article from the popular periodical *Das Magazin,* journalist Trude John draws clear links between the cultural phenomenon of the masculine woman and women's growing participation in sport. Women's masculinization is posited not merely as a matter of appearances and clothing, but as directly related to increasing levels of physical—and by extension, political—equality with men. This chapter examines how popular discourses surrounding women's athleticism in the Weimar period responded to changing ideas about gendered roles and capabilities. As with the conservative backlash against masculine women's fashions in the 1920s German media, critiques of the masculinized female athlete often reached far beyond the realm of sporting commentary to provide a tangible focus for wider discussions and criticisms of troubled gender relations and female emancipation. I argue that the perceived threat to traditional male dominance posed by the sporting woman prompted some commentators to denounce much female physical activity and to overemphasize traditional gender roles in an attempt to recuperate her femininity. Yet I also point to ways in which less conservative commentators held up women's growing physical fitness as a positive sign of progress and modernity, and in particular, to how a female body "steeled by sport" was reclaimed as an aesthetic ideal within the female homosexual subculture of interwar Berlin.

For many women in 1920s Germany, sport represented an opportunity to engage in activities and visual styles that had traditionally been designated "masculine." Because of its close relationship to bodies and physicality, female athleticism—and the masculinized female athlete in particular—provided an important focus for broader concerns about changing gender roles, female sexuality, and acceptable female life trajectories. As Shari Dworkin and Michael Messner observe, "it is the very centrality of the body in sport practice and ideology that provides an opportunity to examine critically and illuminate the social construction of gender."[1] And yet, studies of the Weimar New Woman, as Erik Jensen has highlighted, have all too often neglected physical culture, "even though slender athleticism formed a central and destabilizing part of her image."[2] The following analysis expands upon existing histories of Weimar women's sport by focusing on how the perceived threat of female athleticism was articulated in popular discourses via the specter of masculinization. It draws upon the print media—a major source of 1920s sport coverage—on contemporary publications devoted specifically to questions of women's sporting participation, and on a range of subcultural periodicals.

The Rise of Women's Sport in Germany

The late nineteenth century had seen increasing numbers of middle- and upper-class German women take up activities such as *Turnen* (gymnastics) and cycling, partly in response to concerns about the declining health of bourgeois mothers and mothers-to-be.[3] However, it was the fundamental social, political, and economic changes associated with World War I—including women's participation in war industries, the advent of female suffrage, women's entrance into the German universities, and a significant rise in urban female white-collar employment—that created the conditions for the emergence of a truly modern, muscular, and athletic feminine ideal. This transformation, which also encompassed major reforms in women's sporting attire, was highlighted in the popular media through repeated comparisons between the sporting woman of "today" and her frumpy Wilhelmine predecessor. It took place within the wider context of a massive boom in sporting participation that covered the spectrum of gender, political, religious, and class affiliations.

Sports programs, which before the war had offered a practical response to turn-of-the-century concerns about the physical health and superiority of the German "race" in the face of increasing urbanization and industrialization, were now considered even more central to revitalizing the defeated nation both physically and economically in a context of restricted military involvement. Sport's newfound popularity was also a result of demographic changes: whereas recreational physical activity had once been the prerogative of an elite leisure class, changes to the industrialized workplace such as the increased deployment of labor-saving devices and the introduction of the forty-hour workweek led to a growth in leisure time even amongst the working classes. By the late 1920s almost nine million Germans were members of official sporting organizations, and over 1.2 million of these members were women. This represented a particularly dramatic increase in women's athletic participation compared to the prewar period, leading *Das Magazin* to observe that whereas the female athlete had once been an individual phenomenon, "today she has become a type."[4]

Leading this phenomenon were self-fashioned New Woman celebrities such as actor Hanni Weisse and author Vicki Baum, who made a point of appearing in illustrated magazines engaged in such unconventional activities as boxing, flying, or driving (see Figure 2.1). Although the faddish aspect of women's involvement in nontraditional sports was mocked by some—prominent sporting authority Carl Diem was among those who suggested that the new emphasis on "sport" was driven as much by the desire of certain ladies to appear fashionable as an appreciation of health and fitness—even caricatures could help to reinforce popular associations between sport and modern womanhood.[5] One such cartoon appeared in *Sport im Bild* in 1920, featuring popular film stars such as "Henny" (Porten) wearing boxing gloves and a menacing grin, "Asta" (Nielsen) engaged in a fencing bout, and "Pola" (Negri) as a horse riding "Amazon."[6] Contemporaries were careful to distinguish between women's involvement in such new forms of competitive "sport" and more established areas of female physicality such as gymnastics, or the increasingly popular physical culture (*Körperkultur*) movement, which sought to counter the physical degeneration associated with the industrialization of German society.[7] In particular, it was competitive, physically demanding, and record-oriented activities, such as athletics, swimming, ski-jumping, and soccer, but also typically working-class, masculine sports such as weightlifting or boxing, that attracted the praise, scorn, and general attention of the print media, and that fueled growing concerns about the masculinization of German women through sport. As one *Sport im Bild* journalist commented in 1928, ski-jumping is "neither something for the lady, nor for the woman on skis at all."[8]

Ein boxender Star

Hanni Weisse
der bekannte Filmstar bei seiner
morgendlichen
Lieblingsbeschäftigung

Aufnahmen
von P. Weisse

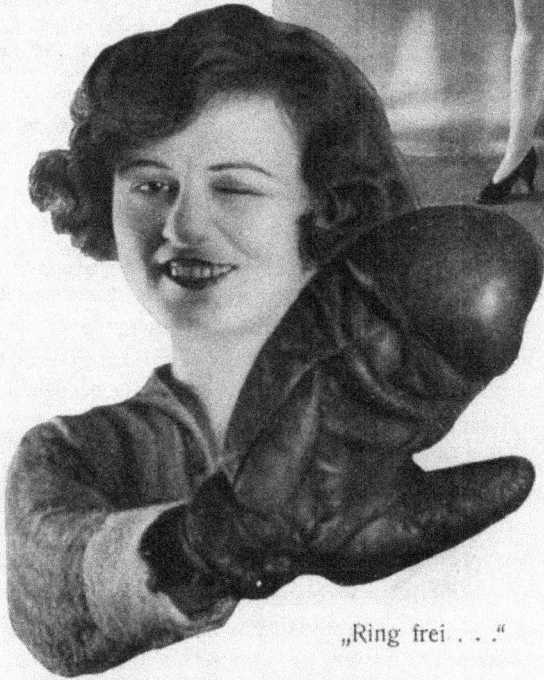

„Ring frei . . ."

Figure 2.1. "A Boxing Star." *Das Magazin,* May 1925, 38.
Source: BPK Bildagentur für Kunst, Kultur und Geschichte

Pushing the Boundaries: Women's Competitive Sport and the Threat of Masculinization

Although the pioneering activities of an elite group of female automobilists and aviators did much to heighten public perceptions of the "New" woman's increased social and spatial mobility, it was more strenuous physical activities that seemed to threaten established notions of gendered difference, and that truly raised the ire of critics. The growing competitiveness and skill of the modern female athlete were met with a heightened sense that women were "catching up" with men physically as well as socially and politically, leading prominent sports journalist Willy Meisl to declare in the *BIZ* that:

> The weaker sex is emulating the stronger sex even in the area of pure physical performance. The man has a strong advantage here, not just naturally, but on account of his centuries-old monopoly on physical training. The era of sport and of emancipation has done away with this privilege, and it is almost astonishing to see what tremendous progress female athletes have been able to make in an unbelievably short space of time.

Meisl's reflections on the fragile status of men's physical superiority are reinforced by accompanying photographs of record-breaking female athletes such as the US swimmer Gertrude Ederle, who recently had swum the English Channel almost one hour faster than the five men who preceded her in this feat.[9] Such examples pointed to the possibility that women might one day overtake men in this last and most important bastion of masculine superiority, and threatened to disrupt all-powerful notions of "natural," biological gender differences.

Historians of other national contexts agree that women's rapid movement into competitive sport during this period was experienced as particularly threatening because it was a time when male dominance in society and politics appeared increasingly under stress. In the US, for example, Behling argues that "women's athletic activity and athleticism, traditionally masculine endeavors, were physical manifestations of suffrage."[10] As Meisl's comments demonstrate, the German media were similarly forthright in linking women's athletic involvement to their political emancipation. Even more explicit was one M. Boden in *Das Magazin*, who appealed to male readers of this general-interest magazine with the words: "She looks like you, dresses like you, fights for her life like you, has the same concerns as you—and therefore also the same rights. Where is that more obvious than in sport?"[11] Conversely, some argued that sport itself had played a pioneering role in women's political development. In this vein, Meisl reflected in an article for *Uhu* on the emancipation of the modern sporting woman from "fragile doll" to companion, comrade, and competitor with men, thereby linking women's equality on the sporting field to increasingly popular ideas about heterosexual camaraderie and companionate marriage. Similar views were shared by contemporary sports experts and educators, as manifested in the edited collection *Die Frau und der*

Sport (Woman and Sport), in which the authors—which included leading Berlin athletic authorities, physical educators, and sports students—insist that after the war, "female athletes came together and demanded equality in the sporting domain as well."[12]

Women's participation in sport was not just important as a symbol of emancipation; it went to the heart of concerns about biological gender difference and racial degeneration. Numerous commentators drew on discourses of *Zivilisationskritik* (civilization criticism), popular since at least the turn of the century, to posit an original, strong female body that had been successively worn down under the conditions of European modernity. Their arguments echoed those popularized several decades earlier by Max Nordau on the topic of "muscle Jews." Nordau had argued that although Jews had suffered physically under a long history of anti-Semitism and ghetto existence, they were not innately degenerate, but rather possessed the potential to evolve back into physically and intellectually superior beings who could work together to form a Zionist nation. These anti-degeneration claims can be compared, as Todd Presner has demonstrated, with the nationalist concerns of German body reform movements such as the *Wandervögel,* and with the celebration of physical strength among sections of the early male homosexual rights movement.[13] Applied to the Weimar female athlete, such "regeneration" arguments allowed some commentators in the 1920s media to proclaim the potential for a stronger version of German womanhood to reemerge under the right conditions.

In this vein, the authors of *Die Frau und der Sport* blame the spread of Christian moral standards for leading to a sedentary female lifestyle in the modern era, and deny any innate differences in athletic ability between men and women:

> The differences for the woman lie not in the anatomical, but in the psychological arena. …
> With the spreading of Christianity, physical exercises were generally rejected as indecent.
> While continual wars meant that the men had to stay physically fit in preparation for
> military service, women's physical activity dropped to zero. Crazy fashions only made the
> situation worse, and the result was a complete weakening of the female sex.[14]

In the modern era, these experts argued, competitive sport provides women with a much-needed counterbalance to the mechanical tasks of modern industrial occupations. Such arguments resonated not only among sports students and educators, but also in the popular press. Their target was primarily the new class of young, unmarried women working in the cities as low-paid, white-collar employees who, it was thought, sought physical activities that would not only complement their confident self-image and boyish bodily aesthetic, but would help "steel" them for the competitive workforce and future motherhood.[15] Physical educators thus sought not only to adapt the goals of physical education to the reality of modern women's lives, but to respond to larger cultural concerns about the health and decline of the nation.

This concerted focus on the modern woman's health and physical strength helped to fundamentally challenge the inevitability of women's status as the "weaker" sex in the Weimar era. Indeed, so frequent were references in the popular media to "Amazonian" female bodies that had been "steeled by sport" that these came to be considered stereotypical features of the Weimar New Woman. This female athlete's increasing proximity to masculine values and bodily ideals was read by many as a serious threat to male social, political, and physical dominance, and disrupted what feminist historians have described as one of sport's most important functions, namely, as "a major site for the naturalization of sex and gender differences" that "continually reproduces men as naturally superior to women."[16] In response, critics devised a range of strategies to defuse the subversive potential of the masculinized female athlete.

Reactions to the Masculinized Female Athlete

Among conservative commentators a popular method of containing this figure was through caricature and ridicule. Female boxers were particular targets of such caricatures, on account of their involvement in a traditionally working-class sport with heavily masculine associations. An early cartoon series from the satirical *Ulk* in 1921 exemplifies this strategy through six images that depict the progress of the modern female physical ideal. Starting with the "Venus of Medici," who decides to leave her pedestal and pursue a sporting career, the reader watches this feminine ideal grow increasingly tough, muscular, and leathery as she proceeds historically from cycling to athletics, wrestling, and boxing, until we are left with a grotesquely bulked-up figure making a vain attempt at feminine humility as she spits out a stream of teeth after knocking out her opponent. As the caption ironically observes: "The modern ideal of female beauty is achieved" (Figure 2.2).

In similar fashion, *Simplicissimus* published an image of a pair of overweight, gorilla-like women boxers in caps and gloves, the winner gazing fiercely at her knocked-down opponent and commenting scathingly: "Are you also a sportsman, fatty—or a sadist?"[17] It is not by accident that artist Karl Arnold places male terms of reference in the mouths of these women, nor that he associates them with such "masculine" qualities as aggression and competition. At the same time, this cartoon critiques the voyeuristic element of women's involvement in "male" sports such as boxing, as it features an audience of well-groomed society ladies and gentlemen sipping wine and engrossed in the spectacle before them. The grotesque creatures on display here could not be further removed from the boxing celebrities described above, whose participation in this nontraditional sport only served to increase their status as glamorous modern women.

Other caricatures played on fears that women's increasing physical equality would encourage too much independence from men, or would hinder their very

Figure 2.2. Steinert, "Women's Sport." *Ulk,* 19 August 1921, 131.
Source: BPK Bildagentur für Kunst, Kultur und Geschichte

ability to "pass" as women. Thus in one cartoon entitled "Emancipation" a group of women shoulder a rowing boat to the caption: "You see, children, when one engages in sport one can do without men altogether!"; a second image shows a group of women walking around a running track naked from the waist up, with the leader declaring in rough Berlin dialect: "—Now don't be shy, girlies! If anyone notices that there are broads here then he's a pig!"[18] These and many similar images commented caustically on the failure of the brutishly masculine female athlete to achieve the female physical ideals of "strength and beauty" (*Kraft und Schönheit*) propagated by physical educators. Seeking to undermine high levels of activity and muscularity in women by showing grotesquely exaggerated female physiques and hinting at "perverse" gender and sexual identities, they provided an effective means of demonizing the female athlete.

A subtler but equally popular way of enforcing limits on women's masculinization through sport was to emphasize "feminine" aesthetics, with journalists quick to offer tips on physical activities that would emphasize a woman's "true beauty," "charm" or "gracefulness." According to 1920s sports theorists, the achievement of "strength and lightness, elegance and dignity" was central to women's sport, which must aspire to more aesthetically pleasing goals than men's.[19] Inherent to such arguments was a condemnation of all activities considered overly masculine, strenuous or aggressive, as journalist Ruth Goetz clarified in no uncertain terms in 1927:

> For scholars and psychologists have often pointed to the damaging influence of tough sports, given that the woman of today has frequently lost her charm on the sporting field. Tennis results in broad hands and flat feet, polo is damaging to the skin, hockey masculinizes the soul and the body. And it is not even necessary to demonstrate the problems [*Widersetzlichkeiten*] that sport causes with respect to beauty.[20]

Standards of feminine beauty also informed assessments of women's athletic attire, which like women's fashions in general, had undergone massive changes since the war. Fashion journalists expressed concern over the introduction of breeches and other practical but "gentlemanlike" garments for sports such as skiing, athletics, tennis, golf, and driving; the women's magazine *Frau und Gegenwart* even declared "~~The skirt~~ trousers VICTORIOUS in sports fashions." In an attempt to compensate for increasing levels of athletic sartorial androgyny, fashion editors included advice on how to wear pants for sport while maintaining an elegant, feminine appearance, noting that "only the boyishly slender may permit themselves the luxury of wearing trousers."[21]

Perhaps more surprisingly, demands for feminine "grace" applied even to the highest levels of competitive sport. Thus female athletes competing in the 800m event at the 1928 Olympics in Amsterdam were denounced in the media as thoroughly unattractive after several women collapsed from over-exhaustion following the race—consequently, the event was scrapped for women until 1960.[22] Implicit in such criticisms was the idea that strenuous physical activity was not only detrimental to a woman's beauty, but endangered her entire physical and reproductive organism, an argument to which I return below.

In Germany it was middle-class women who represented the main target of the media's attacks on women's masculinization through sport, and whose refusal to be satisfied with the traditional bourgeois domestic roles of wife and mother was seen to represent the greatest danger to the German nation. In contrast, it was much easier for wealthy women to participate in the range of cutting-edge sports newly available to women, especially expensive pastimes such as driving and flying. Furthermore, and as was the case with women's fashions in general, the media were more permissive of upper-class women who chose to present themselves in "masculine" sporting attire, or who engaged in daringly masculine and aggressive activities such as boxing or martial arts. The highbrow literary magazine *Der Querschnitt* (Cross Section), for example, had no qualms about publishing an article on the tough sport of Jiu Jitsu authored by the aristocratic Baroness Wöllwarth-Wesendonk, who is photographed wearing full martial arts attire.[23] Similarly, although horse riding was associated with severely masculinized forms of female attire, it remained largely free from derogatory accusations of masculinization not least on account of its upper-class patronage. The middle-class woman, on the other hand, was to engage only in "moderate" activity and heed the expert opinion that "[a]ll that is excessive in women has a repellent effect."[24] Such protective attitudes bear similarities to the philosophy of moderation promoted in the early twentieth-century US, where Susan Cahn has shown that physical activity was directed toward shielding young women from the physical and moral dangers of uncontrolled, "masculine" athletic games, in a way that reflected particularly middle-class values such as refinement, self-restraint, and efficiency.[25]

Narratives of gender transformation provided a further strategy for controlling the threat of the masculinized female athlete. As noted in the previous chapter, these were generally represented in visual form, via a juxtaposition of images of the same woman shown firstly in "masculine" sporting attire during the daytime, and secondly in "feminine," heterosexually appealing clothing in the evening. Cahn observes a similar trend in US media coverage of women's sport from this period, noting that female athletes were expected to assume a masculine persona during competition, but to swap this "mask" for a more appealing and authentic feminine self once the event was over.[26] That such narratives of transformation functioned by reducing female athleticism to a temporary and thus safe transgression is exemplified by the following 1926 article published in fashion magazine *Die Dame,* with the title "The Modern Sporting Lady" (Figure 2.3).

In the first of two images, we see young German motorcyclist Hanni Köhler in tough cycling garb astride her bike with a caption outlining her impressive sporting achievements. In the second image, she is presented in feminine evening dress—or as the caption notes, "in civilian wear" (*in 'Zivil'*). This implicit comparison to the civilian wear of soldiers emphasizes that this is in fact her "normal" or "natural" state, as opposed to the militaristic excesses required by her sport. The accompanying text explains how the modern sporting lady has outgrown her masculinized forebears such as the tomboy, and instead manages to combine the ideal of a healthy body with a genuine claim to femininity:

> Today the true embodiment of the ladylike, of absolute femininity, is the sporting lady. … Her body is steeled and remains flexible, her skin, toughened with wind and weather, maintains with appropriate beauty care its delicacy and fine complexion, and her being does not forfeit grace even as it gains in strength.

As the author reassures readers, this new, "steeled" body only serves to enhance the female athlete's heterosexual attractiveness: "The evening dress of today is best suited to the female body that is accustomed to wearing sports clothes in

Die moderne Sportdame

Figure 2.3. "The Modern Sporting Lady." *Die Dame,* First April Issue 1926, 8.
Source: BPK Bildagentur für Kunst, Kultur und Geschichte

the mornings."[27] A very similar article appeared the following year in *Das Magazin,* describing how the taut, windswept, and sunburned "Sportgirl" by day transforms into the smoking, drinking, Charleston-dancing woman by night, her physical activity only adding to her attractiveness and recreational stamina:

"One sees that a trained body is inexhaustible."[28] On the one hand, such sources point to a liberating reevaluation and expansion of notions of female physicality and beauty, but at the same time they evince a strong coercive streak, for the threat of masculinization is contained by an overemphasis on the potential of the female athlete to transform herself from masculine athlete to feminine, heterosexual partner.

Yet not all commentators came to the same conclusions about the impact of women's newfound athleticism on their capacity to maintain heterosexual relationships. Possibly as a pragmatic concession to the postwar "surplus" of women of marriageable age, some even argued that there were certain women for whom sport itself could act as a substitute for heterosexual life fulfillment: "Not all women will achieve the happiness of marriage. For these women, sport can become their purpose in life."[29] Such examples support Gertrud Pfister's contention that during the Weimar period, sport was seen by some as a means of containing the threat of feminine sexuality by acting as a vehicle for the "sublimation of desires."[30] More importantly, this concerted focus on the female athlete's heterosexual potential highlights what was arguably the greatest fear of all—namely, that "masculinized" activities would lead to "masculinized" sexual desires.

"Her Constitution Is Different from That of the Feminine Woman": Female Athleticism and Homosexuality

I have already noted that 1920s German readers were quite familiar with sexological theories of inversion that equated a masculine gender performance in women with same-sex desire. Consequently, although the threat of homosexuality was only rarely articulated, it lent additional force to critiques of female athleticism in the mainstream Weimar media. Pat Griffin has demonstrated in relation to North American women's sport that "femininity" can sometimes function as a barely disguised "code word for heterosexuality," as the female athlete is "femmed up" to compensate for her athleticism and suspected homosexuality—a strategy at work in the images of motorcycle champion Köhler above. Griffin is not the only historian to highlight links between female athleticism and stereotypes of the "mannish lesbian" in the US at this period; Behling, too, asserts that "(m)annish behavior was clearly linked to female inverts, and athleticism was clearly understood to be masculine." In contrast, Cahn contends that it was not until the 1930s that female athletic mannishness began to connote failed, rather than excessive heterosexuality, and that a more pressing fear among 1920s commentators was that of heterosexual excess and moral deficiency.[31] While these scholars address a distinct national and historical context, they highlight an ambiguity that also surrounds German representations from this period. Certainly, not all critiques of "masculinized" female athletes in the 1920s German media can be attributed to fears of female homosexuality. It was, however, a possibility with which contemporary audiences were quite familiar, and which would have increased the deterrent power of some of the caricatures described above.

In approaching the issue of homosexuality and women's sport, it is important to distinguish between homophobic strategies used by some mainstream media commentators in an attempt to contain the masculinized female athlete, and alternative conceptions of gendered physicality circulating among the emerging female homosexual subcultures of 1920s Germany. A close examination of periodicals published by and for homosexual women at this period reveals that although some contributors echoed the mainstream media's concerns about sport's detrimental impact on health and femininity, others considered a masculinized appearance achieved through physical activity a desirable aesthetic commodity, and an important marker of sexual identity.

In the former camp was Herbert Gerwig, a writer for the "Femina" beauty column of *Garçonne,* whose writings for this regular advertising feature formed part of a small contingent of occasional male contributions to an otherwise female-dominated magazine. In a series of articles, Gerwig emphasizes the aesthetic necessity of wearing a brassiere during sport, warns women against pursuing sport out of a desire for breaking records, and begs them to heed the danger of losing "fundamental feminine values" in favor of "meaningless illusory values … that may at best provide satisfaction for a moment, but which can never provide true fulfillment."[32] In subsequent issues of the same magazine, other (female) contributors likewise urge caution and moderation, rejecting women's involvement in sports such as boxing and wrestling, and suggesting that: "A sport that glorifies maximum performance can only ever be considered minimally appropriate for women."[33] Such excerpts indicate that even publications and subcultures generally supportive of alternative genders and sexualities were influenced by, and participated in, the construction of mainstream aesthetic ideals and debates.

Significantly, however, not all women who identified as homosexual subscribed to such normative feminine ideals. Rather than demonizing female athleticism, these latter contributors posit a masculine, or "virile" gender identification as a central factor in determining how a woman structures her physical activity, a view best illustrated in a series of articles on gymnastics for lesbians that appeared in the short-lived *Frauen Liebe und Leben* in 1928, which replaced the *Frauenliebe* during its ban from public display. Dr. Agnes Strettel explains that just as there are biological differences between men and women that necessitate sex-specific exercises, there are also important differences between masculine and feminine female homosexuals, for whom "the internal secretions of the gonads are of a quite different biological composition." Strettel observes, for example, that the "masculine-oriented lesbian" is far less likely to be interested in emphasizing her bust than in increasing muscle strength. Similarly, Herta Laser advises that exercises known as *Stemmübungen,* which involve tensing the arm muscles while moving them slowly backwards and forwards, are "expedient only for the masculine woman." Yet such a woman, as Laser affirms, may undertake these exercises with impunity, "for her constitution is different from that of the feminine woman, and thus for her such an exercise, which is particularly useful for increasing muscle strength, is never harmful."[34]

As well as pointing to differences between masculine and feminine female homosexuals, both authors draw a general physical distinction between heterosexual and homosexual women, with Strettel observing that

> When a gymnastics system is constructed, it must be clear from the very beginning whether it is intended for the normally oriented or the lesbian woman, or for a man. If one exercises blindly using a cheaply obtained textbook … then one might achieve results that are far from those one desired.[35]

Laser offers the pragmatic contention that the homosexual woman is far more likely than her heterosexual counterpart to spend most of her life in the workforce, and that a youthful appearance therefore represents an important weapon in an increasingly ferocious *Berufskampf* (professional struggle). Although initially faced with greater psychological hurdles in coming to terms with her sexual disposition, Laser argues that the homosexual woman in fact enjoys a slight advantage over her heterosexual counterpart, who must contend with the bodily decline associated with childbearing. This physical superiority is posited as an important weapon in the fight against homophobia, for "it is especially she, for whom youth and beauty is important not least as a weapon against those people who would claim that homosexuality is damaging to one's health, who should care for her body and not neglect it in any way."[36] In this way the lesbian body is portrayed as an ideal, healthy specimen that can be used to counter accusations of homosexual degeneration, with Laser adopting similar arguments to those made by Max Nordau in relation to the "muscle Jew."

Such positive reevaluations of a muscular, athletic female masculinity may be interpreted as a reaction against the implicit demonization of homosexuality in mainstream accounts of women's athleticism. They demonstrate a recognition that for at least some members of the contemporary subculture, a "masculinized" female body represented a desirable physical aesthetic, and an important means of giving visual form to one's gender and sexual identity, not unlike the tuxedos and monocles discussed in the previous chapter. Yet, in distinguishing between masculine and feminine homosexual women in this way, authors such as Laser and Strettel remained subservient to dominant gender paradigms that tended to privilege the masculine and place limits on the feminine. Although such gender-based privileging was also subject to criticism within these magazines, as I explore in the following chapter, it is important to remember that not only were writers and readers of the subcultural magazines influenced by the same debates and aesthetic norms as members of the larger society, but that a homosexual identification did not necessarily correspond to a nonconformist approach to gender, sexuality, or even politics, though it sometimes did.

Given the limited number of subcultural sources dealing directly with women's athleticism, and the absence of letters by readers on these issues, we can only speculate on how important such contributions might have been in affirming individual readers' sense of their physical and gendered selves. Nonetheless, subcultural sources dealing with women's athleticism provide a valuable historical counterdiscourse to the mainstream German media's attacks on the masculinized female athlete, which only grew in intensity as the era drew to a close.

"From Sporting Girl to Sporting Lady": Motherhood and the Female Athlete in the Late Weimar Period

By the late 1920s increasing concern about the conduciveness of women's sport to heterosexual life goals led to an overwhelming media focus on the female athlete's reproductive and domestic duties. Publications such as *Das Magazin* had hinted at this impending domestication for some time: in the article cited at the beginning of this chapter, John goes on to conclude that "woman" may well have been happier in her traditional domestic setting: "But… But… a very quiet question: was she not happier watching over her home and servants and preserving fruit and vegetables?"[37] While the fiercest detractors argued that the female athlete's masculinization would incapacitate her for her true vocation of reproduction, more liberal commentators chose to contextualize athletic activity as a healthy but passing phase of life that would strengthen women for their future roles as wives and mothers. As several historians have observed, at a time when German leaders were anxiously linking the declining birth rate to decreasing national strength, both supporters and detractors shared the common goal of increasing women's capacity to bear more children for the nation, and differed only on how this was to be achieved.[38]

As early as the mid nineteenth century, when women began turning to gymnastics in significant numbers, there had been concern about the negative impact of physical activity on women's reproductive capacity. Pfister has argued that compatibility with motherhood was at the core of debates on women's competitive sport throughout the 1920s, noting that some of the strongest arguments against "excessive" or "masculinizing" sports came from medical experts and gynecologists.[39] However, my research shows that it was not until the late Weimar period that concerns about women's reproductive and domestic responsibilities came to dominate mainstream media commentary on the female athlete; before this, reproduction had been no more important in accounts of women's sport than concerns about their increasingly masculinized appearance, suspect sexuality, or perceived independence from, and physical equality with, men.

This had changed by the early 1930s, when discourses of motherhood and reproduction were clearly shaping mainstream media coverage of women's sport and both supporters and detractors could draw on medical studies in support of their arguments. A particularly reactionary article appeared in *Uhu* in 1931, authored by prominent Leipzig gynecologist Hugo Sellheim, whom Gabriele Wesp identifies as one of the two major contemporary medical opponents of women's competitive sport.[40] Sellheim condemns not only the psychological and emotional immaturity of the sporting woman—illustrated by photographs of exhausted, distressed women comforting one another after losing a race—but the "serious damage" to the female organism and "irreversible" dangers to the female reproductive system caused by women's involvement in competitive sport:

> The willingness to reproduce disappears, for example, and in the event that reproduction does occur, we frequently see a complete and utter failure in respect to the woman's original feminine capacity. Such women have ruined a lifetime of joy in exchange for a few minutes of victorious pleasure.

Sellheim concludes that, whereas competitive sport is only appropriate for men, who must be strengthened to defend house and home, women should concentrate on the well-being of their children and restrict themselves to the domestic realm.[41]

Less sensationalist commentators in the late Weimar period sought a middle path, highlighting women's abilities to be both athlete *and* mother. These cautious supporters could likewise draw on medical evidence, including a 1932 study of ten thousand girls and women that found that sport had no adverse effects on women's health or ability to give birth.[42] Focusing on how women could pass on their sporting abilities to the next generation, they sought to legitimate women's athletic participation, but only for a temporary life phase, which was reevaluated as secondary to the major life goal of motherhood. Such attitudes to women's sport were also popular among physical educators at this period. Thus the authors of *Die Frau und der Sport* argued that women's strength is largely in the form of physical "potential," in preparation for motherhood, and advocated certain precautions including emptying one's bladder before sport in order to avoid pressure on the uterus, not competing on the first day of a menstrual period, and limiting the total number of races.[43]

Although some media outlets took a quite tongue-in-cheek approach toward this push to domesticate the female athlete, such as a 1931 *Simplicissimus* image of a woman hurling herself over a high jump while breastfeeding her baby, a more earnest appeal to the athlete as mother appeared in *Uhu* in October 1932 under the title: "From Sporting Girl to Sporting Mother: A Visit with Happy Mothers who Grew Up as Athletes."[44] Author Edith von Lölhöffel, a medical doctor and lecturer at the German College for Physical Exercises (Deutsche Hochschule für Leibesübungen), argues that sport pursued in moderation provides women with positive benefits and a healthy rather than "masculinized" appearance, and that athletic women are therefore particularly well-equipped to cope with pregnancy. Above all, she suggests, having children can bring them far greater pride and glory than the most spectacular sporting achievements: "two or three children is the average for these sporting mothers, five and eight children the record achievement. And they are prouder of this than the most glorious victory or gold medal."[45] This is illustrated with numerous "before" and "after" photographs of female athletes: one shot of each woman on the sporting field with a caption outlining her achievements, and a second of her as mother training a son or daughter in her former sport. In contrast to earlier commentators, who had focused on the female athlete's transformation from competitor with men by day to object of male desire by night, this article describes a much longer-term transformation, whereby a woman progresses through a stage of youthful athleticism before settling down to become a mother of future athletes. The threat of masculinization is contained within this temporal structure by the woman's eventual return to heteronormative reproductive structures, as she resumes her expected role as wife and mother following a period of youthful experimentation with less conventional gender behaviors.[46]

While efforts were thus made to domesticate the female athlete in the late Weimar period, only seldom was women's athleticism dismissed outright. Indeed, as was the case with women's fashions, sources from the early 1930s demonstrate that it would be wrong to posit a clear-cut reversal of the significant gains made by Weimar sporting women even following the advent of National Socialism, despite an official gender ideology that confined women's role to the domestic sphere. While it is beyond the scope of this chapter to include a detailed analysis of representations of the female athlete beyond 1933, the following section traces some lines of continuity into the early Nazi period, when a number of the magazines examined here were still being published.

The Masculinized Female Athlete beyond the Weimar Era

Even though it would take decades for German women to again engage in such a variety of sports as they had during the heyday of the 1920s, women's athletic involvement did not suddenly come to a halt following Hitler's seizure of power. Firstly, the conviction that an elite group of female athletes could and should represent their nation at the highest levels continued into the Third Reich, as was demonstrated most clearly at the 1936 Olympics.[47] Secondly, the model of healthy, athletic motherhood popularized during the 1920s continued to hold sway in the popular media at least into the early Nazi era, as is illustrated by two photographs published in *Uhu* in May 1933 under the title "Mothers." While the first shows a rather frumpy woman with her head buried inside a pram, the second shows a slim, muscular woman in sporting attire and *Bubikopf* swinging her naked child in the air in naturalistic, *Körperkultur* fashion; clearly, the second image is intended as the more ideal maternal figure.[48]

Another significant point of continuity was the "masculinized" sporting attire and aesthetic popularized during the 1920s, including short haircuts, fitted tricots, shorts, and a boyish physique, all of which enjoyed ongoing popularity in coverage of women's athletic fashions in the early Nazi era. An example of this aesthetic continuity can be seen in two images of German hurdler Ruth Engelhardt-Becker, published in *Uhu* in 1933 (Figures 2.4 and 2.5). As the caption observes, this is indeed "One and the Same Woman: Hurdling Champion Mrs Engelhardt-Becker in Action and at the Domestic Ironing Board." On the one hand, this rather absurd combination of images relies on the established strategy of defusing the female athlete's gender ambiguity by placing her within a clearly domestic setting and referring to her marital status. Yet the images themselves defy such simplistic attempts to "feminize" the female athlete, for although Engelhardt-Becker is shown doing the ironing, her appearance is surprisingly "masculine": her boxer briefs, singlet, and closely cropped hair only serve to emphasize the androgyny of her flat-chested, muscular figure, and undermine the process of domestication that is supposedly taking place.

Ein und
Die Hürdenmeisterin Frau Engelhardt-Becker im Sprung

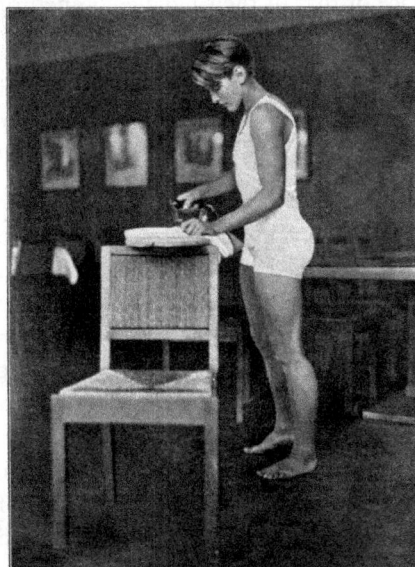

dieselbe Frau
und am häuslichen Plättbrett.

Fot. Pietsch

Figures 2.4 and 2.5. "One and the Same Woman: Hurdling Champion Mrs Engelhardt-Becker in Action and at the Domestic Ironing Board." *Uhu*, April 1933, 10–11.
Source: BPK Bildagentur für Kunst, Kultur und Geschichte

Furthermore, certain "masculinized" values such as camaraderie and competition that had been heavily associated with Weimar women's sport retained legitimacy beyond 1933, and even helped to shape the physical education programs of Nazi girls and women's organizations such as the League of German Girls (BDM). Despite a general focus on female-specific forms of physical exercise aimed at preparing girls for their role as wives, mothers, and upholders of Aryan racial purity, these organizations also drew on the late-Weimar push toward healthy, athletic motherhood, and on the organized, competitive sporting traditions popularized during the 1920s.[49]

Expectations of heterosexual camaraderie and competition also continued to influence sport at a popular level, as is illustrated by an *Uhu* article published in mid 1933. Journalist Heinrich Satter praises young female athletes for their focus on athletic achievement and competition rather than flirtation: "When [the woman] speaks to men on the sporting field, she does so because they understand something of sport, and not because she wants to flirt with them." Yet Satter treads a careful line, on the one hand celebrating women's hard-won achievements and their right to compete against men, but at the same time insisting on what is clearly his main concern, namely, the ongoing potential for successful heterosexual relationships even when men's supposedly superior physicality pales in the face of that of their female competitors. Reflecting on changing gender norms, he asks:

> How does a man live, how does he speak with a woman who, in a sporting sense, can "press him up against the wall," who can run faster, jump further, play better tennis, and is possibly even, if one is not to forget the most extreme cases, stronger, more muscular and tougher than he is himself? Can he get along with her at all?[50]

It *is* possible, insists Satter, for a man to gain and maintain such a woman's attention, and the reason is one of sheer numbers: there are now so many women who have achieved success in nontraditional areas that this is no longer a legitimate source of male shame. An accompanying photograph depicts this new generation of German men and women in identical shorts and tricots, their relationship to one another no longer grounded in notions of essential gender difference but rather in mutual respect, as the caption clarifies: "Sport comrades: the same goal, the same ambition and almost the same appearance" (Figure 2.6).

This far from regressive account of female athleticism and heterosexual relationships from the early Nazi period illustrates how once-revolutionary ideas about heterosexual camaraderie and equality had become incorporated into mainstream sport discourse, and continued to influence discussions of women's sport in the early Nazi period. Admittedly, such levels of optimism about gender equality would not survive for long in such a mainstream forum, as magazines such as *Uhu* were increasingly subjected to Nazi policies of cultural coordination. This is ironically suggested by the editorial decision to follow Satter's article with

Sportkameraden: Das gleiche Ziel, den gleichen Ehrgeiz und fast das gleiche Aussehen.

Figure 2.6. "Sporting Camaraderie between Man and Woman: The Young Generation on the Sporting Fields." *Uhu,* June 1933, 19.
Source: BPK Bildagentur für Kunst, Kultur und Geschichte

a photograph of a young boy in lederhosen and two small girls in dirndls marching in a town parade, with the caption: "The Little Comrade." The juxtaposition between this enforcement of binary gender categories among the next generation and the androgynous "sport comrades" from the first image could hardly be more blatant, and exemplifies both the continuities and contradictions of media coverage of the masculinized female athlete beyond the Weimar era. While it is crucial to acknowledge the ways in which sport was appropriated during the Third Reich as an instrument of racist propaganda and a means of preparing for war, not all images of female athletes from the early Nazi period can be adequately accounted for by the conservative Nazi gender ideology of women as homemakers and mothers; on the contrary, the masculinized female athlete of the Weimar era remained an important figure of "gender trouble" even under fascist rule.

The perceived threat of masculinization dominated media coverage of the female athlete throughout the Weimar period, prompting commentators to develop strategies that would reaffirm the traditional gender order and recuperate her into socially acceptable, heteronormative structures. These included ridiculing "excessive" displays of athletic female masculinity, emphasizing "feminine" moderation and aesthetics, and employing narratives of transformation that juxtaposed images of the masculinized female athlete with her feminine after-hours persona, or that depicted her transition from athlete to mother. Such strategies were aimed at defusing the female athlete's symbolic potential, for her increasing physical competitiveness with men on the sporting field was considered by many to be indicative of her rapid movement into other spheres of German life, including politics and the workforce, or to endanger her capacity to provide the nation with children.

The threat of female homosexuality, although rarely articulated, played an important role in helping to police these limits on women's physicality and contrasted with more positive accounts of the masculine female body developed by members of the homosexual subculture. Such divergent approaches toward the figure of the masculine woman in mainstream and subcultural media outlets are explored further in the next chapter. Yet it was not only homosexual women who came to embrace the strong, athletic models of femininity that were popularized during the 1920s. As a result, even as commentators sought to "return" the female athlete to maternal, domestic settings during the early 1930s against a climate of increasing gender conservatism, it became apparent that the women in question had been irretrievably altered. Short hair, fitted unisex sportswear, boyish, muscular bodies, and ideas about heterosexual camaraderie and competitiveness had become the female athletic norm, and would continue to influence expectations and performances of gender even under National Socialism.

Notes

1. Shari Dworkin and Michael Messner, "Just do … what? Sport, Bodies, Gender," in *Gender and Sport: A Reader*, ed. Sheila Scraton and Anne Flintoff (London: Routledge, 2002), 17.
2. Erik N. Jensen, "Images of the Ideal: Sports, Gender, and the Emergence of the Modern Body in Weimar Germany" (PhD diss., University of Wisconsin, 2003), 5.
3. Ilse Hartmann-Tews and Sascha Alexandra Luetkens, "The Inclusion of Women into the German Sport System," in *Sport and Women: Social Issues in International Perspective*, ed. Ilse Hartmann-Tews and Gertrud Pfister (London: Routledge, 2003), 53; Gertrud Pfister, "Kör-

perkultur und Weiblichkeit: Ein historischer Beitrag zur Entwicklung des modernen Sports in Deutschland bis zur Zeit der Weimarer Republik," in *Sport und Geschlecht*, ed. Michael Klein (Reinbeck bei Hamburg: Rowohlt, 1983), 35–59.

4. "Das Sportgirl heute und vor dreißig Jahren," *Das Magazin*, no. 70, June 1930, 4846f. These figures include approximately 7 million members of the major bourgeois sport organization, the Deutscher Reichsausschuß für Leibesübungen (DRA), and more than 1.2 million members of the working-class organization, the Zentralkommission für Körperpflege und Arbeitersport (ZK); for further statistics of women's sporting involvement at this period see Gabriela Wesp, *Frisch, fromm, fröhlich, Frau: Frauen und Sport zur Zeit der Weimarer Republik* (Königstein/Taunus: Ulrike Helmer, 1998), 12ff., 26, 29, 31; Christiane Eisenberg, "Massensport in der Weimarer Republik: Ein statistischer Überblick," *Archiv für Sozialgeschichte* 33 (1993): 161, 72. On the broader political and demographic context of the Weimar sporting boom see Hermand and Trommler, *Kultur der Weimarer Republik*, 75ff; Pfister, "Körperkultur," 35–59; Theodore F. Rippey, "Athletics, Aesthetics, and Politics in the Weimar Press," *German Studies Review* 28, no. 1 (2005): 85–106. Studies of specific class-oriented, religious, or politically affiliated sporting organizations at this period include Sigrid Block, *Frauen und Mädchen in der Arbeitersportbewegung* (Münster: Lit, 1987); Gertrud Pfister, "Demands, Realities and Ambivalences: Women in the Proletarian Sports Movement in Germany (1893–1933)," *Women in Sport and Physical Activity Journal* 3, no. 2 (1994): 39ff; Gertrud Pfister and Toni Niewerth, "Jewish Women in Gymnastics and Sport in Germany," *Journal of Sport History* 26, no. 2 (1999): 287–325; Marion E. De Ras, *Körper, Eros und weibliche Kultur: Mädchen im Wandervogel und in der Bündischen Jugend 1900–1933* (Pfaffenweiler: Centaurus, 1988).

5. Carl Diem, "Die Frau. Erlebnisse beim Wintersport," *Sport im Bild*, no. 9, 27 February 1920, 236.

6. "Wie sie Sport treiben: Karikaturen von Hans Schweitzer," *Sport im Bild*, no. 40, 8 October 1920, 1082f. On the 1920s cult of athletic celebrities at this period see Antje Olivier and Sevgi Braun, *Anpassung oder Verbot: Künstlerinnen und die 30er Jahre* (Düsseldorf: Droste, 1998), 153f; Hermand and Trommler, *Kultur der Weimarer Republik*, 454.

7. On the development of gymnastics into a largely women-oriented movement by the Weimar era see Wesp, *Frisch, fromm*, 73–101, 178–88. On the *Körperkultur* movement see e.g. Martin L. Müller, "Turnen und Sport im sozialen Wandel: Körperkultur in Frankfurt am Main während des Kaiserreichs und der Weimarer Republik," *Archiv für Sozialgeschichte* 33 (1993): 107–36; Bernd Wedemeyer-Kolwe, *'Der neue Mensch': Körperkultur im Kaiserreich und in der Weimarer Republik* (Würzburg: Königshausen & Neumann, 2004).

8. Henry Hoek, "Skilauf und Dame," *Sport im Bild*, no. 2, 20 January 1928, 97. For analyses of debates surrounding women's involvement in specific sports at this period, including soccer, hockey, and athletics, see Gertrud Pfister et al., "Women and Football—A Contradiction? The Beginnings of Women's Football in Four European Countries," in Scraton and Flintoff, *Gender and Sport*, 67f., 72; Wesp, *Frisch, fromm*, 148, 152, 155ff; Gertrud Pfister, ed., *Frau und Sport* (Frankfurt/Main: Fischer, 1980), 32f.

9. W. M[eisl], "Frauen-Höchstleistungen im Sport: 'Weibliche' Weltrekorde," *Berliner Illustrirte Zeitung*, no. 34, 22 August 1926, 1085. According to Susan Cahn, Ederle's time was in fact two hours faster: *Coming on Strong: Gender and Sexuality in Twentieth-Century Women's Sport* (New York: Free Press, 1994), 32.

10. Behling, *The Masculine Woman*, 192; see also Cahn, *Coming on Strong*, 8, 20, 32f.

11. M. Boden, "Licht Luft Leben Lachen..." *Das Magazin*, no. 37, September 1927, 1364ff.

12. Willy Meisl, "Die Sportsfrau von gestern," *Uhu*, no. 2, November 1927, 18; Dr W. Bergmann, *Die Frau und der Sport* (Oldenburg i.O.: Gerhard Stalling, 1925), 137. Bergmann was the overseer of women's athletics associations in Brandenburg.

13. Todd Samuel Presner, "'Clear Heads, Solid Stomachs, and Hard Muscles': Max Nordau and the Aesthetics of Jewish Regeneration," *Modernism / modernity* 10, no. 2 (2003): 269–96; Max Nordau, "Muskeljudentum," *Die Jüdische Turnzeitung,* no. 2 (1900): 10–11.

14. Bergmann, *Die Frau und der Sport,* 19f., 48ff., 19 cited here.

15. On the New Woman's attention to physical health and fitness see also Grossmann, "*Girlkultur,*" 62–80.

16. Susan Birrell and Cheryl L. Cole, "Double Fault: Renee Richards and the Construction and Naturalization of Difference," in *Women, Sport, and Culture,* ed. Susan Birrell and Cheryl L. Cole (Champaign: Human Kinetics, 1994), 392.

17. Karl Arnold, "Berliner Bilder XXIV. Damenringkampf," *Simplicissimus,* no. 21, 20 August 1923, 268.

18. M. Frischmann, "Emanzipation," *Simplicissimus,* no. 13, 23 June 1930, 149; Jeanne Mammen, "Frisch, fromm, fröhlich, frei!" *Simplicissimus,* no. 23, 7 September 1931, 273.

19. Bergmann, *Die Frau und der Sport,* 50, 60f. Such arguments were criticized as superficial by some, including sports students Annemarie Kopp and Carla Verständig, whose opinions are cited alongside those of numerous other 1920s female sports students and educators in Pfister, *Frau und Sport,* 125–34.

20. Ruth Goetz, "Footing," *Das Magazin,* no. 32, April 1927, 814.

21. Hertz, "~~Der Rock~~ Die HOSE SIEGT in der Sportmode," 13; Ola Alsen, "Der Anzug der Skiänläuferin," *Sport im Bild,* no. 8, 20 February 1920, 208. On women's sporting fashions in the Weimar era see also Wesp, *Frisch, fromm,* 188–205; Pfister, *Frau und Sport,* 27f., 31, 39, 110ff.; Wolter, *Hosen, weiblich,* 103–95; Kessemeier, *Sportlich, sachlich, männlich,* 209ff.

22. This event is discussed in Pfister, *Frau und Sport,* 38; Wesp, *Frisch, fromm,* 157; Jensen, "Images," 455–71.

23. Baronin Inga Wöllwarth-Wesendonk, "Jiu-Jitsu," *Der Querschnitt* 5, no. 8 (1925): 703ff. See also Bertschik's examination of representations of women drivers and pilots in *Mode,* 247–52.

24. Bergmann, *Die Frau und der Sport,* 64.

25. Cahn, *Coming on Strong,* 8f., 15, 27f., 30, 81f.

26. Ibid., 214.

27. "Die moderne Sportdame," *Die Dame,* no. 14, 1st April Issue 1926, 8.

28. Boden, "Licht Luft Leben Lachen..." 1367.

29. Bergmann, *Die Frau und der Sport,* 75. On the female "surplus" in interwar Germany see Peukert, *Weimar Republic,* 86–89.

30. Pfister, *Frau und Sport,* 29f.

31. Pat Griffin, "Changing the Game: Homophobia, Sexism and Lesbians in Sport," in Scraton and Flintoff, *Gender and Sport,* 196; Behling, *The Masculine Woman,* 195; Cahn, *Coming on Strong,* 165–72, 327–39.

32. Herbert Gerwig, "Normen weiblicher Schönheit: Die Büste und ihre Mängel," *Garçonne,* no. 6, 17 March 1931, 13.

33. Ada v. Niendorf, "Der Frauensport und seine Wirklichkeit," *Garçonne,* no. 8, 15 April 1931, 13f.; see also H. Peukert, "Der Sport und die Dame," *Garçonne,* no. 26, 23 December 1931, 6.

34. Dr. Agnes Strettel, "Heim-Gymnastik für lesbische Frauen," *Frauen Liebe und Leben,* no. 2, 1928, 20ff.; Herta Laser, "Richtiges Lüften und Frauenturnen," *Frauen Liebe und Leben,* no. 1, 1928, 8.

35. Strettel, "Heim-Gymnastik," 20.

36. Laser, "Richtiges Lüften," 6.

37. Trude John, "Die männliche Frau," *Das Magazin,* no. 24, August 1926, 760.

38. Pfister, *Frau und Sport;* Jensen, "Images," 109–112, 442–55.

39. Pfister, *Frau und Sport,* 29, 34–40; Gertrud Pfister, "Sport for Women," in *Sport and Physical Education in Germany,* ed. Roland Naul and Ken Hardman (London: Routledge, 2002), 168ff.

40. Criticizing Sellheim's lack of empirical evidence, Wesp notes his rather obnoxious argument that pregnancy was the best form of physical exercise for women: *Frisch, fromm,* 161f.

41. Geheimrat Hugo Sellheim, "Macht der Sport die Frau glücklich? Ein Epilog zu den Deutschen Frauen-Meisterschaften in Magdeburg 1931," *Uhu,* no. 1, October 1931, 18–24.

42. This and other contemporary medical studies in support of women's sport are detailed in Pfister, *Frau und Sport,* 36 cited here.

43. Bergmann, *Die Frau und der Sport,* 18f., 61.

44. Olaf Gulbransson, "Die Frau von 1932 wird immer weiblicher," *Simplicissimus,* no. 39, 28 December 1931, 459; Edith von Lölhöffel, MD, "Vom Sportmädel zur Sportmutter: Besuch bei glücklichen Müttern, die als Sportlerinnen aufwuchsen," *Uhu,* no. 1, October 1932, 25–30, 108.

45. Lölhöffel, "Vom Sportmädel," 108.

46. Cahn observes a similar trend in US media coverage of this era, whereby tomboy athletes grow up to become champions, but on the way trade their boyish ways for feminine charms: *Coming on Strong,* 214.

47. On the continuing role of women's competitive sport as a symbol of German strength at the international level, see Wesp, *Frisch, fromm,* 242.

48. "Mütter," *Uhu,* no. 8, May 1933, 58f.

49. On the physical education principles of women's organizations under National Socialism see Regina Landschoof, "Frauensport im Faschismus," in *Frauensport im Faschismus,* ed. Regina Landschoof and Karin Hüls (Hamburg: Ergebnisse, 1985), 35–72; Wesp, *Frisch, fromm,* 240–61.

50. Heinrich Satter, "Sport-Kameradschaft zwischen Mann und Frau: Die junge Generation auf den Sportplätzen," *Uhu,* no. 9, June 1933, 20.

Chapter 3

"MY EMIL IS DIFFERENT"
Queer Female Masculinities in the Weimar Media

My Emil is different,
My Emil is nice!
She's in love with me
Never leaves me in the lurch!
She's my everything in this world!
She's not for sale, not even for cash!

....

Oh Emil, that's a real man,
A real fast worker.
I'm so happy that I've got him!
Emil, my Emil, loyal to the grave!

     Eny, "Sie liebt nur Emil," *Die Freundin,* October 1930

*I*n this poem, written in rough Berlin dialect and published in the homosexual women's magazine *Die Freundin,* "Emil's" brand of masculinity—faithful, reliable, and loving—is presented as not only far superior to that of the average guy, but as achievable only by a woman. This chapter examines how popular stereotypes of the masculine woman were reevaluated within the subcultural media, and how contributors to magazines such as *Die Freundin* and *Garçonne* actively negotiated identity categories such as "virile"/"feminine," "homosexual," and "transvestite," in order to produce positive models of nonheteronormative or "queer" existence, visibility, and sexual relationships. These subcultural sources offer a valuable counterpoint to the hysteria surrounding the masculinization of women in the mainstream Weimar media, where women such as Emil, whose gender performances were identifiably masculine, were represented in overwhelmingly negative, stereotyped terms, as a threat to patriarchal social structures and as "perverse" figures inviting social ridicule. By examining the much more enabling and nuanced ways in which female masculinity was embodied and debated within newly emergent female homosexual communities, we can gain a deeper understanding of how female masculinity has developed as a gender with its own complex history.

As noted in the introduction, *Die Freundin* and *Garçonne* were the two longest running and most widely distributed homosexual women's publications of the Weimar era, although several smaller magazines were also published at this period. *Die Freundin* was affiliated with the homosexual rights organization League of Human Rights (BfM) and the homosexual women's organization Ladies' Club Violetta (Damenklub Violetta). It was published by the Radszuweit-Verlag from 1924 to 1933, except for an unexplained absence in 1926 and during a yearlong ban beginning in mid 1928, when it was placed on the list of *Schund- und Schmutzliteratur*—a catalogue of alleged pornographic, obscene, and culturally dubious literature purportedly designed to protect youth from unwanted influences—and consequently banned from public display on newsstands. The slightly higher-brow *Garçonne* was published between 1930 and 1932 by the Bergmann-Verlag and was the successor magazine to *Die Frauenliebe* (1926–1930). It was affiliated with the political German Friendship Association (DFV) and the more socially oriented Ladies' Club Monbijou (Damenklub Monbijou), organizations that competed for members and superiority with the BfM and Violetta. Like *Die Freundin, Garçonne* was banned from public display on newsstands during 1931/32 but continued to publish despite a subsequent drop in advertising, publicity, and sales, until the enterprise finally fell apart in 1932.[1] Both magazines regularly featured a range of political and educational articles; large entertainment sections including short stories, novellas, and poems; classifieds sections and advertisements for subcultural organizations and events; photographs of "virile" and "feminine" homosexual women and occasional nude or erotic portraits; and regular columns and supplements on topics such as transvestism. Although the magazines—like the metropolitan subculture itself—were more accessible for Berlin-based women than those in the provinces, their reach and influence extended far beyond their Berlin publication base, an aspect that is explored further in chapter 5.

The homosexual magazines offer an unparalleled window onto Weimar sexual subcultures, and onto some of the new forms of female subjectivity enabled by the expansion of democratic citizenship and the liberation of the cultural arena following the 1919 November Revolution.[2] For many years scholarship on these sources was largely restricted to chapters in anthologies or unpublished theses, mostly in German; however, two recent studies have contributed greatly to our knowledge of these publications. As well as providing a useful survey of the homosexual magazines and their major contributors, Heike Schader's 2004 monograph *Virile, Vamps und wilde Veilchen* focuses particularly on the magazine fiction, examining the representation of sexuality and desire, the depiction of feminine-identified women, and the masculine/feminine relationship paradigm favored by many homosexual women at this period. However, it is her earlier work on female "virility" that is most pertinent to this analysis, as she concludes that this subcultural label for female masculinity acted as a crucial marker of identification and visibility for many homosexual women in 1920s Germany.[3] While I agree with this assessment, my analysis also brings transgender iden-tificatory possibilities into sharper focus, arguing that these cannot always be subsumed under the label "homosexual."

More recently, Marti Lybeck's research on female homosexuality in Wilhelmine and Weimar Germany provides an excellent analysis of the emergence of early German female homosexual "publics," contextualized against broader historical developments relating to class, female emancipation, and an increasingly liberal-ized public sphere. Her reading of the subcultural magazines as evidence of a community torn "between desire and social belonging"—between new possibili-ties for same-sex eroticism on the one hand, and the longing to be acknowledged as respectable and valued citizens on the other—is highly informative; however, it is her discussion of female masculinity in relation to homosexual identification and desire that is of primary concern here. Lybeck's diagnosis of the middle-class female homosexual community of 1920s Germany as deeply informed by "mas-culinist" ideologies, often at the expense of feminine identificatory possibilities, in many respects aligns with my findings in the following analysis. I disagree, though, with her use of the terms "masculine masquerade" to designate women who "passed" as men in public, and "masculine mimicry" to denote women who adopted "some of the conventional signs of masculinity."[4] While it is crucial to be alert to the constructedness of gendered identity constellations *particularly* during such intense moments of historical flux as the Weimar period, such ter-minology runs the risk of conceptualizing masculinity as inherently foreign to female bodies and by extension, a natural expression of male ones, rather than as a range of gender characteristics and performances that can be just as legitimately performed by women as by men.

Despite differences in format, content, and intended audience, there were points of crossover between mainstream and subcultural publications. Some au-thors, including Grete von Urbanitzky, wrote for both mainstream magazines and homosexual audiences; general-interest publications reviewed novels and films with homosexual themes (including Radclyffe Hall's *Well of Loneliness* when it appeared in German in 1929, and Leontine Sagan's film *Mädchen in Uniform*);

and prominent sexologists contributed articles to the likes of the popular *Uhu*. Although it is unlikely that the subcultural magazines were read much beyond their core audience of homosexual women and "transvestites" of both sexes, it is quite probable that these same readers also purchased mainstream periodicals such as the *BIZ* or *Das Magazin*. By reading subcultural and mainstream publications together in this chapter, I highlight the extent to which these media sources drew on shared cultural reference points, as well as how they reflected vastly different audience needs, fears, and desires.

Writing Histories of Queer Female Masculinities

Historians of sexuality have criticized as anachronistic the use of twentieth-century terms such as "gay" or "lesbian" to describe historical subjects, and this acknowledgement of the historical contingency of sex-gender signifiers has led to ongoing debates about how to approach the study of individuals and communities in the past whose experiences may or may not have included nonconformity to heteronormative structures, same-sex relations (whether emotional, political, or sexual), transgender identifications (including cross-dressing and passing), and other nonnormative performances of gender and sexuality. From the perspective of lesbian history, Judith Bennett suggests the term "lesbian-like" in order to open up history-writing to more of the "ordinary" women whose lives did not comply with dominant narratives of marriage and motherhood, while Martha Vicinus categorizes historical lesbianisms according to specific forms of same-sex behavior, including passing, romantic friendships, and cross-dressing.[5] While their methods differ, such approaches remind us, as Doan observes, of the importance of distinguishing between questions that concern us now and what the historical record allows us to conclude. At the same time, they are forthright about seeking to write histories that have meaning for lesbian/bisexual/queer women today, warning that to avoid terms such as "lesbian" altogether risks creating "a pure, inviolable, and irrelevant past: a fetish instead of a history."[6]

One of the biggest problems with existing histories of the masculine woman is that scholars have often paid inadequate attention to the historical and geographical specificities that shaped how women in the past viewed and constructed their own sex-gender identities. Both lesbian and transgender historians have each tended to lay claim to narratives of female masculinity in the past in order to serve their own political agendas in the present. Responding to this trend, scholars such as Halberstam, Jay Prosser, and Nan Boyd demand that we not only distinguish more carefully between "lesbian" and "transgender" histories, but also that we acknowledge instances where a focus on either "lesbian" or "transgender" in isolation cannot provide adequate tools for historical analysis. Halberstam's model of "perverse presentism" illustrates this approach: she explicitly refrains from reading past female masculinities as synonymous with early forms of lesbianism, and calls on historians of sexuality to instead "account for historical moments when the difference between gender deviance and sexual deviance is hard to discern."[7]

It is this refusal to pin down evidence of past female masculinities to narratives of *just* gender or *just* sexuality, and the insistence on acknowledging the complex interplay of these factors with other identity constructs such as class, race, and ethnicity, that I believe offers the most historically useful and accurate approach. Rather than contributing simply to lesbian *or* transgender history, this chapter highlights how sex-gender "inversion" and the figure of the masculine woman were represented in interconnected but unstable ways within the Weimar media. In an attempt to provide an analysis that is simultaneously true to the historical documents, alert to theoretical debates about gender and sexuality, and of relevance to readers in the present, I use a combination of historically specific and more recent terms to describe aspects of sexual and gender identity that arose in Weimar-era discussions of the masculine woman. Of course, queer and postmodern scholarship has rightly problematized notions of essential "identity," whether sexual or otherwise. I consider it productive and historically relevant to discuss gender and sexuality in relation to ideas about identity, whilst acknowledging that this is a fluid and contested construct.

This chapter expands upon existing studies of gender and sexuality in Weimar Germany by examining the limited capacity of sexological categories such as "homosexual" or "transvestite" to describe the contemporary spectrum of queer female masculinities, and by highlighting the extent to which ideas about sexual otherness played into mainstream representations of the masculinized woman. It is divided into three parts: the first contrasts the ways in which popular stereotypes of the masculine woman were represented in the mainstream and subcultural media; the second section focuses on media appropriations of sexological discourses, which mainstream and subcultural commentators used to come to very different conclusions (the survey of medical discourses on inversion in the introduction provides an important frame of reference here); and the final section examines the subcultural magazines for evidence of what might now be termed "transgender" experience, including accounts of women passing as men and of female-to-male transvestism. This last section, in particular, demonstrates how the subcultural media provided a forum in which contemporaries could negotiate subtle but all-important distinctions between various embodiments of female masculinity.

Amazons and Intellectuals:
Sexualized Stereotypes of the Masculine Woman

In previous chapters I have argued that the masculine woman was represented in the Weimar popular media in stereotyped ways that, at their most derogatory, were often informed by associations with homosexuality. Here I examine two key stereotypes of the masculine woman, the Amazon and the intellectual, as they appeared in the popular and subcultural media. I argue that the mainstream media represented these figures as threatening because of their implicit rejection of men and disruption of social and gender norms, and illustrated this threat through references to homosexuality. In contrast, subcultural commentators drew on these stereotypes in more positive and enabling ways that reflected the needs of their queer audiences.

A legendary figure associated with ancient female separatist warrior societies and female strength, the Amazon was referenced by countless commentators in the 1920s media as a symbol of the modern, independent woman. Appearing everywhere from posh fashion magazines to satirical and homosexual publications, in its more positive forms the "Amazon" label was used to celebrate women's achievements on the sporting field and to signify respect for the strength, independence, record-breaking achievements, and elegance of the new breed of female automobilists, pilots, and equestriennes. It was even used in advertising copy to appeal to the spending power of the New Woman—a cigarette advertisement featuring a female automobilist in the latest driving attire declared that "[t]he Amazon type is, in a sense, the model of the modern woman."[8] According to Inge Stephan, the Amazon myth has traditionally enjoyed particular significance during periods of historical upheaval, such as revolutionary France, when individuals such as Olympe de Gouges and Mary Wollstonecraft sought to harness the revolutionary goal of equality for women as well as men.[9] It is no accident that commentators in the 1920s returned to this legendary figure to express their concerns and hopes about Germany's womanhood, for the Weimar Republic represented a similar moment of historical crisis that involved a fundamental redefinition of women's role in society.

Consequently, the Amazon stereotype was also used to critique the masculinized modern woman and her rejection of heterosexual life goals. The satirical *Simplicissimus* published a number of cartoons in this vein entitled simply "The Amazon"; in one such image a grotesquely muscular woman declares her outright rejection of heterosexual relationships: "I'd like to see the hurricane that could sweep *me* into the harbor of marriage!"[10] One of the most detailed popular culture critiques of this figure can be found in Wolfgang von Lengerke's 1928 novel *Die Amazone Gloria* (Gloria, the Amazon), a chapter of which was published in *Das Magazin*. Lengerke's novel charts how a modern New York socialite becomes disenchanted with men and founds a feminist colony in Texas along with other women who have left their husbands and children, only to see it slowly destroyed by a contagious wave of female homosexuality. In such ways, mainstream commentators conflated the image of the Amazon with negative, overtly sexualized stereotypes of the masculine female homosexual and the political emancipist.[11]

Subcultural audiences shared this fascination with the Amazon, but were more likely to interpret this figure—including her rejection of heteronormative values—in a positive light. The Amazon type featured in periodicals for homosexual women in various forms: in fictional narratives, where she stood for strength and youth; as a sexological subcategory of the masculine woman; and as one of a long line of historical role models that also included Catherine the Great, the legendary "Pope Johanna," Joan of Arc, Sweden's Queen Christina, and Germany's Charlotte von der Pfalz. Moreover, such historical figures—often the subject of feature articles—were themselves frequently described as "Amazonian" in ways that tended to conflate ideas about female masculinity and homosexuality. Thus a writer for *Die Freundin* tells of how Catherine the Great became both more masculine and more homosexual with age, "so that she also required girlfriends for her gratification"; others such as French singer Julie Maupin were even said to have embodied masculinity in a superior fashion to most men:

> (P)hysically a perfectly beautiful woman, but spiritually and psychologically all man in the best sense, more man in any case than most people who are only physically men but without any other trace of masculinity, and her sexual tendencies also seem to have been exclusively directed toward women.[12]

In harking back to such historical role models of female masculinity and homosexuality, contributors to the 1920s magazines overlooked what might have seemed their obvious precursors, the female emancipists of the 1890s. Lybeck usefully situates this oversight in terms of a disavowal of the more feminine identification of the earlier generation of "New" women that, like that of "normal" women, continued to be associated with stereotypes of feminine lasciviousness, deception, and frivolity—even within the emerging homosexual community.[13] Positioning the masculine Amazon as a strong and positive role model, the subcultural magazines worked toward affirming readers' nonheteronormative gender and sexual identities and providing these with a proud and unique history, even as feminine homosexual identifications were devalued in the process.

A second major stereotype of the sexually "other" masculine woman was that of the intellectual and/or artistic woman. Women had first gained entry into German universities in 1908, and somewhat earlier in Switzerland, although they formed part of a much longer tradition of upper- and upper middle-class female intellectuals reaching back at least as far as the salons of the Enlightenment. As noted in the introduction, intellectual women had been theorized in the late nineteenth and early twentieth centuries by sex researchers such as Havelock Ellis and Otto Weininger as unusually masculine, particularly those involved in the emancipation movement, which was considered a veritable breeding ground for female inversion. Smith-Rosenberg observes that in the US at this period, "the creation of a new medico-sexual category, the Mannish Lesbian, linked women's rejection of traditional gender roles and their demands for social and economic equality to cross-dressing, sexual perversion, and borderline hermaphroditism."[14] In 1920s Germany this was likewise a hot topic, reflected not only in mass media coverage but also in the publication of academic monographs such as Alice Rüle-Gerstel's 1932 *Das Frauenproblem der Gegenwart: Eine psychologische Bilanz* (The Woman Question of the Present: A Psychological Summary), in which the author investigates the links between female sexuality, the women's movement, biology, and sociological trends such as women's work. This linking of female intellectualism and emancipation was particularly targeted at middle-class women, whereas at least as far as the sexologists were concerned, the working-class masculine or "invert" woman was far more likely to be associated with criminality.[15]

The mainstream Weimar media willingly perpetrated associations between female intellectualism and masculinity, and as with representations of the Amazon, depictions of academic, emancipated women ranged from the admiring to the malicious. Illustrating the former approach was a 1921 *Dame* article on sculptor Renée Sintenis, which observes how—"like all good female artists"—she has a "somewhat masculine element" which shows itself physiologically in her "tall, boyish build" as well as her powerful work.[16] Not surprisingly, in the context of this high-end women's fashion magazine, Sintenis's homosexual leanings are ignored. In contrast, representations of pipe-smoking female intellectuals and artists in satirical journals such as *Simplicissimus* or *Ulk* hint strongly at sexual as well as gender inversion. In one of numerous such cartoons, entitled "The Poet" (1927), a masculine noun is used to describe a Gertrude Stein–like figure seated at her desk with horn-rimmed glasses, sharp features, pageboy haircut, and heavy-set suit. Her feminine partner stands supportively to one side as the poet pens verses that would, as the caption scathingly claims, evoke the envy of Goethe himself (Figure 3.1). Such images evince a strong discomfort in relation to women whose creative or intellectual capacity "crossed over" into traditionally masculine territory, disturbing the conventional binary of "masculine" creative production versus "feminine" reproduction.[17]

Despite being politically aligned more closely with the male-dominated homosexual rights movement than the women's emancipation cause, the homosexual women's magazines regularly featured fictional representations of emancipated female artists and intellectuals, as well as theoretical contributions on female emancipation. *Die Freundin* even published an excerpt from Weininger's notoriously misogynistic chapter on "emancipated women"—a move that Lybeck describes as typical of publisher Friedrich Radszuweit's "masculinist" political stance, and correspondingly, of that magazine's tendency to associate "masculine" achievement with female homosexuality at the cost of female solidarity.[18] In contrast, the more feminist *Frauen Liebe und Leben* (the *Frauenliebe* substitute during 1928) directly linked the modern woman's masculine fashions to her political emancipation: "the question arises as to whether these masculinizing tendencies in women's external appearance are pushing in the same direction as the societal-intellectual emancipatory efforts of a subsection of modern women."[19] Such contributions reinforced the popular association between female intellectuals or emancipists

Figure 3.1. "The Poet." *Ulk,* 2 December 1927, 375.
Source: BPK Bildagentur für Kunst, Kultur und Geschichte

and masculine gender identity, but—as the following examples emphasize—in a generally more positive fashion than was typical of the mainstream media.

Thus at least one homosexual-identified writer directly criticized the "outdated," malicious image of the unattractive bluestocking in the popular media, countering that the women's movement was in fact full of nice, good-looking, clever, and charming women.[20] Meanwhile, in the romantic short stories that made up the bulk of these magazines, masculine female intellectuals and artists generally appear as well-dressed, independent, and stoic, but also rather dark and introspective figures, often from an upper-class background, and with a tendency to pine for their feminine lovers. Following on from older subcultural representations of the female intellectual, such as Aimée Duc's 1903 novel *Sind es Frauen?* (Are These Women?), which described a group of "third sex" female students in turn-of-the-century Zurich (an attractive destination for this earlier generation of German-speaking "New Women," who were not yet admitted to the German universities), Weimar homosexual authors constructed female intellectuals as articulate, independent, highly educated, and politicized women not short on erotic appeal.[21] As well as serving as sexual role models, the upper-class background of many such characters presumably functioned as a form of escapism for the largely lower- and middle-class readership of the 1920s homosexual magazines.

A short novella entitled "Club of Girlfriends" exemplifies subcultural appropriations of the female intellectual stereotype, albeit in lightly satirical fashion, portraying a lineup of middle-class working women who have adopted the masculine fashions and subcultural aesthetic and erotic codes discussed in chapter 1. One of the protagonists, a musician and teacher named Lisa Gerlach, is described as "a striking apparition, who makes an unforgettable impression even at first glance." Tall and sharply dressed in black suits in the English riding style, "[o]ne could call her beautiful were it not for the too strongly emphasized self-confidence, exaltation, capriciousness, and strong, unrestrained passion that speak in her face." Gerlach's friend Klara Semmler, PhD, a poor but hardworking high school teacher, likewise prefers a stern aesthetic that consciously differs from mainstream models of feminine beauty:

> Her face is angular and severe, it could never have been pretty or even just attractive. ... But in it are two very clear, intelligent, almost grey-white eyes with a sharp light, her build is short and stocky. She always wears the same long grey Havelock coat, which could just as easily belong to a young man as a woman, a high choker collar, cuffs, and a black-and-white spotted tie. It has happened more than once that someone seeing her from behind, in the crush of the tram or the hustle and bustle of the city or by twilight, has called out to her: "I say, you there, young man."[22]

In another story, a lesbian sculptor named Myriam Brenk represents a wealthier, upper-class version of the artistic woman, a tall, austere figure who smokes while working and speeds through the city in her dark red Mercedes with her chauffeur in the passenger seat.[23] Such stories represented the female intellectual in more three-dimensional and erotically appealing ways than the mainstream press; however, their conflation of female masculinity and intelligence did not go without criticism in the subcultural magazines.

On the contrary, some readers protested vigorously against the implication that feminine homosexual women were less intelligent than their masculine counterparts. This issue arose with a vengeance within the context of an impassioned reader debate in *Garçonne* in 1931 on the topic of faithfulness, in which virile and feminine-identifying women discussed the rights, responsibilities, strengths, and flaws of the masculine homosexual woman. (Later that year, *Die Freundin* also featured a similar series of articles and letters debating the behavior and appearance of masculine homosexual women, and discussing the possibility of sexual relationships between two masculine or two feminine women—a possibility that, as Gudrun Schwarz observes, the sexologists excluded as a matter of principle.[24])

Käthe Wundram set the ball rolling, provocatively suggesting that the virile homosexual woman is generally more intelligent and interested in subjects such as politics and literature, whereas the sole life goal of the feminine homosexual woman is love—and thus it is she who commits the greater crime if she is unfaithful to her masculine partner. This view carries strong traces of Weininger's theory that whereas masculine women are intelligent and emancipated, feminine women lack the capacity for agency, intelligence, or an ego.[25] Wundram's remarks attracted heated replies from both feminine- and masculine-identifying women. Representing the former camp, Lo Hilmar condemned Wundram's underestimation of the feminine woman as "typically male, in that she prefers to belittle all that is feminine."[26] Ilse Schwarze, a self-identified masculine woman, likewise dismissed Wundram's perspective as outdated, shameful, misogynistic, and incompatible with modern relationship models such as companionate marriage, which depend on equality between partners: "What happens to camaraderie when the masculine woman believes herself to be so intellectually superior to her feminine companion?" In a separate contribution, she also drew on her own experiences with highly intelligent feminine women, while remarking scathingly upon masculine female acquaintances "who are not forced to groan under the burden of a large intellect."[27]

As several scholars have observed, the act of assigning "virile" and "feminine" roles to homosexual women is rarely questioned in these contributions, rather, it is the content and implications of these gender roles that is at stake.[28] Schwarze, for example, focuses on how virile and feminine women can come together to form progressive sexual relationships, arguing that there is no need to mimic that which is undesirable about hierarchical heterosexual partnerships: "Is it good that men in 'normal' marriages cheat on their wives?—That they assume the right to do so, just because they are men? Is it really necessary that the masculine woman adopt this arrogant view for herself?"[29] Likewise, a feminine-identified contributor to the *Freundin* lamented that it was not necessary for her masculine counterparts to take on what she termed the "worst masculine characteristics": "Same-sex love would be meaningless if all you wanted to be were full men!"[30] Clearly, the gendering of characteristics such as intelligence and unfaithfulness as masculine hit a nerve within the contemporary subculture, as women sought to balance feminist political beliefs with personal and erotic identities as virile or feminine homosexual women, and in many cases, an ongoing investment in relationship structures based on gendered difference.

The arguments cited here point to a community trying to negotiate what it meant to be a homosexual woman at this period, and to what extent this was determined by ideas about gender. It is important to note that these questions attracted different answers according to the socioeconomic background of the women concerned. Thus Kokula suggests that whereas virile/feminine structures played a particularly important role among the lower- and middle-class female homosexuals who were the chief audience of magazines such as *Die Freundin* and *Garçonne,* upper-class women often adopted slightly more androgynous styles. This argument has parallels to studies of female sexual subcultures in other contexts, notably the mid twentieth-century US, where scholars have distinguished between working-class butch/femme structures and middle-class androgynous or feminine "romantic friendships."[31] However, Lybeck's research helps to complicate this assumption for the Weimar context, as her analysis of the periodicals reveals that not only did masculine/feminine erotic structures often cross class lines at this period, reflecting increased degrees of intermingling by women of different backgrounds within new same-sex spaces, but that "masculinity" served as an important ideology and source of social respectability even amongst ostensibly feminine-identified homosexual women: "They accepted the public sphere as a space gendered masculine and inserted themselves into it through a strategy of masculinity."[32] Erotic gender differences, then, were less a case of specific female "types" than of relatively subtle distinctions among outwardly "masculine" women.

Judith Butler has famously described "queer" genders such as "butch" and "femme" as "copies" for which there is no "original," arguing that they help to highlight the constructedness and performativity of gender by showing that gendered behaviors are neither natural, preexisting, nor inevitable expressions of biologically "sexed" bodies.[33] It is clear from this *Garçonne* debate that some homosexual women in 1920s Germany were convinced that female masculinity represented an inborn and superior psychological and even moral state. However, others showed a much greater awareness of the constructedness and contingency of gendered characteristics, and questioned the relevance of heteronormative structures and hierarchies as the basis of homosexual relationships. In doing so, they preempted much later debates in a range of national contexts surrounding butch-femme models of lesbian sexuality.[34] In negotiating popular stereotypes of the masculine woman, the subcultural magazines offered their audiences a more differentiated account of the relationships between masculinity, homosexuality, and feminist political goals than did the mainstream press, which tended to resort to derogatory caricatures of man-hating female inverts. The extent of this representational trend is explored further in the next section, which examines the impact of sexological discourses on broader cultural discussions of female masculinity.

"Adam's Missing Rib!" Sexological Theories of Female Masculinity in the Popular and Subcultural Media

The popular press played a vital role in the dissemination of sexological knowledge during the Weimar era, and it was not unusual for mass culture representations of the masculine woman to assume a quite detailed audience familiarity with sexological theories about female sex-gender inversion. While the popular media at times provided audiences with sympathetic portrayals of "third sex" otherness, more often the female invert was depicted as inherently perverse, inviting reactionary responses to her implicit rejection of heterosexual and reproductive duties. In contrast, the subcultural magazines articulate a more complex relationship between female masculinity and homosexuality, with commentators using scientific arguments to argue that such sex-gender phenomena were natural, congenital conditions deserving of legal protection and social respect.

The familiarity of mainstream audiences with a range of sexological knowledges was highlighted in reader responses to the previously mentioned *BIZ* reader competition "What Do You Say about Fräulein Mia?" in which a female white-collar worker sports an exaggeratedly masculine outfit, short hair, and assertive stride (see Figure 1.7). Many of the one-liner responses to this competition—which came from all over Germany, reflecting the *BIZ*'s nationwide readership—incorporated medicalized ideas about sexual and gender inversion, although generally in ways that favored wit and rhyme over scientific accuracy. "Those fellows at Steinach's must have implanted her with the wrong monkey?" was the answer awarded the considerable first prize sum of five hundred marks, directly referencing Viennese biologist Eugen Steinach's hormone experiments and gonad transplantations in rodents, which Hirschfeld had used in developing his theory of sexual intermediaries.[35] Other respondents variously mocked "third sex" theories of inversion as an inborn condition ("When the Lord God sees her—he'll laugh and say: Did I make three back then?"; "Adam's missing rib!") or thematized the role of clothing as an expression of gender ("Clothing alone does not make the man: it's naked facts that decide the matter!") or used language to play with ideas about hermaphroditism and intersexuality: "Fräulein Mia seems to find herself in the hermaphrodite weeks!" (*Zwitterwochen*—a linguistic play on the rhyming word for honeymoon, *Flitterwochen*, a term that simultaneously emphasizes this figure's divergence from heteronormativity); "The most makeshift dwelling: half gentleman's room; half ladies' room/woman" (a play on a historic German term for "woman," *Frauenzimmer*). A few drew on familiar stereotypes of homosexual causality to suggest that female inversion was a response to failed heterosexuality, while others were less concerned with sexological categories than with women's perceived rejection of their maternal duties: "By the time her kid finds the breast it will have starved!" Positing Mia as a sign of the changing times ("At least in our days the guessing game 'boy or girl?' ended at the latest at birth"), many responses highlighted the constructed nature of gender performance ("By Jove, a made man!"; "Self-made man"), but often only in order to reaffirm an underlying or "essential" femininity ("Boy, boy, you'll turn back into a girl in the end!"; "Put a mouse on her tie and just see how soon she forgets her masculinity"). The editors noted the mixture of serious protests and humorous replies that this competition attracted, but clearly endorsed the latter approach as the preferable solution to such inappropriate gender displays.[36]

That the first prize in this competition could go to a response referencing cutting-edge hormone research and its impact upon understandings of gender and sexuality demonstrates a strong interest in such topics on behalf of the 1920s German reading public. The interest in hormone research also extended to other questions such as aging, as the popular media keenly reported on scientific efforts to find the key to youth, a quest thematized in Vicki Baum's popular novel *stud. chem. Helene Willfüer* (Helene). *Uhu* published several articles at this period that employ sexological theories to help explain the phenomenon of female sex-gender inversion. In a 1924 piece entitled "The Riddle of the Glands: The Mysterious Effects of Inner Secretion," Dr. Curt Thomalla argues that sexually intermediate forms are the result of hormones or "inner secretions" rather than degeneration. Although reminiscent of Hirschfeld's theory of sexual intermediaries, which likewise explained nongenital gender abnormalities with reference to hormonal development, Thomalla's agenda proves to be less progressive: he describes such individuals as "diseased" and proposes hormone manipulation as a potential "cure" for homosexuality. The image selected to illustrate this article depicts four "women" in full male attire whose "inner secretions" have led them to select male occupations and acquire police permits to dress as men (Figure 3.2). Although the sexual tendencies of these individuals are not articulated, the audience is encouraged by means of association to connect their masculine appearance with theories of congenital and hormonal inversion.[37]

Another *Uhu* article, "M plus W: On Primitive Masculine and Feminine Characteristics," combined the hormone research of Steinach and Hirschfeld with philosophical theories of gender ranging from Plato to Weininger. Author and Steinach student Dr. Paul Schmidt explains to his readers that all gendered characteristics, whether physiological or behavioral, are caused by hormonal secretions, but he also elaborates on the influence of historical and demographic factors. He thus expresses surprise that the current generation of women—who as a result of the postwar "excess" of women must compete harder for the attention of men—has "abandoned" the obvious signs of womanhood, such as long hair or Rubenesque curves. Schmidt blames this "merging of the sexes" on the

Figure 3.2. "The Influence of Inner Secretion on Body and Soul." *Uhu,* November 1924, 89.
Source: BPK Bildagentur für Kunst, Kultur und Geschichte

masculinization of women rather than the feminization of men, and suggests possible reasons why female masculinity might appeal to the cultural imagination at this particular historical moment:

> Is it to fulfill the age-old longing for the hermaphrodite, the organism that is really of both sexes? Is it emancipation, the "revolutionizing of woman"? Is it the wish of women to replace men's male friendships of the war years? Or is it a natural adaptation to a time that allows for ... no superfluous luxuries of feeling?

Although Schmidt explains the current wave of female masculinization using a mixture of biological, political, and Zeitgeist arguments, his findings are conservative, emphasizing heterosexual complementariness and reproduction as the ultimate, inevitable goal of sexuality, and dismissing the masculine woman as a temporary historical aberration who will not harm the vitality of the "true" heterosexual couple.[38]

While popular magazines thus addressed sexological approaches toward female masculinity at a general level, they tended to avoid directly confronting the still largely taboo topic of homosexuality. In contrast, satirical magazines such as *Ulk* and *Simplicissimus* published numerous images during the mid to late 1920s caricaturing the female homosexual and targeting gender as well as sexual inversion. Often these images took the form of drawings by contemporary artists such as Jeanne Mammen, to which the magazine editors added snappy captions suggesting specific, and frequently homophobic interpretations. References to homosexuality were employed in order to reinforce critiques of the selfish modern woman interested only in her own pleasure, and to showcase her disregard for both men and reproductive responsibilities—as a typical caption declared: "It's a shame about the men—one just doesn't have any use for them."[39] Thus the 1926 *Ulk* spring cover depicted two figures in suits and ties walking arm in arm across a meadow; the monocle, cigarette, and severe skirt suit of the first point clearly to her sex-gender inversion, while the sex of the second figure is difficult to determine, but again suggestive of sex-gender alterity. A perturbed stork bites the ankle of the second figure, rejecting the infertility of this "third sex" couple at the most symbolically reproductive time of year (Figure 3.3).[40]

Such caricatures point toward a growing public awareness of the masculine visual styles favored by many within the female homosexual subculture at this time, although as noted in chapter 1, stereotypical images of the masculine female homosexual had been infiltrating mainstream publications since at least the early 1920s. To an extent, they also reflect the widespread voyeuristic fascination with the queer clubs of the metropolis, which were increasingly frequented by heterosexual visitors of both sexes—McCormick notes that certain homosexual bars and cafés were even listed in tourist guides to Berlin's night life. Although this phenomenon was critiqued in often scathing tones by mainstream and subcultural commentators alike, it undoubtedly contributed to a more widespread awareness of homosexual visual styles.[41]

By around 1930, sexual suspicion was increasingly extended to feminine as well as masculine women alone together in public, as caricatures thematized fears that female homosexuals were becoming indistinguishable from "normal" women. A typical example featured two feminine women enjoying themselves on a carousel while a third looks on rather enviously, but convinces herself that: "I'm not riding the carousel without a man—after all, I'm not perverse!" Others feature feminine women who are "read" as heterosexual by men until their sexual advances are rejected; occasionally playing up the titillating aspect of lesbian sexuality for heterosexual men: "You know what, let's pretend we're 'girlfriends,' that makes the men more ambitious."[42] This increasing sexual suspicion can be linked to what Chauncey has termed the "resexualization" of women in mainstream ideology at this period, whereby concern shifted from the fact of women's sexual activity to their choice of sexual partners, reflected in the sexological shift

Figure 3.3. "Spring 1926: Even the Stork Is Confused!" *Ulk,* 12 March 1926.
Source: BPK Bildagentur für Kunst, Kultur und Geschichte

from "inversion" to "homosexuality." Although Chauncey argues that in the US this newly sexualized conceptualization of womanhood focused on the "sexually precocious and profoundly heterosexual" flapper, the images examined here show that mainstream German audiences were growing ever more alert to the sexological and cultural phenomenon of the female homosexual, in both masculine and feminine variants, and that this figure was increasingly perceived as a threat to traditional heterosexual structures.[43]

Homosexual magazines were likewise keen to publish articles that referred to recent scientific research on gender and sexuality. They demonstrate a more sympathetic approach toward sexological variations than does the mainstream press, aware that they were publishing for an audience that identified to varying degrees with such nonnormative categories. Contributors to these magazines consistently argued that homosexuality, transvestism, and other sex-gender phenomena were natural, congenital, and hormonal conditions that reflected the endless variety of "sexual intermediaries" existing throughout the natural world. By distancing such conditions from theories of perversion or degeneration, subcultural commentators sought, often quite explicitly, to contribute to contemporary homosexual and transgender rights activism, such as the campaign to abolish Paragraph 175 of the Criminal Code prohibiting male homosexual acts. These overtly political motives reflect the organizational links between the female homosexual magazines and various branches of the homosexual rights movement. The magazines also functioned as a reference point for further information on sexological and sexual-political topics, through the publication of book excerpts, reviews, and advertisements, and by publicizing lectures on topics such as "The Normal and the Abnormal Woman" or "The Masculinization of Woman."

One of the most extensive sexology-informed examinations of the masculine woman within the subcultural magazines was a series of ten articles entitled "Bachelorette and Bachelor" (Junggesellin und Junggeselle) written for *Garçonne* in 1930/31 by a German professor of entomology and ethnology, Ferdinand Karsch-Haack, known within the Weimar homosexual rights movement for demonstrating the occurrence of same-sex activity in non-Western cultures as well as the animal kingdom.[44] In this series Karsch-Haack decisively links gender and sexual alterity in his taxonomy of the *Männin,* an umbrella concept he uses to describe female individuals who are, he argues, neither fully woman nor man, but a combination of both, and whose counterpart is the more or less feminized man. He divides this concept into three categories, the first of which is "the lesbian" or "Sapphic woman," encompassing masculine women with an "exclusive" and "inborn" tendency toward their own sex. These "born bachelorettes" prefer masculine occupations and can, argues Karsch-Haack, be found in significant numbers among female emancipists and in the military—a claim that echoed the findings of Krafft-Ebing and Ellis. Within this category, Karsch-Haack distinguishes further between the more feminine "lesbian" and the more masculine "man-woman" or "virago," but he adds that any cross-dressing tendencies within this category remain secondary to sexual identity. In contrast, the second subcategory of *Männin*, the so-called *Transmutistin*, is characterized by an overwhelming need to simulate a male appearance, and may be either heterosexual or homosexual. Here Karsch-Haack rejects Hirschfeld's term "transvestite" as being too strongly focused on cross-dressing, whereas he suggests that his own term is better able to encompass other factors such as voice, makeup, perfume, hairstyle, gait, and nicknames. His third category treats the Amazon, for whom he argues neither sexual object choice nor clothing is central, but rather the desire to rule.[45]

Such texts by male "experts" appeared frequently in the homosexual magazines, and while not all subcultural commentators abided by such taxonomies of the masculine woman, this kind of direct and detailed engagement with sexological themes constituted an important means of disseminating "scientific" findings to the women most directly affected by them. In addition, it was not uncommon for lay members of the subculture to speak out on sexological topics, demonstrating a close and often critical familiarity with a range of scientific and philosophical texts. Some had clearly adopted theories such as Hirschfeld's taxonomy of sexual intermediaries as fact—as one commentator forthrightly observed: "Every thinking and unprejudiced person knows that the pure man and the pure woman are only abstractions; in reality there are transitional forms."[46] Hirschfeld was cited with particular frequency, reflecting the widespread respect for his work as a sex researcher and campaigner for Berlin's "third sex" community. Yet there were many contributors to the homosexual magazines who did not hesitate to criticize or ignore sexological theories that appeared to undermine their cause. In coverage of several contemporary murders by homosexual women in the United States, for example, commentators sought to combat the homophobia that was preventing the perpetrators' fair trial, and pleaded for international solidarity among "Garçonne-oriented" women in campaigning against their death sentences. In doing so they resisted the classifications of sexologists such as Ellis, who had linked working-class female inversion to criminality.[47]

The magazine short fiction also played an important role in the critical communication of sexological knowledges. By incorporating theories of sex-gender inversion into fictional characterizations of masculine women, such theories became personified and naturalized within a medium that sought to have a direct emotional impact on the reader. Sometimes the inclusion of sexological ideas occurred in a relatively straightforward fashion, such as when fictional characters turn to scientific works in their search for sexual enlightenment. In Selli Engler's long-running novella in *Die Freundin*, "Poor Little Jett," one of the protagonists reaches for books by Otto Weininger and Anne v. d. Eken (author of the 1906 study *Mannweiber—Weibmänner und der § 175* [Man-Women—Women-Men and Paragraph 175]), which the author goes on to cite at length on topics such as female emancipation and the role of the "man-woman" within the women's movement. A similar story features an enlightened father who, suspecting his daughter's homosexual tendencies to be hereditary, introduces her from an early age to sexological texts:

> Professor Hannsen had recognized early on that his daughter took after her mother. He didn't consider this a misfortune, but he wanted to protect her from marrying, only to recognize her disposition later on. So he enlightened his daughter, obtaining for her books and magazines on homosexuality, for he suspected that he would die an early death.

This narrative trope of sexological discovery would have been familiar to homosexual readers of this period, having featured in Radclyffe Hall's widely publicized *Well of Loneliness* as well as the German lesbian saga *Der Skorpion,* examined in chapter 5, while ideas about hereditary homosexuality appeared in a number of other short stories as well.[48]

Theories of female inversion were also incorporated into the short fiction in more subtle ways, for instance by attributing elements of biological and psychological masculinity to the queer heroine. Just as Krafft-Ebing, Ellis, and Hirschfeld had described the boyish childhoods, muscular builds, and masculine characteristics of the female invert, authors of 1920s lesbian fiction described characters in terms that merged understandings of masculine gender and homosexuality. A typical example is the masculine heroine "Gert" in Ruth Kampe's 1932 novella "The Child," published in *Garçonne.* Complementing his/her masculine nickname, "Gert" wears decidedly masculine clothing, has a passion for driving and smoking, and exhibits sexual superiority over a younger, feminine partner. S/he displays a rather chauvinistic brand of pride and jealousy when said girlfriend proposes sleeping with "another" man in order to have a baby ("You cannot serve two masters"), and rejects feminized signs of emotional vulnerability ("How dreadful, her masculine features were thoroughly disfigured from crying!"). Countless similar heroines likewise sport muscular, energetic builds, severe features, and sharp hairstyles, and exhibit characteristics coded as "masculine," such as energy, egocentrism, intelligence, melancholy, humor, and a highly developed capacity for agency. As with Gert, these masculine visual styles and characteristics are frequently reinforced by the use of male nicknames ("Ferdi," "Heinz," etc.), pronouns, and other expressions and terms of endearment usually reserved for boys or men (*"Bubi," "Junge," "Kerl"*); indeed, it was not unusual for a character to be described as a "smart looking lad," or as having a "delightful boy's body."[49] Furthermore, while I have shown that the ideal of a female body "steeled by sport" was also prominent within broader cultural discourses during the 1920s, it is clear from the subcultural magazines that a "boyishly slender" female body remained an important means of encoding female homosexual desire even into the 1930s.

Through such positive reevaluations of masculine physical and behavioral characteristics in women, subcultural authors moved beyond the often hollow and pathologizing taxonomies of the sexologists, which, as Halberstam has argued, often "glossed over differences that may have made all the difference to women within the sexual subcultures in question, and … missed subtle differences between types of female masculinity."[50] Writers in the homosexual magazines created characters that were erotically attractive, enthusiastic about sex, and human in their flaws and strengths. At times, like "Emil," the masculine female homosexual was considered to "do" masculinity better than a man; at other times she was represented as an attractive synthesis of masculine and feminine attributes: "O you, my beloved, strong boy! How you are like a man but with the soul of a girl."[51]

Of course, subcultural authors were not above resorting to types, and the construction of virile and feminine characters in the short stories often followed patterns that relied on erotic codes and shorthand familiar to a female homosexual audience. Schader identifies a range of virile types, from exotic "Ben-Hur" and "Don Juan" characters to financially dependent "Gigolos" and tuxedo-clad, upper-class "Gentlemen," who are complemented in the magazine fiction by feminine types including the "vamp" and the "exotic woman."[52] To this list I would add the boyish *Bubi*, a type that embodied youthful playfulness and sexual enthusiasm and was often depicted in relationships with powerful and wealthy older women, and the Amazons and intellectuals described above. Yet even when they resorted to types, authors of magazine short fiction diverged from both sexological and mainstream discourses surrounding the virile homosexual woman, not least by emphasizing the erotic impact she had on her surroundings.

The content of the subcultural magazines demonstrates that women in the 1920s homosexual community were quite prepared to resist sexological theories that threatened to undermine their relationships. Rather than accepting the sexological notion that feminine homosexual women were susceptible to heterosexual advances, for example, subcultural authors were more likely to depict feminine characters leaving boyfriends or husbands in order to be with virile women, while a few insisted in no uncertain terms that heterosexuality was just as impossible for the feminine homosexual woman as for her virile counterpart. As one fictional masculine protagonist announced to her feminine girlfriend: "You see, dear Monika, you are every bit 'too feminine' as I am 'too little.' It is just as impossible for you to be truly happy with a man as it is for me."[53] Similar views were also expressed by nonfiction contributors, although with little consensus as to whether the feminine woman was more or less feminine than her heterosexual counterpart. Such critical interventions into sexological discourses show that while subcultural commentators were willing to adopt those theories that suited their political and emotional goals, they were also engaged in actively constructing and negotiating ideas about masculinity and femininity in order to better reflect the aspirations and realities of their audience.

From "Passing" to "Transvestism": Homosexual and Transgender Masculinities

Subcultural commentators were thus both critical and selective in their appropriation of sexological discourses, as they worked to create a more nuanced and positively connoted spectrum of queer female masculinities than either the mainstream media or medical texts could offer. This final section focuses specifically on those versions of female masculinity that might today be classified as "transgender." I examine, firstly, media discourses surrounding biological women who "passed" in their everyday lives as men, and secondly, subcultural debates surrounding the topic of female-to-male "transvestism"—a term coined by Hirschfeld in 1910, and which by the Weimar period was starting to inform processes of cross-gender identity construction for at least some masculine women.

"Women in Men's Clothing": Narratives of Passing Women

Histories of women who "passed" as men—a phenomenon often expressed in the 1920s German media via the phrase "women in men's clothing" (*Frauen in Männerkleidung*)—have often fallen under the banner of either "lesbian" histories that privilege the sexual relationships of the "women" involved, or more recently, "transgender" histories that privilege gender identity. Schader's research on the homosexual magazines falls into the former camp, as she argues that it was the absence of a cultural concept of female homosexuality that led some women prior to the early twentieth century to live as men.[54] Yet this explanation does not adequately account for those individuals who continued to pass as men in 1920s Germany despite the presence of a thriving urban homosexual subculture. My intention here is not to write a history of women who lived as men at this period—which would require the analysis of quite different sources—but rather to examine how the mainstream and subcultural media negotiated narratives of passing, not least as a means of reflecting upon post–World War I gender relations. The term "passing" is not unproblematic: in one of the more insightful discussions of this phenomenon, Hanna Hacker criticizes the sexism involved in associating qualities such as strength, initiative, and assertiveness with masculinity; meanwhile she also observes that the passing woman has been viewed as a symbol of genuine feminist protest against the historical boundaries of femininity. She defends her analytical use of this term, however, on the basis of its potential to encompass multiple meanings that go beyond "cross-dressing," and it is in this sense that I employ it here.[55]

Whereas the popular Weimar media used narratives of female-to-male passing to deal at a very literal level with the masculinization of women, the subcultural magazines attempted to satisfy numerous, and at times conflicting goals in their coverage of this phenomenon. These long-term performances of gender often lasted for decades or even until death, and formed part of a centuries-old tradition that was particularly prevalent in Western Europe.[56] Both mainstream and subcultural reports of female-to-male passing tended to follow a typical structure, due not least to the fact that the subcultural magazines often reprinted stories on this phenomenon from the major newspapers, although frequently adding editorial comments. In most cases, these narratives focus on the moment of exposure, and interpret the months or years of successful passing prior to that moment through the lens of this gender "deception," rather than respecting the self-identifications of the individuals in question, who had often lived long successful lives as men prior to this point, working difficult jobs, marrying, and sometimes also raising families. In addition, many of the reports highlight pragmatic or financial reasons for the "choice" to live and work as men, whether to escape a criminal past, avoid destitution by entering more lucrative "male" professions, or avoid sexual harassment when traveling alone. This follows a pattern that Garber has identified as the "progress narrative" of transvestism, whereby the reader's discomfort is smoothed over by stories that recuperate social and sexual norms: "s/he did this in order to a) get a job, b) find a place in a man's world, and c) realize or fulfill some deep but acceptable need." Similarly, Dekker and van de Pol argue that a woman who "became" a man was widely perceived as striving for something higher and better, which was generally met with understanding by the wider society.[57] Presumably, newspaper editors in 1920s Germany thought that audiences would more easily stomach tales of gender "deviance" when the individuals concerned were victims of modernization or poverty.

Yet various incongruencies in these reports hint at less pragmatic, more psychological reasons for passing that might be better termed "transgender" or "pre-transsexual." The confused and inconsistent use of pronouns suggests at least some awareness that for certain individuals, passing was more than just a fleeting "disguise" or "masquerade," particularly for those who continued to pass despite being "exposed" as women. Furthermore, it was not unusual for reporters to praise the success of the passing woman's masculine performance: one "Marie Kuntz" was said to smoke a pipe, chew tobacco, and exhibit "an absolutely masculine manner, which she had 'acquired' over the years." Perhaps the clearest examples of transgender awareness can be found in reports of women passing as male soldiers, for as *Die Freundin* observed, "These women perceived the world in the masculine way and consequently wanted to be in no way inferior to men."[58] A piece on "Transvestites in the World War" used the example of passing soldiers to not only counter sexological assumptions that there were statistically far fewer female-to-male than male-to-female transvestites, but also to demonstrate the strength of their "masculine" convictions:

> When the male courage of the transvestite woman, who in any case wants to be at least temporarily a man, goes so far that they are aware that their body may well be laid out by a bullet, then this is evidence that transvestism in women—if perhaps rarer, is also stronger and more irresistible than in men.[59]

At least in some cases, then, the subcultural magazines interpreted narratives of passing in order to affirm the authenticity of transgender lives.

Media coverage of two particularly prominent 1920s cases of female-to-male passing exemplifies the different reception of this issue in the mainstream and subcultural press. The first involved the British fascist leader "Colonel Barker," who caused a stir across Europe when revealed in 1928 to be biologically female. Halberstam and Doan have perceptively examined the Barker affair in relation to ideas about female masculinities, female inversion, and homosexuality in early twentieth-century Britain, including the relationship between Barker's fascist politics and his/her various sexual, gender, and class identities.[60] In Germany, the Barker case was so well known that journalists referenced it as shorthand for other reports of passing women and men alike. *Frauenliebe* (the predecessor to *Garçonne*) covered the case in some detail, and the contradictory tone of this report reflects the at times blurred boundaries within the contemporary subculture between "virile" and passing women.

On the one hand, the reporter describes the case in rather condescending terms as a "great farce" and Barker as a "valiant Amazon who had led a strange double life." Yet the article is also sympathetic to the possibility that an individual's sexual or gender identity can change over time. Thus we read that before becoming "Colonel Barker," the masculine "Mrs Pearce Crouch" was a lesbian who was hardly out of place in upper-class English society, and who only later succumbed to her natural "disposition," for which she should hardly be punished: "For what should one punish the brilliant transformation artist, to whom blind fate has attributed the wrong sex? What crime has she committed?"[61] In contrast, mainstream media coverage of the Barker affair was both less forgiving and less flexible: *Uhu* published a full-page photo of Barker in female attire (albeit with masculine styling, including a crisp white shirt, dark tie, and long, simple skirt), which it juxtaposed against a smaller, by implication less authentic photo of Barker as a "man," with slicked-back hair and army medals (Figure 3.4). The caption continues this visual undermining of Barker's masculine identity by referencing his/her supposedly "true" gender: "the London fascist leader, who lived and worked for years as a man, married and divorced as a man, before now turning out to be a woman."[62]

The second case involved the German "Josef Maria Einsmann," who according to the daily Cologne newspaper *Kölner Tageblatt* had lived as a man in Mainz for twelve years with a wife and two illegitimate children, which he cared for as his own until he was "exposed" in 1931. In this article, which *Die Freundin* reprinted in 1931, the *Tageblatt* reporter equates Einsmann's passing with inauthenticity, secrecy, and masquerade, speculating on the feelings of a married couple "who had to disguise themselves on a daily basis, who for not a single minute could behave as those they truly were, who even within their own walls had to preserve their secret from their growing child." Yet additional editorial comments by

Eine besonders interessante
Zwischenstufe M+W

Phot. Pacific & Atlantic

Phot. Central News

„Capitain Barker", der Londoner Faschistenführer,
der jahrelang als Mann gelebt und seinen Beruf ausgeübt hatte, als Mann verheiratet und geschieden war,
bis er sich jetzt als Frau entpuppte

25

Figure 3.4. "'Captain Barker,' the London Fascist Leader." *Uhu,* May 1929, 25.
Source: BPK Bildagentur für Kunst, Kultur und Geschichte

Freundin writer Paul Weber take quite a different tone, contrasting the "us" of his subcultural audience with the "them" of the heterosexual mainstream, emphasizing Einsmann's masculinity, and framing his story in terms of a successful transgender man who has done his duty by his beloved wife and their children: "For all of us this matter is no 'exceptional case,' but rather the dream of what the reality of a thoroughly masculine woman can look like."[63] Elsewhere, Weber continued this line of argument by describing Einsmann as a "caring family man," and explaining that it was his "inner impulses" that drove him to pass as a man, whereas the authorities have now forced "her" to wear "unnatural" female clothing.[64]

Such efforts to legitimize transgender identifications were echoed by various subcultural commentators when they described passing women as successful with the "opposite" sex, as female "husbands," or as "fathers."[65] Although they report that some "wives" were aware of their partner's condition, others clearly remained oblivious until their own or their "husband's" death. Karsch-Haack highlighted this difficulty of categorizing relationships between passing women and other women, which he suggests could be variously described as "Sapphic," "normal" or "legal marriages." This nuanced approach aligns with Halberstam's more recent observation that "relations between women" and "same-sex relations" are poor descriptors for the physical relations between masculine women and their lovers.[66] However, such openness to transgender identifications was by no means typical of all subcultural coverage of female-to-male passing, which often followed the mainstream media in insisting on an individual's "true" sex.

Whereas the mainstream press tended to focus on a passing woman's female anatomy in order to neutralize her gender transgression, some subcultural writers sought to reinterpret passing narratives through the lens of female homosexuality. These reports show particular interest in the "homosexual" relationships between passing women and their wives or girlfriends, often with little regard for how the individuals concerned may have perceived these relationships—for as Prosser points out, had such individuals been able to realize their transsexual identifications, their "homosexual" desires might well have become "heterosexual."[67] Thus a report on an Argentinean woman who had passed as a man for twenty-three years before being "discovered" upon her death insists on describing "her" relationship with her wife as a "marriage partnership between woman and woman."[68] In a similar vein are numerous short stories that feature homosexual women who temporarily pass as men, during which time a woman (either heterosexual or homosexual) falls in love with them. The narrative reaches a climax as the passing woman reveals her male "disguise" to her female lover, and in the romanticized style of much of the magazine fiction, the two live happily ever after as a homosexual couple. This formula emphasizes female gender and homosexuality as the core of the passing woman's identity, and undermines her masculine identity as a temporary masquerade.

Fictional narratives of passing women were far less common in the mainstream media, but at least one short story published in *Uhu* in 1927 used this phenomenon to encourage reflection on changing gender relations between women and men. "Peter's Brother Paul: A Peculiar Story" tells of a young mother who accompanies her son Peter to a school camp disguised as his long-lost brother Paul. "Paul" endears himself to Peter's schoolmates and becomes the troubled object of affection of a boy named Alfons, before being revealed as a woman when she needs to be rescued from a lake. In terms of its gender politics, this story evinces contradictory motives. On the one hand, it uses the trope of passing to contain the dual threats of female masculinity and male homosexuality within safe, temporary limits, similar to the lesbian romances described above or the trouser roles examined in the next chapter. Thus Paul's performance of masculinity is viewed in reductive terms as boyish and vulnerable, while Alfons's realization that his love for "Paul" is actually heterosexual symbolizes his development from boy to man.

At the same time, the narrative engages in a sympathetic reflection on the transformations taking place in modern heterosexual gender relations. Consequently, the revelation of "Paul's" gender is greeted not by anger or disgust, but by the reflection of class teacher Mr. Kleinschroth that he is witnessing "a living slice of cultural history." Kleinschroth admires "Paul" as the epitome of twentieth-century "new" womanhood: "young, agile, boyishly slender, a school leaving certificate in the handbag, a mother but asexual, and only exposed by accident." The narrative ends normatively in the sense that it recuperates both femininity and heterosexuality, but it also points to the possibility of social transformation, as Kleinschroth reflects that this new generation of young men will grow up better able to deal with "the woman problem of their day ... for the modern woman exists, but the modern man has not yet been invented."[69] One of the most progressive mainstream representations of the masculinized woman, this story uses the passing woman as a catalyst for new, more equal ways of relating between men and women.

The "Female Transvestite" and the "Virile Homosexual Woman"

Even more than with representations of the passing woman, subcultural discussions of female-to-male transvestism highlight a moment of historical transition in the conceptualization of sexually "other" female masculinities. Halberstam notes that the claims to male identity made by passing women such as Barker "cannot be easily dismissed and should be understood not as simply transsexual but at least as the beginning of the emergence of a transsexual identity." At the same time, she emphasizes that the distinctions between some historical transgender and lesbian identities can become quite blurry and mark the "gender fiction" of clear distinctions.[70] This categorical blurring is certainly evident in debates within 1920s German sexual subcultures, particularly as commentators attempted to distinguish between new ideas about "transvestite" identities and older ideas about sex-gender "inversion" or "virile" female homosexuality. In debating these terms and their relevance to the contemporary subculture, contributors undertook important definitional work that would lay the basis for post–World War II conceptualizations of "queer" female masculinities.

Die Freundin and *Garçonne* regularly published extensive columns and supplementary sections on transvestite issues, suggesting high levels of cooperation and crossover between transvestite and homosexual subcultures at both an organizational and community level. In addition, there were strong financial and pragmatic reasons for publishing transvestite supplements in homosexual magazines with established distribution channels and connections to homosexual rights organizations—at least one attempt to establish an independent magazine for transvestites failed to attract readers and was, according to *Freundin* publisher Friedrich Radszuweit, a financial failure.[71] Contributors to these sections debated the meaning of the still-new classification "transvestism," but generally this term was understood in a Hirschfeldian sense as going beyond cross-dressing to encompass other aspects of gender identity that would today be understood under the banner of "transgender" or "transsexual," and it is in this sense that I use it here.

Like Hirschfeld's study *Die Transvestiten* (The Transvestites, 1910), these magazine supplements focused primarily on male-to-female transvestite issues, with only rare commentaries by self-identified "female transvestites."[72] Many of the male-to-female transvestites who contributed to the transvestite supplements were also at pains to point out the large proportion of heterosexuals in their ranks, with estimates ranging from 35 to 99 percent. By insisting, in sometimes quite homophobic fashion, upon the "real" masculinity of heterosexual transvestite men, who succumb to their inner femininity only in private but have wives and families in public, they sought to counter powerful cultural stereotypes of the effeminate, homosexual male transvestite. As Hirschfeld had done in *The Transvestites,* these male-to-female transvestites distinguished between homosexuality and transvestism, and prioritized gender over sexual object choice as the basis for identity.[73]

In contrast, female-to-male transvestites were by and large assumed to be homosexual, by sexologists and members of the subculture alike. Such classifications were based on understandings of biological sex rather than gender identification: thus a "homosexual" female transvestite was a biological woman who identified as masculine and had sexual relationships with women. (Rare mentions of "heterosexual" female-to-male transvestites include Karsch-Haack's aforementioned survey of female masculinities in *Garçonne,* a short story in *Die Freundin,* and an article suggesting that there are at most ten transvestites per one hundred heterosexual women.[74]) This convergence of homosexual and transgender identities echoed earlier sexological discourses of female sex-gender inversion, and was underlined by editorial decisions that blurred the boundary between the masculine homosexual woman and the female transvestite. The "transves-

tite" supplements often included photographs of masculine women in suits
and ties who were indistinguishable
from many of the cover models of the
homosexual magazines (see Figures 3.5
and 1.3), while an article on women's
trousers was not atypical in collapsing
the clothing of "the virile homosexual
or transvestite-oriented woman" into a
single category.[75] Schader even suggests
that one of the reasons the transvestite supplements were included within
publications targeting an otherwise female homosexual audience was that
many of the women buying and reading the magazines themselves identified
in some way with this category, such
that the image of the virile homosexual
woman at this period "blends seam-
lessly into the image of the female
transvestite."[76] While there is some evidence to support this claim, it brushes
too quickly over a range of contradictory sources that highlight ongoing
definitional and identificatory struggles
surrounding such categories.

Figure 3.5. Cover image, *Garçonne,*
October 1930.

Source: Deutsche Nationalbibliothek, Leipzig

Subcultural contributors who identified as "masculine" or "virile" were often
quite clear about how closely or not they chose to identify with transvestism.
Claiming to speak on behalf of masculine women, "Hansi" explicitly criticized
the tendency within the *Freundin* to categorize all masculine women as female
transvestites:

> I hereby declare that we are not transvestites, with only a few exceptions, we masculine
> women do not wear suits or shirts and ties in order to wear men's clothing. We want to
> remain women, which is why we also always wear skirts. It is only the masculine touch that
> we emphasize. Female transvestites are as rare to find as homosexual male transvestites.[77]

The rarity of self-identified female-to-male transvestite–authored contributions to
the supplement sections would seem to confirm Hansi's claim about the relative
numbers of individuals who chose to identify as masculine rather than transvestite, although as Schader points out, many of the short stories feature homosexual
female-to-male transvestites.[78] It is, moreover, difficult to determine the number of women engaged in contemporary transvestite organizations. Contribu-

tors "E. K." and transvestite club leader Lotte Hahm, both of whom also seem to have identified as homosexual, were among the few self-identified female-to-male transvestites to appear in the *Freundin* column. Like Hansi, E. K. clearly distinguishes between a masculine female homosexual aesthetic and transvestite sartorial preferences, but does so from a transvestite perspective. Thus he argues that although the general trend toward masculine women's fashions has made his life easier, only full masculine attire will suffice: "What good are tuxedos to me when they are not accompanied by trousers. I will do without the tuxedo, but not the trousers." Meanwhile, Lotte Hahm, who appeared regularly in the Berlin scene magazines pictured in tuxedo jacket and pants, seems to have embraced a multiplicity of identifications with little apparent conflict as leader of both a transvestite group and the League of Ideal Women's Friendship (Bund für ideale Frauenfreundschaft).[79]

These debates about visual styles highlight some of the competing understandings of female masculinity among members of the contemporary subculture, as well as the emergence of new identificatory possibilities. On the one hand, many masculine-identifying women seem to have retained conceptual links to older sexological models of sex-gender inversion that saw gender expression and sexual object choice as two sides of the same coin. Yet they did not simply appropriate such pathologized models, but rather reworked them into a positively and erotically connoted masculine female homosexual aesthetic that, as seen in chapter 1, also functioned as an important marker of subcultural visibility. At the same time, we can trace an increasing distinction between female homosexual and transvestite identities, whereby a homosexual identification is determined primarily by sexual object choice, whereas a transvestite identification prioritizes cross-identifying tendencies.

In his essay on female sexual inversion, Chauncey argues that it was not until the turn of the twentieth century that the medical concept of homosexual desire emerged as a discrete sexual phenomenon, so that whereas cross-dressing had once been seen as an integral aspect of sexual inversion, under the banner of transvestism it was now being increasingly distinguished as a separate sexual identity. The sources examined here demonstrate that this reconceptualization was taking place not just within the medical profession, but also within contemporary "third sex" subcultures. Furthermore, the German evidence supports Chauncey's argument that the shift in focus from sex-gender inversion to sexual object choice occurred first in relation to men, and followed a slower, more complicated path in relation to women.[80] In the Weimar subcultural magazines, the frequently articulated view that most female transvestites were also homosexual, on the one hand, and indications of growing pressure on contributors to distinguish between the masculine appearances of female transvestites and homosexuals, on the other, each point to a transformation in sexological categories that was still underway.

This analysis of sources on passing and transvestism highlights the importance of incorporating ideas about transgender identities into the history of female masculinities in early twentieth-century Germany. It is generally accepted that transsexual surgery first became a real or accessible possibility in the 1940s, despite evidence of much earlier surgical "conversion" procedures dating back as far as the 1880s. Yet the sources examined here show that there were plenty of individuals living long before this date who demonstrated "clear transsexual fantasies and cross-identifications," as scholars have also shown in other national contexts.[81] And although examples of self-identified "transvestites" seeking surgical transformation of their "male" or "female" bodies are very rare in the subcultural magazines, several commentators did make important conceptual links between sex "reassignment" procedures performed on intersex or "hermaphrodite" individuals, and wider social issues facing transvestites in 1920s Germany. Paul Weber, a homosexual/transvestite rights activist and writer for *Die Freundin,* used for example a report on the surgery of intersex Danish painter Lille Elven/Lili Elbe to highlight the ongoing injustices facing *all* transvestites.[82] Through such interventions, members of Weimar sexual subcultures foreshadowed the conceptual move toward a more clearly articulated transsexual identity in subsequent decades.

In *Undoing Gender,* Butler advocates a critical and ongoing reevaluation of what constitutes the "human" to include those traditionally excluded from mainstream political and historical discourses, including women, people of color, gays and lesbians, and transgender and intersex subjects. Gender plays an important role in this reevaluation, as she argues that the process of extending social and legal recognition to drag, butch, femme, or transgender subjects is not a question of creating new genders, but rather of establishing "a new legitimating lexicon for the gender complexity that we have been living for a long time."[83] Within this schema, female masculinity can be understood as a gender category that, despite its necessarily mediated and imperfect relationship to real, embodied subjects, at the same time extends to those subjects necessary social and historical recognition—in Butler's terms, the necessary prerequisites for a "livable life." By examining how 1920s German commentators distinguished between various embodiments of female masculinity, as well as the slippages that occurred between such categories, we can begin to trace the historical emergence of queer forms of self-identification—from "transsexual" to "butch," "boi dyke" to "drag king"—that still hold meaning for individuals today.

This chapter has attempted to reach beyond one of the still-dominant sources in the history of sexuality, the writings of the sexologists, in favor of examining the writings of individuals who were themselves active participants in the emerging queer subcultures of interwar Germany. I have argued that the stereotyped and overwhelmingly negative representation of sexually "other" female masculinities in the mainstream Weimar media contrasted starkly with the far more differentiated spectrum of female masculinities available in subcultural publications. Although both media forms drew on similar cultural and political resources in their depictions of the masculine woman, including stereotypes of the Amazon and the female intellectual, political discourses of female emancipation, narratives of passing, and the writings of the sexologists, I have argued that they did so with very different motivations. The mainstream media used the German public's increasing familiarity with sexological discourses and ideas of a "third sex" to attack the masculine woman's alleged rejection of men and motherhood, situating her as a disruptive and perverse figure responsible for social failings such as Germany's low birth rate. In contrast, subcultural commentators sought to establish more positive and enabling discourses of female masculinity, whether by reevaluating the role of masculine women in the female emancipation movement, drawing on sexological texts in order to defend the naturalness and legal status of a range of sex-gender identifications, or depicting the fictional masculine heroine as a figure of desire. The following chapter continues this comparative analysis in relation to the theatrical trouser role, a cultural phenomenon that raises additional questions of cross-dressing, transgression, and masquerade.

Notes

1. On the links between the magazines, the homosexual rights organizations, and the women's clubs see Ilse Kokula, "Lesbisch leben von Weimar bis zur Nachkriegszeit," in *Eldorado: Homosexuelle Frauen und Männer in Berlin 1850–1950. Geschichte, Alltag und Kultur,* ed. Michael Bollé (Berlin: Rosa Winkel, 1984), 149f.; Lybeck, "Female Homosexuality," chap. 6; and Petra Schlierkamp, "Die Garconne" (169ff.) and Katharina Vogel, "Zum Selbstverständnis lesbischer Frauen in der Weimarer Republik: Eine Analyse der Zeitschrift 'Die Freundin' 1924–1933" (162ff.), both in Bollé, *Eldorado.*
2. On female subjectivity and citizenship in Weimar Germany see Canning, "Claiming Citizenship," 233ff.
3. Schader, *Virile;* also: "Virile homosexuelle Frauen im Spiegel ihrer Zeitschriften im Berlin der zwanziger Jahre," in *Verqueere Wissenschaft?* ed. Ursula Ferdinand, Andreas Pretzel, and Andreas Seeck (Munich: LIT, 1998).
4. Lybeck, "Female Homosexuality," 46 cited here. Other studies examining these sources include Kirsten Plötz, *Einsame Freundinnen: Lesbisches Leben während der zwanziger Jahre in der Provinz* (Hamburg: MännerschwarmSkript-Verl., 1999) and several unpublished theses held at the Lesbenarchiv Spinnboden in Berlin.
5. Judith M. Bennett, "'Lesbian-Like' and the Social History of Lesbianisms," *Journal of the History of Sexuality* 9, no. 1–2 (2000): 11–13; Martha Vicinus, "'They Wonder to Which Sex I Belong': The Historical Roots of the Modern Lesbian Identity," *Feminist Studies* 18, no. 3 (1992): 467–97. The debate about what constitutes "lesbian" history is, of course, a much larger one; useful summaries can be found in Laura Doan, "Topsy-Turvydom: Gender Inversion, Sapphism, and the Great War," *GLQ: A Journal of Lesbian and Gay Studies* 12, no. 4 (2006): 523ff; Martha Vicinus, *Intimate Friends: Women Who Loved Women, 1778–1928* (Chicago: University of Chicago Press, 2004), xv ff.

6. Doan, "Topsy-Turvydom," 526; Bennett, "'Lesbian-Like,'" 13f. cited here.

7. Halberstam, *Female Masculinity*, 161, see also 50–59, 149–51. See also Jay Prosser, "Transsexuals and the Transsexologists: Inversion and the Emergence of Transsexual Subjectivity," in *Sexology in Culture: Labelling Bodies and Desires*, ed. Lucy Bland and Laura Doan (Cambridge: Polity, 1998), 116–31; Nan Alamilla Boyd, "The Materiality of Gender: Looking for Lesbian Bodies in Transgender History," *Journal of Lesbian Studies* 3 (1999): 74ff.

8. "Der Typ der Amazone...," *Die Dame*, no. 20, 2nd June Issue 1931, 33. See also Bertschik's analysis of popular Weimar discourses surrounding the "Amazon" in *Mode*, 243–55.

9. Inge Stephan, "'Da werden Weiber zu Hyänen...' Amazonen und Amazonenmythen bei Schiller und Kleist," in *Aus dem Verborgenen zur Avantgarde: Ausgewählte Beiträge zur feministischen Literaturwissenschaft der 80er Jahre*, ed. Hiltrud Bontrup and Jan Christian Metzler (Hamburg: Argument, 2000), 97–104.

10. "Die Amazone," *Simplicissimus*, no. 14, 1 July 1921, 184.

11. Wolfgang von Lengerke, *Die Amazone Gloria* (Berlin: Weltbücher Verlag, 1928).

12. Prof. F. Karsch-Haack, "Katharina II. Kaiserin von Rußland—die nordische Semiramis," *Die Freundin*, no. 14, 25 July 1927, 4; Prof. F. Karsch-Haack, "Junggesellin und Junggeselle (4. Fortsetzung)," *Garçonne*, no. 5, 15 December 1930, 3.

13. Lybeck, "Female Homosexuality," 49.

14. Smith-Rosenberg, "The New Woman," 271f.

15. Dr. Alice Rüle-Gerstel, *Das Frauenproblem der Gegenwart: Eine psychologische Bilanz* (Leipzig: S. Hirzel, 1932). Other studies on this topic from the first decades of the twentieth century include the MD Hartung's "Homosexualität und Frauenemanzipation" ("Homosexuality and Women's Emancipation," 1910) and Anna Rüling's "Frauenbewegung und homosexuelles Problem" ("Women's Movement and the Homosexual Problem," 1904), reproduced in Leslie Parr, ed., *Lesbianism and Feminism in Germany, 1895–1910* (New York: Arno, 1975). On the sexological linking of working-class female "inverts" and criminality see Chauncey, "Sexual Inversion," 100f.; Halberstam, *Female Masculinity*, 78.

16. Lotte Zavel, "Die Bildhauerin Renée Sintenis," *Die Dame*, no. 14, Ende April 1921, 7.

17. In the context of Weimar artistic production, Maria Tatar provides an inspiring analysis of how artists such as Otto Dix displaced the reproductive functions of the female body with the "creative energies of male autogeny," connecting the wartime destruction of the male body to the postwar symbolic destruction of the female body in images of sexual murder: *Lustmord: Sexual Murder in Weimar Germany* (Princeton: Princeton University Press, 1995), 68–97.

18. Lybeck, "Female Homosexuality," 382. On the political positioning of the lesbian magazines in relation to the women's and homosexual rights movements see also Hacker, *Frauen und Freundinnen*, 119–39; Mecki Pieper, "Die Frauenbewegung und ihre Bedeutung für lesbische Frauen (1850–1920)," in Bollé, *Eldorado*, 116–24.

19. Otto Weininger, "Geschlecht und Charakter. Von Otto Weininger. 'Die emanzipierten Frauen,'" *Die Freundin*, no. 2, 14 January 1931, 2f.; Dr. Eugen Gürster, "Hosenrolle und Frauenemanzipation," *Frauen Liebe und Leben*, no. 2, 1928, 17.

20. Karla Mayburg, "Kameradschaft und Liebesfreundschaft: Noch eine Entgegnung!" *Garçonne*, no. 26, 23 December 1931, 3.

21. Martin and Breger have shown Duc's novel to be fertile ground for the study of turn-of-the-century female masculinities; see also Lybeck's social and cultural history of female university students in 1890s Zurich: Breger, "Feminine Masculinities"; Martin, *Femininity*, 54–70; Lybeck, "Female Homosexuality," chap. 3.

22. Marie-Luise v. Bern, "Der Klub der Freundinnen," *Die Freundin*, no. 9, 30 April 1928, 2. Lybeck notes that the satirical aspect of this novella is directed primarily against the "old-fashioned" form of same-sex socializing represented by the elite women's club: "Female Homosexuality," 331.

23. Lia Walter, "Myriams Sieg," *Die Freundin,* no. 49, 7 December 1932, 3.
24. Gudrun Schwarz, "'Mannweiber' in Männertheorien," in *Frauen suchen ihre Geschichte: Historische Studien zum 19. und 20. Jahrhundert,* ed. Karin Hausen (Munich: C. H. Beck, 1983), 62–76. The *Freundin* debate can be found in the issues from November–December 1931.
25. Käthe Wundram, "Die Treue der maskulinen und die der femeninen [sic] Frau," *Garçonne,* no. 15, 22 July 1931, 1f.; cf. Weininger, *Geschlecht,* 79–93 and 182–96.
26. Lo Hilmar, "Treue gehört zur Liebe," *Garçonne,* no. 18, 2 September 1931, 1.
27. Ilse Schwarze, "Ist Männlichkeit gleichbedeutend mit Intelligenz? Vierte Erwiderung zum Thema: Die Treue der maskulinen und die der femininen Frau," *Garçonne,* no. 20, 30 September 1931, 1; Ilse Schwarze, "Offener Brief an Thea Neumann," *Garçonne,* no. 24, 25 November 1931, 3.
28. The broader terms of this debate on faithfulness, including gender and generational implications, are examined in Lybeck, "Female Homosexuality," 474–88; Schader, *Virile,* 102ff. and 124ff.; Schader, "Virile homosexuelle Frauen," 141ff.; Schlierkamp, "Die Garconne," 169–79.
29. Schwarze, "Ist Männlichkeit gleichbedeutend mit Intelligenz," 2.
30. Tony, "Die Freundin hat das Wort: Brief an S.," *Die Freundin,* no. 49, 9 December 1931, 5f.
31. Kokula, "Lesbisch leben," 149; see e.g. Elizabeth Lapovsky Kennedy and Madeline Davis, *Boots of Leather, Slippers of Gold: The History of a Lesbian Community* (New York: Routledge, 1993). While the historical German terms *viril* and *feminin* can be loosely aligned with the Anglo-American descriptors "butch" and "femme," I avoid using the latter terms here on the basis that they first emerged within the historical context of the 1950s US and would skew a study of women in 1920s Germany.
32. Lybeck adds that many of the middle-class women who were beginning to identify as homosexual at this period experimented with a range of relationship ideologies, desires, and gendered personae that cannot be reduced to binary gender structures: "Female Homosexuality," 49, 359ff., 413ff., 580 cited here.
33. Butler, *Gender Trouble,* 180.
34. These debates emerged strongly in the 1970s, when butch-femme models were criticized for privileging heterosexual relationship models; more recently they have been reinterpreted by some as a form of resistance to the dominant sex-gender system. For a critical summary see Halberstam, *Female Masculinity,* 121f.
35. Steinach had castrated and then transplanted the genital organs of various species in order to observe the effects on gendered behavior. The results of these experiments are recorded in Eugen Steinach and Josef Loebel, *Sex and Life: Forty Years of Biological and Medical Experiments* (London: Faber, 1940); on Steinach see also Anne Fausto-Sterling, *Sexing the Body: Gender Politics and the Construction of Sexuality* (New York: Basic Books, 2000), 146–69. Hirschfeld describes his application of Steinach's experiments to theories of gender and homosexuality in *Sexuelle Zwischenstufen,* 104.
36. "Was sagen Sie bloß zu Fräulein Mia?/Das Ergebnis unserer Preisfrage in Nr. 46," *Berliner Illustrirte Zeitung,* no. 51, 18 December 1927, 2127f.
37. Dr. Curt Thomalla, "Das Drüsenrätsel: Das geheimnisvolle Wirkung der inneren Sekretion," *Uhu,* no. illeg., November 1924, 82–91, 142–44.
38. Paul Schmidt, "M plus W: Über männliche und weibliche Ureigenschaften," *Uhu,* no. 8, May 1929, 20–26, 26 cited here.
39. "Abseits vom Taumel," *Simplicissimus,* no. 47, 20 February 1928, 642.
40. *Ulk,* no. 11, 12 March 1926, cover. Other examples of this trend include "Teegeflüster," *Ulk,* no. 19, 7 May 1926, 139; "Tanzbar 'Silhouette,'" *Simplicissimus,* no. 11, 28 October 1929, 372; "Träumerei," *Simplicissimus,* no. 46, 14 February 1927, 617; Jeanne Mammen, "Freundinnen," *Simplicissimus,* no. 3, 20 April 1931, 32; "Liebe," *Simplicissimus,* no. 31, 28 October 1929, 371.

41. McCormick, *Gender and Sexuality,* 56. A typical cartoon thematizing such voyeuristic practices is E. Thöny's "Vergnügungsreisende aus der Provinz," *Simplicissimus,* no. 18, 28 July 1930, 208; for a subcultural critique of such practices see P. W., "Schauobjekte," *Die Freundin,* no. 3, 18 January 1933, 1.

42. "Frühlings Erwachen," *Ulk,* no. 28, 11 July 1930, 222; "Spekulation," *Simplicissimus,* no. 18, 28 July 1930, 209; see also "Verlorene Liebesmüh," *Ulk,* no. 8, 25 February 1927; "Die falsche Adresse," *Simplicissimus,* no. 22, 27 August 1929, 282.

43. Chauncey, "Sexual Inversion," 106f.

44. For more on Karsch-Haack, see Robert Aldrich and Garry Wotherspoon, *Who's Who in Contemporary Gay and Lesbian History* (London: Routledge, 2001), 238f.

45. This series was published in *Garçonne* from November 1930 to March 1931, and in most of these issues constituted the major feature article. *Die Freundin* also published a shorter, similar series by Karsch-Haack on "Historical Men-Women" ("Historische Männinnen") in 1927.

46. Helga Karig, "Relativität der Minderwertigkeit," *Frauenliebe,* no. 50, n.d. 1927, 3. See also Lybeck's analysis of how subcultural commentators drew on the "respectable" language of science in order to situate themselves within the public sphere: "Female Homosexuality," 370ff.

47. See e.g. P. B. B., "Rundschau: Morgen! Eine lesbische Frau wird hingerichtet," *Garçonne,* no. 5, 2 March 1932, 3f.; "Aus Liebe zur Freundin den Mann erschlagen!" *Die Freundin,* no. 7, 2 April 1928, 2.

48. Selli Engler, "Arme kleine Jett (13. Fortsetzung)," *Die Freundin,* no. 47, 19 November 1930, 4f; see also Hansi, "Eine Frau von Format," *Die Freundin,* no. 46, 18 November 1931, 5f.; Charlotte Rex, "Bis ins dritte und vierte Glied," *Die Freundin,* no. 9, 26 February 1930, 4ff.; Demona, "Jugend," *Die Freundin,* no. 9, 2 March 1932, 2ff.

49. Ruth Kampe, "Das Kind," *Garçonne,* no. 1, 6 January 1932, 2, and subsequent installments: *Garçonne,* no. 2, 20 January 1932, 1f., *Garçonne,* no. 3, 3 February 1932, 2. On the use of male nicknames by homosexual women see Hirschfeld, *Berlins drittes Geschlecht,* 81–88; Schader, *Virile,* 109.

50. Halberstam, *Female Masculinity,* 77.

51. Lo Hilmar, "Liebe! (Eine Geschichte in drei Briefen)," *Garçonne,* no. 1, 15 October 1930, 12.

52. In addition to the gender-oriented categories of "virile" and "feminine," Schader discusses a range of other binaries employed in the representation of sexual relationships, including young-old, rich-poor, teacher-student, and familiar-exotic: *Virile,* 109–19, 122–36.

53. Nora Marlen, "Dith und Monika," *Die Freundin,* no. 29, 22 July 1931, 4.

54. Schader, "Virile homosexuelle Frauen," 138f.

55. Hacker, *Frauen und Freundinnen,* 140f.

56. For histories of female-to-male passing see e.g. Rudolf Dekker and Lotte van de Pol, *Frauen in Männerkleidern: Weibliche Transvestiten und ihre Geschichte* (Berlin: Verlag Klaus Wagenbach, 1989); Lehnert, *Wenn Frauen,* 39–49; Geertje Mak, "'Passing Women' im Sprechzimmer von Magnus Hirschfeld: Warum der Begriff 'Transvestit' nicht für Frauen in Männerkleidern eingeführt wurde (trans. Mirjam Hausmann)," *Österreichische Zeitschrift für Geschichtswissenschaften* 9, no. 3 (1998): 384–99; Julie Wheelwright, *Amazons and Military Maids: Women who Dressed as Men in the Pursuit of Life, Liberty, and Happiness* (London: Pandora, 1989). "Performance" is used here in the sense articulated by Butler, who emphasizes that although gender is "performative," that does not mean that it can be donned and abandoned at will: Judith Butler, *Bodies that Matter: On the Discursive Limits of "Sex"* (New York: Routledge, 1993), x.

57. Garber, *Vested Interests,* 69; Dekker and van de Pol, *Frauen in Männerkleidern,* 95.

58. "Das Geheimnis um Marie Kuntz," *Die Freundin,* no. 3, 28 January 1931, 2; P. W., "Frauen als Soldaten," *Die Freundin,* no. 4, 25 January 1933, 1.

59. Emi Wolters, "Die Welt der Transvestiten: Transvestiten im Weltkriege," *Die Freundin,* no. 15, 13 April 1932, 6.

60. Doan, *Fashioning Sapphism,* 82–94; Halberstam, *Female Masculinity,* 91–95.

61. "Der weibliche Hauptmann," *Frauenliebe,* no. illeg., 1928, 1f.

62. Schmidt, "M plus W: Über männliche und weibliche Ureigenschaften," 25.

63. "Josef Maria Einsmann," *Die Freundin,* no. 35, 2 September 1931, 2f.

64. Paul Weber, "Das Urteil gegen Frau Einsmann," *Die Freundin,* no. 36, 7 September 1932, 2.

65. For reports of female husbands and fathers see e.g. "Ein sensationeller Ehescheidungsprozeß," *Die Freundin,* no. 29, 16 July 1930, 4f.; "Was die 'Freundin' plaudert: Ein Doppelleben," *Die Freundin,* no. 18, 19 September 1927, 4.

66. Prof. F. Karsch-Haack, "Junggesellin und Junggeselle (7. Fortsetzung)," *Garçonne,* no. 3, 3 February 1931, 4; Halberstam, *Female Masculinity,* 56f.

67. Prosser, "Transsexuals," 119.

68. "'Seine' Frau und ihr 'Mann,'" *Die Freundin,* no. 28, 9 July 1930, 2.

69. Hofer-Dernburg, "Peters Bruder Paul: Eine merkwürdige Geschichte," *Uhu,* no. 1, October 1927, 25–32, 32 cited here.

70. Halberstam, *Female Masculinity,* 95, see also 153.

71. Friedrich Radszuweit, "Transvestiten!" *Die Freundin,* no. 24, 11 December 1929, 5.

72. See e.g. Elly R., "Die Welt der Transvestiten: Die Transvestitenfrage," *Die Freundin,* no. 1, 2 July 1929, 4.

73. See e.g. Toni Fricke, "Der Transvestit: Aus dem Empfindungsleben eines 'Transvestiten'!" *Die Freundin,* no. 2, 12 September 1924, 1–2 of "Transvestit" supplement; Fred Ursula, "'Wär' ich doch eine Frau...'" *Die Freundin,* no. 3, 21 February 1927, 5; Maria Weis, "Der Transvestit: Das Wesen des Transvestitismus," *Frauenliebe,* no. 19, n.d. 1930, 4.

74. J. Schröder, "Die Zwillinge," *Die Freundin,* no. 6, 5 February 1930, 4; E. Raven (Leipzig), "Die Welt der Transvestiten: Das Empfindungsleben der Transvestiten. Ein Beitrag zur Aufklärung über Transvestitismus (Fortsetzung und Schluß)," *Die Freundin,* no. 50, 14 December 1932, 6.

75. Annemarie Groverius, "Meinungsaustausch über Modefragen: Die Frau in Hosen," *Die Freundin,* no. 15, 8 August 1927, 6.

76. Schader, *Virile,* 110.

77. Hansi, "Die Welt der Transvestiten," *Die Freundin,* no. 23, 8 June 1932, 6.

78. Schader, *Virile,* 110.

79. E. K., "Meinungsaustausch der Transvestiten," *Die Freundin,* no. 13, 11 July 1927, 6. For more on Hahm see Schader, *Virile,* 76f.; Lybeck, "Female Homosexuality," 365ff.

80. Cf. Chauncey, "Sexual Inversion," 88ff.

81. Halberstam, *Female Masculinity,* 86. Bernice Hausman dates the emergence of a transsexual identity to the 1940s on the basis that this was when medical technologies for sex reassignment became available: *Changing Sex: Transsexualism, Technology, and the Idea of Gender* (Durham, NC: Duke University Press, 1995). However this chronology has been criticized as too late and too rigid by various scholars, including Halberstam and Prosser ("Transsexuals," 118–27).

82. Paul Weber, "Aus Mann wird Frau," *Die Freundin,* no. 13, 1 April 1931, 5; see also Paul Weber, "Die Welt der Transvestiten: Lili Elbe tot!" *Die Freundin,* no. 39, 30 September 1931, 6; Marie Weis, "Der Transvestit: Aus Mann wird Frau," *Garçonne,* no. 6, 17 March 1931, 12.

83. Judith Butler, *Undoing Gender* (London: Routledge, 2004), 31.

Chapter 4

THE TROUSER ROLE
Female Masculinity as Performance

Across the boards of the stage or those of real life the ladies parade in their trouser roles, delighting their fellows with their fabulously trained bodies, the beauty of their movements, the charm of their smile.

Trude John, "Hosenparade," *Das Magazin,* August 1930

*T*he most literal and least controversial embodiment of female masculinity in Weimar popular culture involved women dressing and acting as men for the sake of theatrical or cinematic performance, a phenomenon known as the "trouser role" or *Hosenrolle.* Clothing functions as a powerful signifier of gender, and cross-dressing in particular can have a symbolic significance that goes far beyond the garments themselves: Chris Straayer observes that the "representation and containment of gender by clothing and other visual systems offer gender as a construction susceptible to manipulation by cross-dressing, drag, and masquerade."[1] The "manipulation" of gender proscriptions within the culturally sanctioned boundaries of the *Hosenrolle* during the Weimar era drew on a historical tradition that stretched back to at least the eighteenth century on the German stage, and fulfilled a cathartic function at a time of significant gender role upheaval within German society. As a piece of clothing historically gendered "male," trousers represent an important symbol of virility and can be used to signify the accessing of masculine privileges and protections, enabling actions that would be impossible in a skirt or dress. This chapter argues that, like coverage of women's "masculin-

Notes for this section begin on page 148.

ized" fashions, reports on the *Hosenrolle* in the 1920s and early 1930s German media responded to the mass reading public's need to engage on a nonthreatening and familiar level with the masculinization of woman. By situating the masculine woman within the strict spatial and temporal constraints of an overtly fictional theatrical performance, audiences were provided with a safe—and simultaneously titillating—brand of female masculinity that only rarely challenged the dominant social order.

Yet as the above excerpt demonstrates, the term *Hosenrolle* was used by some contemporaries to describe gendered "performances" in life as well as on stage. Thus this chapter also interrogates the policing of these boundaries between fiction and reality, as well as instances when the onstage, carnivalesque boundaries of the *Hosenrolle* phenomenon broke down and merged with offstage, lived experience, opening up a space in which social transformation could occur. The widespread fascination with the trouser role in Weimar Germany is evident from a large body of contemporary magazine photography and commentary, which is examined here alongside a 1925 study by social commentator Alfred Holtmont, as well as several cinematic examples of this phenomenon, including Leontine Sagan's 1931 film *Mädchen in Uniform* (Girls in Uniform). While magazine coverage of the *Hosenrolle* generally functioned to contain the politically disruptive potential of the masculinized woman, I argue that the theatrical appropriation of male clothing and prerogatives within the hugely popular new medium of film could provide a powerful means of challenging traditional gender and social hierarchies, and of articulating nonheterosexual desires.

Preferring a gender-neutral language, I have chosen to refer to female "actors" rather than "actresses," and note here that all of the actors described in this chapter were women. The term *Hosenrolle* is used interchangeably with the English "trouser role" (sometimes also referred to as a "breeches role") to refer to women cross-dressing in order to "pass" as men within the boundaries of a theatrical or cinematic narrative, although the actor's "actual" sex was mostly known to the audience and visible despite the disguise. The suspension of disbelief required by such gender crossings was generally sustained throughout the narrative—only rarely, such as in the 1933 film *Viktor und Viktoria* (Victor and Victoria), did women cross-dress only to be revealed as women *within* the narrative, although such roles are also important within the history of the *Hosenrolle*. I avoid using the term "transvestism" here except where it explicitly appears in the sources, in order to separate popular discussions of the *Hosenrolle* from sexological and subcultural discourses. In describing women in trouser role representations as "cross-dressing," I follow Susanne Benedek and Adolphe Binde's use of this term, which focuses not on pathologizing or psychologizing approaches that look toward individual motivation, but rather on the semiotics of the visual representation. I also draw on Garber's distinction between "established" and "subversive" cross-dressing, whereby the former serves to stabilize binary gender relations and the latter to disrupt them.[2] Cross-dressing per se, as these scholars insist, is not necessarily a subversive act; rather, its transgressive potential depends on factors including representational context, parody, self-reflexivity, and audience positioning.

In their coverage of the *Hosenrolle,* Weimar media commentators drew on a centuries-old European history of women cross-dressing in order to perform male theatrical roles. Whereas in the sixteenth century most theatrical and operatic roles were conventionally performed by men, by the seventeenth century women had begun to replace boys not only in women's roles but also in certain male parts. Indeed, having boys play women's parts had begun to represent an unacceptable breach of gender boundaries by this period, whereas similar restrictions would not apply to female travesty until much later. In France, the rise of the *Hosenrolle* has been linked to the Revolutionary and Napoleonic wars, when numerous plays featured women who went to war as men, often in aid of husbands or lovers. On the operatic stage, music historians connect the rise of the trouser role in the eighteenth and nineteenth centuries to increasing opposition to the (mostly Italian) practice of creating *castrati,* musically talented boys castrated in order to play women's roles and other characters requiring a high voice. The *castrati* had not only provided a means of circumventing earlier religious prohibitions on female performance, but also held their own peculiar erotic appeal, evidenced in the enthusiastic reactions of commentators ranging from Montesquieu to Goethe. As the numbers of *castrati* declined, female singers began to replace them in both female and male roles, although this was only one of several factors in the rise of the *Hosenrolle,* which soon became an operatic fixture in its own right. The clean features and vocal range of the mezzo-soprano, which could be perceived as on the verge of breaking, were considered particularly appropriate for the portrayal of the passionate but still sexually immature phase of male adolescence, and suited the general audience preference for higher registers. Prominent operatic *Hosenrollen* include Cherubino in Mozart's *Marriage of Figaro* (1786), Hänsel in Humperdinck's *Hänsel and Gretel* (1893), and the passionate young Octavian in Strauß und Hofmannsthal's *Der Rosenkavalier* (1911); the figure of the pageboy was a further well-loved trope.[3]

While the operatic *Hosenrolle* continued strongly into the twentieth century, the golden era of the theatrical trouser role was during the late eighteenth and nineteenth centuries, when women began to be cast in major, heroic men's roles on the "legitimate" stage, often in Shakespearean plays and most frequently in the role of Hamlet. The most famous nineteenth-century female Hamlet was the Parisian Sarah Bernhardt, who first performed the role in 1899. Such roles gave older actresses the opportunity to demonstrate their professional virtuosity at a time when women's roles were both fewer and less varied than men's, and were so common that by the end of the century "it was unusual to find an actress who had not performed [breeches] parts."[4] While the tradition of the serious theatrical *Hosenrolle* had faded somewhat by the Weimar era, it was rejuvenated by the new medium of film, heralded by Danish actress Asta Nielsen's 1921 turn as Hamlet in the German film of the same name.[5]

The *Hosenrolle* as "Safety Valve"

In addition to its long stage history, cross-dressing by men and women in Europe had a centuries-old history within carnival and other folk traditions. These festivals sought to turn the everyday world upside down by inverting and parodying social norms and hierarchies, including class, gender, and political and ecclesiastical rank. In his work on French Renaissance scholar François Rabelais, Mikhail Bakhtin famously described this medieval and Renaissance carnival culture as involving the "temporary suspension of all hierarchic distinctions and barriers among men and of certain norms and prohibitions of usual life."[6] His optimistic formulation of the transgressive nature of carnival has since led scholars to speculate on the political potential—or lack thereof—of such "carnivalesque" role reversals, of which gendered cross-dressing forms an important aspect.

Terry Eagleton suggests that the fact that carnival was licensed by the authorities made it merely a form of social control of the lower classes, "a permissible rupture of hegemony, a contained popular blow-off as disturbing and relatively ineffectual as a revolutionary work of art." Rather than protesting against the established order, then, rites of reversal can also function to strengthen and contain dominant social hierarchies.[7] They do so, as Natalie Zemon Davis observes, by providing "an expression of, and a safety valve for, conflicts within the system," serving to relieve the system when it has become authoritarian, but without undermining the basic order of the society itself. Yet such carnivalesque rituals could also have transgressive potential. Thus Zemon Davis argues that rites of gender inversion did not always function in practice to keep women in their place and thereby reaffirm the existing social structure, but could also contribute to efforts to change the distribution of power within society: "As literary and festive inversion in preindustrial Europe was a product not just of stable hierarchy but also of changes in the location of power and property, so this inversion could prompt new ways of thinking about the system and reacting to it."[8] Similarly, Stallybrass and White conclude that while carnival is often a "stable and cyclical ritual with no noticeable politically transformative effects," in conditions of heightened political tension it can "act as catalyst and site of actual and symbolic struggle." Consequently, they argue that the "politics of carnival" can only be assessed through close analysis of particular historical moments and cultural contexts.[9] Such ideas about the conservative and subversive possibilities of carnivalesque transgression have informed analyses of masquerade and drag by gender theorists such as Butler, Garber, and Straayer, and offer important insights into the regulatory and transformatory functions of the Weimar-era *Hosenrolle*, which sought to reassure audiences through strictly controlled performances of gender inversion, but on occasion exceeded the boundaries of these performances in ways that dramatically challenged existing social hierarchies.

Whereas the popularity of the trouser role was in decline in other European countries at this period, the frequency of *Hosenrolle* representations in the Weimar media point to the ongoing popular and erotic appeal of this phenomenon in 1920s Germany.[10] These representations generally consisted of photographs of young, attractive women starring in current plays or films, and created a safe distance between the spectator and the spectacle of the masculine woman by drawing clear boundaries around her theatrical cross-dressed performance. By providing a forum in which commentators could speculate on the extent to which women were exceeding the socially acceptable limits of gender masquerade, *Hosenrolle* images lent a degree of moral clarity to the much more complicated web of anxieties and desires surrounding the ongoing "masculinization" of German womanhood in areas as diverse as politics, the professions, education, fashion, athletics, and sexual relationships. At the same time, trouser role representations prompted Weimar commentators to seek ways to limit "offstage" gender transgressions and thereby regain a sense of control over larger social and demographic changes.

Photographs of women in trouser roles in 1920s German magazines covered a diverse range of dramatic genres. *Die Dame* featured actors Elisabeth Bergner and Margaret Köppke in boyish, tight-legged period costume, stars respectively of the 1926 film *Der Geiger von Florenz* (The Violinist of Florence) and play *Kaiserin von Neufundland* (Empress of Newfoundland); the satirical *Ulk* featured caricatures of a cross-dressed Emmy Sturm as a "sweet cavalier" and of Asta Nielsen as Hamlet; and *Das Magazin* published numerous images of female actors and singers dressed as soldiers, sailors, Eton boys, and street urchins (see Figure 4.1), as well as a photograph of a black woman in uniform with the questionable title "chocolate Hussar."[11] In his 1925 study *Die Hosenrolle* (The Trouser Role), Holtmont noted that such costumes were typical of the operetta trouser role, which frequently included sailors, soldiers, pages, and students.[12] Captions carefully clarified for readers that such boyish costumes did not lessen, but rather enhanced the feminine erotic appeal of the women in question, for in each case the success of the image depends on the reader seeing *through* the costume. Thus accompanying an image of a carefully coiffed "street urchin" dressed in torn overalls and loosely flowing shirt was the explanation: "The diva, as our picture shows, certainly does not always need to appear in full dress in order to make an impression. This street urchin costume is at least as charming as a great evening dress. (Though to be sure, it is also very well made.)"[13] Editors further ensured that readers were in on the "truth" of the masquerade by using the actors' real names and titles such as "Miss." These were clearly not women genuinely trying to pass as men; their erotic appeal lay rather in the divide between onstage (mas-

Der Junge

Aufnahme des amerikanischen Stars Miß Percy im kleidsamen Dreß einer Rolle

Phot. Fox Film

Figure 4.1. "The Boy: Photograph of the American Star Miss Percy in Flattering Costume." *Das Magazin,* June 1925, 67.

Source: BPK Bildagentur für Kunst, Kultur und Geschichte

culine) performance and offstage (feminine) reality. The reader rests assured in the knowledge that the depiction of onstage gender transgression will be rectified once the actor leaves the theater—an assurance that extends to the static medium of the magazine photograph.

Yet these clear onstage/offstage boundaries did not always hold true, and the possibility that the *Hosenrolle* actor could step off the stage in her male costume became a powerful metaphor for women's expansion into various realms of male privilege. Whereas the images described above were presumably included as editorial fillers for the enjoyment and mild titillation of audiences, feature articles on the *Hosenrolle* made explicit links between on- and offstage cross-dressing and its implications for German society. In one such article by Martha von Zobeltitz, published in *Sport im Bild* in May 1924, only one of the accompanying drawings features a woman engaged in cross-dressed theatrical performance; the others show women—in "masculine" dress, but clearly identifiable as female—participating in outdoor sports such as ice skating, hunting, athletics, and riding. This visual merging of the overtly theatrical trouser role with an increasingly masculinized contemporary femininity is confirmed in the content of the article, which addresses sexual relationships, sport, and fashion alongside questions of dramatic performance. Beginning with the—apparently feminist—assertion that a marriage need not be unhappy when the woman is wearing the symbolic trousers, Zobeltitz suggests numerous practical and erotic reasons why a woman might choose to wear pants: "Either because she wants to be equal with the man—for career or athletic reasons—or because she wants to transfer her charms into a new milieu, whether on the stage in a professional sense, or privately on the parquetry floor." Journalist Trude John likewise acknowledged the trouser role's function as a symbol of female emancipation when she argued, in tongue-in-cheek fashion, that while the "weak" sex might look better in pants, such superficial trouser-wearing is a poor substitute for real power or progress.[14]

A more detailed exploration of the links between the *Hosenrolle*, female emancipation, and the masculinization of Germany's womanhood can be found in Holtmont's study, which has received little critical attention to date. Holtmont uses his topic as a springboard to speculate on issues of feminist politics, the physical and intellectual significance of gender, philosophies of gender difference, ideas about female masculinity and homosexuality, and the possibility of gender equality. In explicitly linking women's onstage masculine performances to the female emancipation movement Holtmont echoed the arguments of earlier scholars such as Ellis and Weininger, who had argued that it is only women's inner masculine component that drives them to seek emancipation. The first half of his book surveys historical, literary, mythological, and anthropological examples of female-to-male cross-dressing, which Holtmont situates as precursors to the modern theatrical *Hosenrolle*; these include famous personalities such as George Sand and Joan of Arc, the development of trouser fashions for women, Amazonian myths and societies, and folk and religious gender-crossing traditions. The second half consists of a detailed history of women's participation in the theater and the development of the trouser role.

Less cautiously than the journalists cited above, Holtmont traces the historical development of the *Hosenrolle* in relation to women's position in society, arguing that whereas early operatic or ballet trouser roles relied on base titillation, by the nineteenth century there was an increasing demand for "pronounced men's roles" that reflected the increasing progress of women's emancipation. This led to an intellectualized version of the *Hosenrolle*, as feminine charms were abandoned in favor of realism and virtuosic genius: "[A]n innermost conviction that it is genius independent of sex that results in the full intellectual realization of a character seems for the majority of outstanding women who play men's roles to be the driving force and motivation."[15] Bullough and Bullough have shown that it is no coincidence that such "serious" gender impersonation became a staple of the nineteenth-century stage, at a time when gender divisions were becoming increasingly formalized.[16] Indeed, Holtmont suggests that from the nineteenth century onward it is precisely in the successful concealment of feminine charms that audience pleasure lies: "the overcoming of all the instruments of power of the female body in favor of an idea, this all only served to double the pleasure."[17]

Importantly for this examination of the masculine woman in Weimar Germany, Holtmont also extends his historical analysis to the present situation. Contemplating "the unquestionable transformation of the modern woman into a new type in world history," and clearly sympathetic to the goals of the women's movement, he links women's ongoing masculinization to their increasing social and political mobility in 1920s Germany.[18] The *Bubikopf* phenomenon, with its symbolic connections to emasculation and castration, provides a visual expression of women's emancipation, sending the message that they are no longer willing to live in "slavish pregnancy" to men. Not content to settle with social commentary, Holtmont calls for a utopian system of gender equality whereby all individuals should be allowed to develop their talents according to ability rather than gender. Despite a damning assessment of female homosexuality, he suggests that it should become possible to speak of the "masculine character" of a woman who is in all other respects clearly and charmingly female.[19] Holtmont's study thus uses the *Hosenrolle* both as means of interpreting contemporary gender relations and as a powerful symbol of transformatory potential.

Precisely because of the *Hosenrolle*'s significance as a symbol of female emancipation, commentators sought to establish clear boundaries around this phenomenon in order to contain its threatening potential. Frequently they employed strategies similar to those already identified in relation to women's "masculinized" fashions and sporting activities, including (over-)emphasizing the "true," authentic femininity and heterosexuality of the women in question, as well as the transience of their masculine gender performances. Thus women could dress as men in order to please and titillate their menfolk, but they should not equate this with masculine privilege in either private or political life. "[T]o dress as a boy is for every female creature a charming game that makes the men laugh," insists John, even as she notes that it is "paradoxical" that women are dressing as men in order to attract men—a subdued reference to the homoerotic and narcissistic processes involved in reading femininity through male costume.[20] Two photographs published in *Das Magazin* in 1927 illustrate how gender crossing can be made to adhere to respectable boundaries: here a small image of a French soubrette named "Rahna" dressed in top hat and tails is juxtaposed against a much larger portrait of the same woman wearing a white, low-cut evening dress, pearls, makeup, and a submissive smile (Figure 4.2).[21] As with the narratives of transformation described in previous chapters, this image emphasizes Rahna's "true" femininity by showing her in attractive feminine attire in the main photograph, whereas the smaller image suggests a less authentic masculine gender performance.

Holtmont likewise situates trouser role performers as erotic spectacles designed to appeal to the heterosexual male gaze, but as detailed above, his analysis goes deeper than that of the magazine journalists, charting how the function of the *Hosenrolle* has been adapted throughout history in order to suit changing audience needs. The trouser role, he argues, holds a particular resonance for contemporary German society given the preference for "androgynous" female fashions and activities. This argument leads him to the unusual conclusion that the increasing masculinization of female fashions, with their demonstrated appeal for the male sex, could in fact contribute to the preservation of the race at a time when most social commentators feared quite the opposite result.[22] Such positive emphasis on the heterosexual attractiveness of the trouser role actor provided one means of keeping her gender transgression within safe boundaries, even as it admits the sexually dangerous possibility that gender ambiguity was central to her appeal.

On the flip side, scorn and ridicule were used to police actors and other women who ignored the boundaries of the theatrical performance and chose to "cross-dress" in their private lives as well as on stage. Writing for the conservative illustrated weekly *Die Woche*, Ludwig Sternaux contrasted the erotically and artistically desirable trouser role actor with other, less pleasing forms of real-life female masculinity, such as the city women who holiday in the Bavarian provinces in barely fitting pants: "For that, too, is a trouser role, though a very questionable one. And it has nothing to do with art."[23] Sternaux's insistence on a clear distinction between theatrical cross-dressing and the masculinization of women's fashions was echoed in the previously cited *BIZ* article "Now that's Enough!": "We do occasionally enjoy seeing an actress in the theater playing a trouser role if she is suited to such things, but neither on stage nor during sport can just any woman risk being seen in trousers." Accompanying this tirade are photographs of two actors who have failed to embody such distinctions, "cross-dressing" offstage

R a h n a

Die elegante französische Soubrette der Haller-Revue, für die
der Volksmund das Beiwort „die Buttergleiche" gefunden hat

Figure 4.2. "Rahna." *Das Magazin,* September 1927, 1337.

Source: BPK Bildagentur für Kunst, Kultur und Geschichte

as well as on. The captions underline this boundary crossing through references to the personal lives of the actors concerned: "Not a man, but rather the English actress Dolores (in private—not in a role)"; "The actress Johanna Sutter (civilian image)" (see Figure 1.6).[24]

A central problem with *Hosenrolle* actors who carried their masculine personas off the stage was not simply that they crossed a boundary between fiction and reality, but that their transgression also suggested the possibility of sexual inversion, at a time when sexologists and the media were paying increasing attention to convergences of masculine identity and homosexual orientation in women. Just as Garber emphasizes the transvestite's ability to effect multiple crossings and excesses—of race, class, rank, and sexuality in addition to gendered crossings—numerous scholars have noted the social censure surrounding European trouser role actors whose cross-dressing combined with suspected homosexual activity.[25] Thus the emphasis on the essential femininity of the trouser role actor described above is simultaneously an assurance of her heterosexuality: by undermining the possibility of an "authentic" masculine gender performance, images such as those of "Rahna" were intended to displace the threat of homosexuality.

At the same time, *Hosenrolle* performances raised taboo questions of homoerotic spectatorship, providing respectable female spectators with a rare opportunity to openly admire another woman's body and voice "in an atmosphere of heightened emotion and powerful sensual arousal."[26] Sexologists had already been discussing the links between trouser role performers and homosexuality for some decades: Ellis reflected that it is "noteworthy that women seem with special frequency to fall in love with disguised persons of their own sex"; while Krafft-Ebing suggested that many female actors and singers were themselves inverts, "particularly those who excel in trouser roles, for here they are in their element and play their true, that is masculine character."[27] In Weimar popular culture the sheer prevalence of *Hosenrolle* representations in magazines, on stage, and on the screen is evidence of their appeal to female as well as male audiences; however, heterosexual men continued to be discursively located as the only legitimate desiring subjects of these roles.

On the other hand, homosexual magazines from this period are more attentive to the possibility that *Hosenrolle* performances could involve more than a "playful masquerade." Not only was Holtmont's monograph advertised within these magazines as one of several contemporary publications of interest to transvestites, but numerous contributors expressed interest in the idea that *Hosenrolle* performances might be driven by the need to express an essential gender identity or sexual, psychological, or biological drive. Sex researcher Karsch-Haack observed with irony that whereas "cross-dressing" within the context of occupational or sporting activities is now considered socially acceptable, more personal motives for gender transgression are met only with condemnation and sexual stereotyping: "Dressing up as a result of an inner drive? No! The boundary of what is permissible must be sharply drawn at this point! For: the inner drive is suspicious, it encompasses the danger of sexual seduction, of sexual excesses!"[28] In other articles for these magazines, Karsch-Haack proceeds to describe how the gender-crossing of performers such as Julie Maupin and Felicitas von Vestvali (also known as Anna Marie Stägemann) extended to "masculine" activities such as fencing and dueling, and at times coincided with homosexual desires. Unlike the mainstream media journalists cited above, however, Karsch-Haack defends the inner motives of trouser role performers as a natural consequence of sexological variance and suggests that transvestism can assist both homosexually and heterosexually desiring people who feel strongly that they should have been born as members of the "opposite" sex.[29] Other subcultural commentators likewise linked the *Hosenrolle* to a range of sex-gender phenomena that they defended as natural, biological conditions deserving of legal protection. Eugen Gürster in *Frauen Liebe und Leben,* for example, argued that it is only those actors already in possession of an essential masculine tendency and physicality who are attracted to male roles, and likewise cites the example of Vestvali, whom he argues not only possessed a "strongly masculine physique and intensive alto voice," but *instinctively* (the emphasis is Gürster's) took refuge in the short, close-fitting male habits of *Hosenrollen* such as Hamlet or Romeo.[30]

Members of Weimar sexual subcultures also used the trouser role trope as a means of challenging mainstream boundaries for cross-dressing. One letter to *Die Freundin* directly contrasted the social acceptability and erotic attraction of theatrical trouser role performances with the lack of understanding for transvestites in the wider community, especially male-to-female transvestites. The author observes that while most men find a well-built woman playing boys' roles on stage "pretty and charming," the man in women's skirts is dismissed as a figure of ridicule, even though both cross-dress for similar reasons:

> [T]he masculine lady dresses in men's clothes because she finds it fun, the feminine man in women's clothes because he also finds it fun. Few people can think so objectively that they can understand that for both it is the same sex change that is longed for. Unfortunately there are transvestites who look neither good nor inconspicuous as ladies, and equally there are ladies who would be better to refrain from wearing men's clothing in the presence of others. These people should pursue their particular nature at home.[31]

At one level, this letter conforms to discriminatory social norms concerning appropriate gendered aesthetics, as the author restricts cross-dressing in public to those who manage to look both pleasing and convincing in their cross-dressed attire. Importantly, however, the trouser role also functions here as a means of pleading for wider social acceptance of transvestism, as the author criticizes the hypocrisy of socially condoning cross-dressing in some spaces but not others.

This example is also illuminating for the way it highlights the discrepancy in public opinion surrounding (acceptable) female and (intolerable) male cross-dressing, a distinction that was thematized repeatedly in Weimar-era discussions of the *Hosenrolle* in mainstream and subcultural publications alike. Zobeltitz expressed a popular opinion when she wrote in *Sport im Bild* that while a woman dressed as a man may appear both touching and comic, a man dressed as a woman is always somewhat ridiculous, and even borders on the repugnant.[32] Studies of cross-dressing explain such asymmetrical treatment with reference to dominant gender hierarchies, arguing that it has traditionally been considered less acceptable for men to reject their "natural" authority by appearing as women than for women to strive toward a "higher" goal by disguising themselves as men. Holtmont adopts just such a viewpoint in his contemporary study when he argues that male-to-female cross-dressing entails loss of status through effeminization, emasculation, and softening, whereas female cross-dressing is linked to empowerment, emancipation, and virtuosity. According to Holtmont, this desire to ascend to a "higher" intellectual and physical state entails a woman's transition from passive receptor to active procreator.[33] From a more personal perspective, male-to-female transvestites wrote to the subcultural magazines bemoaning their degraded status in comparison to female-to-male cross-dressers, who were seen to enjoy considerable levels of social respect not just within the homosexual women's clubs, but within society generally.[34] Despite its symbolic associations with political emancipation, then, female-to-male cross-dressing was perceived as the lesser of two evils, whereas male-to-female cross-dressing signaled a crisis of masculinity that necessitated an even fiercer policing than women's gender transgressions.

A final and powerful means of containing the gender transgression of the trouser role actor was to confine theatrical cross-dressing to women playing boyish or adolescent male roles. This had two functions: firstly, it reduced the threat of political emancipation by reinforcing women's status as lesser political beings, represented by the immature youth. Secondly, a focus on sexually immature characters reduced the threat to heteronormative gender relations symbolized by the trouser role actor. Prior to becoming psychologized and sexualized in the late nineteenth century, adolescence was widely seen as a pre- or asexual phase of a young man's life, and this youthful androgyny was considered to be best portrayed on stage by having a woman play the role. Women brought greater acting experience to their roles than young boys; their higher voices were considered suitable for the characters of boys yet to undergo puberty; and their presence, as noted above, introduced a level of sexual ambiguity and erotic appeal involved in "reading" a cross-gendered performance. It is no accident, as Garber observes, that the character of Peter Pan, the boy who will never grow up to become a man, has often been played by women, for the transvestite often traverses age as well as gender boundaries, and androgyny has frequently been associated with adolescence.[35] A woman playing a boyish, asexual character represented a far lesser cultural threat than if she were to assume the rank and sexual experience of, say, a middle-aged male political leader. These cross-dressed boy roles could well be important within the context of the play, but increasingly, as Naomi André points out, "they were not characters that had the maturity and valor needed to be the primary contender for the hand of the soprano heroine."[36]

Weimar commentators repeatedly attempted to restrict women in trouser roles to this "safe" period of adolescence. It was not unusual for journalists to condemn the serious Shakespearean trouser roles of the nineteenth century as "failed experiments," whilst simultaneously delighting in the eroticism of "the little *Rosenkavalier* in his pageboy dress" or Asta Nielsen's "hermaphrodite Hamlet."[37] Holtmont describes with pleasure the erotic experience of watching a woman playing a youthful street urchin: "a tingling sensation awakes in the audience member when these highly physical roles are played by an actress."[38] In his analysis of French trouser role actors, Berlanstein suggests that this preference for women in adolescent roles was a remnant of the eighteenth-century "one-sex" model of gender and anatomy. Thomas Laqueur has shown that whereas women in the eighteenth century were viewed scientifically as lesser, imperfect males rather than the biological "opposites" of men, this model was replaced during the nineteenth century with the ideology of separate spheres and gender binarity. Building on this framework, Berlanstein argues that the representation of youth was one area in which the one-sex conceptualization survived, so that "(m)ale imitators were never disguised as mature men, husbands, or fathers but took the part of boys."[39] Yet whereas Berlanstein argues that this dramatic tradition declined in fin-de-siècle France due to a crisis of masculinity that saw intellectuals calling for a new, muscular youth that could defend the nation, the popularity of *Hosenrolle* images in the Weimar mass media tells another story. Despite an arguably even deeper crisis of masculinity in World War I–defeated Germany, it seems that German audiences needed the *Hosenrolle* more than ever. By restricting the *Hosenrolle* to young, attractive women playing adolescent male roles and excluding more "dangerous" embodiments of female masculinity such as the masculine female emancipist or the virile homosexual woman, Weimar commentators engaged in a process of containment that sought to provide audiences with a means of clarifying changing gender roles and expectations within their own lives.

It is important to emphasize the political implications of allowing women only a reductive form of masculinity in 1920s Germany, only a few years after they had achieved the right to vote and at a time when, having proven their abilities during the war, they seemed to threaten men's dominance within a newly industrialized workforce. The theatrical preference for adolescent masculinity can also help to explain the ongoing popularity even into the 1930s of "boyish" styles such as the *Bubikopf,* which represented a less threatening variant of masculine women's fashions than the tuxedos or monocles of the mid 1920s: journalists repeatedly commented on the "childish" or "youthful" gloss that the *Bubikopf* lent even to older women. The New Woman herself, as Petro points out, was considered by some critics to be renouncing femininity and regressing to an adolescent and deeroticized femininity, thus deviating from the path of "normal" female sexual development.[40] Weimar media coverage of the *Hosenrolle* responded to a cultural need to engage with models of female masculinity that did not endanger male political and social dominance, at a time when this very dominance, along with women's commitment to traditional female ideals of marriage and children, seemed increasingly under threat.

The *Hosenrolle* in Weimar Cinema

Films produced in Weimar Germany provide another important source of representations of both the trouser role actor and the masculine New Woman. More so than photographs or fashion drawings, film involves a personal and three-dimensional relationship with the spectator, playing to the audience's fantasies, desires, and need for self-identification. Many of the films produced at this period of German history were pioneering in their approach to gender and sexuality; according to film theorist Richard Dyer they often exhibit a "general openness about sexuality."[41] The early silent film *Anders als die Andern* (Different from the Others, 1919, dir. Richard Oswald), for example, includes an explicit appeal in favor of homosexual rights, and features a lecture by Magnus Hirschfeld on the naturalness of the homosexual condition. Feminist film scholars also emphasize women's increased visibility in cultural production and consumption at this period, showing that for the first time, women were specifically addressed as privileged audiences for the new media of photojournalism and cinema, "engendering a new stage in the critical reevaluation of the female image."[42] An important part of this reevaluation involved audiences engaging with trouser role representations—characters whose gender ambiguity challenged conventional understandings of the spectatorial gaze. This section examines several cinematic *Hosenrolle* performances, seeking to identify instances where female-to-male cross-dressing functioned not simply as a "safety valve," but as an instrument of social change.

Many of the Weimar-era films that engaged with the trouser role trope can hardly be considered subversive; rather, like the magazine images examined above, they functioned to confine female-to-male cross-dressing and acting to strict times and places. Such "safe" trouser role representations included Asta Nielsen's star turn as *Hamlet* (1920, dir. Svend Gade and Heinz Schall) and Elisabeth Bergner's role in *Der Geiger von Florenz* (1925/26, dir. Paul Czinner).[43] The musical comedy *Viktor und Viktoria* (Victor and Victoria, 1933, dir. Reinhold Schünzel), produced in the year that Hitler came to power, is of particular interest in this context for the way it plays with and extends the traditions of the *Hosenrolle*. This film features a woman named Susanne ("Viktoria") who substitutes for a sick male actor (Viktor), who in turn works in a cabaret earning a living as a female impersonator. Offstage, "Viktoria" must carry on the masquerade of passing as a man in order not to ruin the show, while onstage she must "double pass"—play a man who is impersonating a woman. Barbara Creed observes that such comedies of sexual disguise highlight the performative nature of gender, as actors use the artifice of special effects, including costumes, wigs, and makeup, in order to perform various gender roles with ease and authority.[44] As in the later US version starring Julie Andrews, *Victor/Victoria* (1982, dir. Blake Edwards), the humor relies on the audience's knowledge of "Viktoria's" "true" gender, as she struggles, often comically, to assert herself in a man's world.[45]

The German film ends even more normatively than the remake, with both Viktor and "Viktoria" finding heterosexual partners and "Viktoria" relinquishing her onstage/offstage stage transvestism. In this the film strongly exhibits elements of the "temporary transvestite" formula identified by Straayer in the context of Hollywood cinema. According to this formula, films that engage with transvestism typically "offer spectators a momentary, vicarious trespassing of society's accepted boundaries for gender and sexual behavior." Yet while these films generally support heterosexual desire at the narrative level, they sometimes challenge it at more ambiguous levels, including that of the visual, allowing for other, "queered" readings of the cinematic text.[46] Thus Dyer points to the "queerness" of a kiss between two women in *Der Geiger von Florenz,* each of whom is aware that the other is a woman, despite one of them being in male costume.[47] Similarly, "Viktoria's" performance of masculinity leads to the repeated emergence of queer desires that temporarily disrupt the heteronormative narrative. Women in "Viktoria's" stage audience fall in love not only with her (feminine) stage persona, but also gasp with approval as she "reveals" at the end of her act that she is fact a "man"; afterwards they gaze admiringly across the dining room at the strapping figure of "Mr. Viktoria" in a tuxedo, and even invite her to intimate afternoon teas with clear romantic intent, which the heterosexual Viktoria must then fend off.

There are parallels here to the oft-cited scene in the 1930 film *Morocco* (dir. Josef von Sternberg), in which Marlene Dietrich's character Amy Jolly appears on a cabaret stage cross-dressed in a tuxedo and top hat and proceeds to flirt with both male and female audience members. This scene features gestures and movements that, as Andrea Weiss points out, "were inconsistent with the narrative and even posed an ideological threat within it," so that when Dietrich flirts briefly with a woman, this is "a flirtation with the lesbian spectator as well."[48] Such moments of subversion, as Creed has shown, expose "contradictions in the ideology, despite the fact that the narrative structures of the Sternberg-Dietrich films ... ultimately relocate her within a patriarchal discourse."[49] Like Dietrich in *Morocco,* "Viktoria's" assumption of a typically masculine dress and manner excludes the possibility of conventional sexual objectification by the audience—the traditional fate of the female screen star in Hollywood narrative cinema, as feminist film theorists such as Laura Mulvey and Mary Ann Doane have demonstrated.[50]

Yet unlike Dietrich, whose character never attempts to "pass" as male even as she confidently assumes male privileges and a "masculine" desiring gaze, "Viktoria" remains ever uneasy in her male costume, posing no lasting threat to either patriarchal or heteronormative social hierarchies.

In contrast to "Viktoria's" playful but ultimately subservient approach to the social norms of female-to-male cross-dressing, the main character Manuela von Meinhardis (played by Hertha Thiele) in Leontine Sagan's *Mädchen in Uniform* (1931) oversteps these boundaries with dramatic consequences. Just as Garber argues that the figure of the transvestite has the potential to act as an agent and not just a marker of cultural change, Manuela uses the carnivalesque privileges of the *Hosenrolle* performance not only to voice her nonheterosexual desire, but to shake the entire hierarchy of the authoritarian institution in which the film is set.[51]

Mädchen in Uniform was a novelty within Weimar cinema, both written and directed by women and produced using an all-female cast, an aspect that was widely commented upon in media coverage of its release.[52] It was highly successful in Germany and went on to screen across Europe and in the US and Japan. The film tells of the growing love of sensitive new pupil Manuela for her boarding school teacher, Fräulein von Bernburg, played by Dorothea Wieck. With her mother recently deceased, Manuela craves affection from the widely adored Bernburg, who in turn is opposed to the school's totalitarian Prussian codes and is more affectionate and motherly toward the girls than are her colleagues. Bernburg interchangeably nourishes and discourages Manuela's infatuation, which is even more intense than that of her fellow pupils, most of whom likewise have a "crush" on their teacher. While the school's direction tolerates a degree of intimate female friendships, Manuela challenges the carefully maintained order when, still dressed as Don Carlos after a school production of the Schiller play of the same name, and drunk on punch and success, she announces her love for Bernburg. She does so not only in front of her fellow students, but also before the institution's authoritarian headmistress, played by Emilie Unda. This scene provides the film's turning point, as the headmistress declares the events "a scandal" and banishes Manuela to solitary confinement. Distraught and heartbroken, Manuela escapes and climbs the school's forbidding staircase, and is about to throw herself from the top when she is stopped by her fellow students and Fräulein von Bernburg, all of whom are disobeying orders in coming to her aid. As B. Ruby Rich describes, this "averting of imminent tragedy is a triumph for the forces of love and community, signaling the coming of a new order."[53]

For many years, *Mädchen* was interpreted first and foremost as a prophetic protest against authoritarian, militaristic rule in the years immediately prior to the Nazi seizure of power. Since the film's rediscovery by feminists in the 1970s many critics have also stressed the centrality of lesbianism to the film's plot: most prominent is Rich's argument that the film is "not only antifascist, but also anti-patriarchal in its politics."[54] Nor was its homosexual aspect lost on contemporary reviewers. Although some critics played down the erotics of the relationship between Manuela and Bernburg, a 1932 piece in the fashion magazine *Die Dame* describes the progression of "the teenage veneration of a girl for her teacher into an erotic complex," while a review in *Die Freundin*, which could be expected to focus on the film's homosexual themes, describes the "lesbian orientation of the orphaned and pubescent Manuela von Meinhardis," and praises Dorothea Wieck's portrayal of Fräulein von Bernburg's internal "struggle between her self-control and her orientation."[55] More recently, queer film scholars have undertaken important analyses of the ways in which female homosexuality is portrayed in this film. Dyer examines the relationship between Manuela and Bernburg as one of "feminine" lesbian identification, noting how this emphasis on the feminine in the cinematic narrative marked a departure from the Berlin theatrical version of Christa Winsloe's play, *Gestern und Heute* (Yesterday and Today). In that version, Bernburg had been played by Margarete Melzer, who was later described by Thiele (Manuela) in an interview as "an absolutely masculine type."[56] Meanwhile, Straayer conducts an innovative reading of the characters of Manuela and the rebellious Ilse von Westhagen as examples of young but sexualized "baby butches"; other analyses have focused on whether this is a "coming out" film, or on the relationships between maternal, erotic, and anti-authoritarian themes.[57]

The scene of primary interest here, in which Manuela assumes the costume of Don Carlos and publicly announces her love for Bernburg, has also received scholarly attention. Rich highlights the transgression involved in the act of naming that which, although known and tolerated, cannot be expressly pronounced; Dyer emphasizes the significance of Manuela "coming out" as homosexual while occupying "male" space; and Straayer likewise emphasizes the significance of Manuela being temporarily "butched up" in this scene.[58] In other words, despite its otherwise overwhelmingly "feminine" representation of female homosexuality, the film includes a prominent enactment of female masculinity at a critical moment in the narrative, and does so in order to enable the expression of same-sex desire. The gender-bending tradition of the *Hosenrolle,* so well accepted that it can be performed even within the context of a strict, militaristic boarding school, is crucial in enabling this turning point.

Prior to Manuela donning the flattering cavalier tights and floppy feathered hat of Don Carlos for the lead role in the school play, the viewer has already been privy to numerous "feminine" expressions of homosexual desire within the school environment: we watch as love letters are sent between the girls; the initials "E.v.B." (Elisabeth von Bernburg) are stitched into dresses and scratched into arms; palpable excitement surrounds Bernburg as she kisses each of the girls goodnight in their dormitory, paying particular attention to Manuela; and numerous acts of kindness demonstrate Bernburg's affection for her young, motherless student. However, it is Manuela's male costume that acts as a catalyst for the public voicing of these desires, actively positioning her as both a figure of homo-erotic desire and a desiring subject in her own right. Manuela uses the privileges of her male costume to access forbidden erotic and cultural spaces, embodying a female masculinity that spills over the limits of the "temporary transvestite" narrative. Even before the play begins, the artifice of the costume and the tradition of the *Hosenrolle* have begun to create a carnivalesque erotic zone that eschews normal social boundaries, evident when a clearly smitten fellow student starts to incessantly stroke Manuela's legs as she rehearses her lines backstage, declaring without any fear of reprimand or scandal: "Oh Manuela, you're so beautiful!" (see Figure 4.3). Manuela, on the other hand, has thoughts only for Bernburg, whom she aims to impress with her performance. The erotic potential of the *Hosenrolle* embodied by Manuela in these backstage scenes contrasts with the comic performance of masculinity by a fellow student named Marie, who presents a podgy and somewhat ridiculous figure with her small, bushy beard, overly tight costume and lack of acting talent.

Once Manuela takes the stage, we watch as her Don Carlos declares his undying love for his queen (Figure 4.4). The parallels between Manuela's passion for Bernburg and this fictionalized taboo passion of a young man for his father's wife have been explored in some detail by Rich, who argues that Sagan deliberately annexes the theme of forbidden love via the "sanctity of German high culture," whereby it is no accident that the Queen Mother Elizabeth and Fräulein von Bernburg bear the same first name.[59] The overwhelmingly positive and subtly eroticized reactions of the teaching staff to Manuela's performance further evidences the lapsing of social hierarchies permitted by the *Hosenrolle*—even the headmistress comments on her student's "beautiful legs." However, the distance between fiction and reality crucial to maintaining this carnivalesque space disintegrates when, following the play, Manuela gets drunk on punch and makes a speech, declaring her undying love for Fräulein von Bernburg: "She loves me! I'm not afraid of anything!" As evidence of mutual affection, Manuela even reveals that the revered teacher has given her one of her own petticoats. Unlike her fellow pupil Ilse, who shortly beforehand, also in male costume, had stood among her peers toasting Manuela and the play's success, Manuela stands on an elevated stage separated physically from the others, emphasizing her difference from her fellow pupils and their schoolgirl crushes. Although it might have been possible to dismiss this speech as drunken revelry if only fellow pupils had been present, Manuela continues in the spirit of Don Carlos's masculine bravado even after she spots the headmistress entering the room, and declares: "Yes, *everyone* should know it!" By directly challenging this central authority figure and explicitly naming her homosexual desire, Manuela goes beyond the point where her conduct can be dismissed as an innocent crush: her desire explodes the theatrical boundaries of the *Hosenrolle* masquerade. This disrespect for the line between truth and

MÄDCHEN IN UNIFORM - Deutschland 1931
Regie: Leontine Sagan
Quelle: Filmmuseum Berlin - Stiftung Deutsche Kinemathek

Figure 4.3. Manuela during rehearsal, *Mädchen in Uniform*. (Germany, 1931) Dir. Leontine Sagan.

Source: Filmmuseum Berlin – Stiftung Deutsche Kinemathek

MÄDCHEN IN UNIFORM - Deutschland 1931
Regie: Leontine Sagan
Quelle: Filmmuseum Berlin - Stiftung Deutsche Kinemathek

Figure 4.4. Manuela as Don Carlos, *Mädchen in Uniform.* (Germany, 1931) Dir. Leontine Sagan.
Source: Filmmuseum Berlin   Stiftung Deutsche Kinemathek

fiction has dramatic consequences, as Manuela's confinement and subsequent attempted suicide lead pupils and teachers alike to question and ultimately defy the school's authoritarian hierarchies.

The suspension of established truths and hierarchies during carnivalesque rituals enables, as Bakhtin explains, an unusually frank and free type of communication that is impossible in daily life, abolishing conventional notions of distance and norms of etiquette: "This carnival spirit offers the chance to have a new outlook on the world, to realize the relative nature of all that exists, and to enter a completely new order of things."[60] That such utopian social reevaluation is not always the result of carnivalesque activities is evident from most of the examples discussed in this chapter, which functioned primarily to defuse the threat of women's masculinization, enabling a letting-off of steam in order that things may return to "normal." Against this predominantly conservative trouser role tradition, the subversive and transformative consequences of the gender masquerade in *Mädchen in Uniform* become all the more significant. What begins as a typical, conventionally harmless *Hosenrolle* performance is transformed into an erotic spectacle, and Manuela's masculine costume becomes a precondition for her "real-life" declaration of same-sex desire and love.

Disrupting heteronormative expectations to various degrees through their appropriations of the *Hosenrolle* trope, films such as *Mädchen in Uniform* and *Viktor und Viktoria* spoke to contemporary German cultural anxieties about changing gender roles and ideas of sexual morality. The challenges they posed to normative understandings of gender and sexual desire directly addressed the female spectator as well as the conventional male gaze, emphasizing the cultural importance of this new figure in Weimar public life. Although the appearance of these films shortly before the National Socialists came to dominate cultural life highlights just how quickly such transgressive representations can be undermined and repressed by more conservative forces, they also provide some grounds for optimism. As McCormick points out, the extreme popularity of films such as *Mädchen in Uniform* provides "proof of the fact that popular culture at the end of the Weimar Republic was not invariably reactionary, as so many critics have assumed."[61] Encouraging reflection on questions of sexual desire and difference that were rarely articulated within such a mainstream arena, Sagan's film in particular demonstrates the potential of gender masquerade to disrupt and challenge the stability of the heterosexual project and its powerful normative equation of gender with (hetero)sexuality. At the same time, this cinematic text highlights the symbolic significance of gender in the maintenance of social hierarchies—a symbolism at the heart of Weimar-era anxieties about the "masculine woman."

Representations of the *Hosenrolle* in Weimar popular culture responded to a need to experiment and engage with new gender models and ideas about women's increasing political and social mobility within a safe forum. By emphasizing the clear temporal and spatial boundaries of the theatrical trouser role, Weimar journalists sought to rein in the threat of uncontrolled female "masculinization" that seemed to be penetrating other areas of social life, from fashion to sport and from marriage to the workplace. They did so by condemning gender transgressions that fell outside of restricted, theatrical contexts; by reiterating the femininity and heterosexuality of the trouser role actor; by confining her masculine performances to the stage or the bedroom; by trivializing her sexual and political power to the level of an adolescent boy; and by condemning the possibility of homosexuality. Indeed, despite the homoerotic subtexts involved in reading heterosexual desire through cross-dressed costume, and despite the fact that women read the popular Weimar magazines as avidly as men, journalists persisted in situating the desiring subject of the *Hosenrolle* performance as a heterosexual man. Such discursive strategies testify to the widespread fear that the cross-dressed woman—so closely related in symbolic terms to the masculine New Woman—would defy social taboos and hierarchies by stepping off the stage and accessing real-life masculine privileges.

Notes

1. Chris Straayer, *Deviant Eyes, Deviant Bodies: Sexual Re-orientations in Film and Video* (New York: Columbia University Press, 1996), 43.

2. Susanne Benedek and Adolphe Binde, *Von tanzenden Kleidern und sprechenden Leibern: Cross-dressing als Auflösung der Geschlechterpolarität?* (Dortmund: Edition Ebersbach, 1996), 14; Garber, *Vested Interests.* Cf. Straayer's use of these terms, whereby transvestism involves attempting to pass as a member of the opposite sex, while cross-dressing "exaggerates the opposite sex's assumed gender codes to appear obviously, inadequately disguised": *Deviant Eyes*, 47.

3. On the history of the trouser role and its connections to the *castrati* see e.g. Naomi Adele André, *Voicing Gender: Castrati, Travesti, and the Second Woman in Early-Nineteenth-Century Italian Opera* (Bloomington: Indiana University Press, 2006), 2ff., 12; Corinne E. Blackmer and Patricia Juliana Smith, eds., *En travesti: Women, Gender Subversion, Opera* (New York: Columbia University Press, 1995); Elke Krafka, "Die Hosenrolle am Theater—Kostümierung oder Grenzüberschreitung?" in *Sakkorausch und Rollentausch: männliche Leitbilder als Freiheitsentwürfe von Frauen,* ed. Andrea Stoll and Verena Wodtke-Werner (Dortmund: Edition Ebersbach, 1997).

4. F. Michael Moore, *Drag! Male and Female Impersonators on Stage, Screen, and Television: An Illustrated World History* (Jefferson, NC: McFarland, 1994), 18; see also Stefanie Hetze, "Die Hosenrolle im Theater," in *Frauen in Hosen: Hosenrollen im Film. Texte und Materialien,* ed. Madeleine Bernstoff and Stefanie Hetze (Munich: Münchner Filmzentrum e.V., 1989), 6.

5. See e.g. Jan Berg, "Asta Nielsen: Darstellung von Weiblichkeit und Weiblichkeit als Darstellung," in *Idole des Deutschen Films: Eine Galerie von Schlüsselfiguren,* ed. Thomas Koebner (Munich: Edition Text und Kritik, 1997), 65.

6. Mikhail Bakhtin, *Rabelais and his World,* trans. Helene Iswolsky (Bloomington: Indiana University Press, 1984), 15.

7. Eagleton in Peter Stallybrass and Allon White, *The Politics and Poetics of Transgression* (London: Methuen, 1986), 13.

8. Natalie Zemon Davis, *Society and Culture in Early Modern France: Eight Essays* (Cambridge: Polity, 1987), 143, see also 130.

9. Stallybrass and White, *Politics and Poetics,* 14ff.

10. According to Lenard R. Berlanstein, the trouser role had all but died out in interwar France, as changing understandings of sexuality "created new and unacceptable tensions around transvestite behavior," even though "masculine" women's fashions were similarly popular in France and Germany: "Breeches and Breaches: Cross-Dress Theater and the Culture of Gender Ambiguity in Modern France," *Comparative Studies in Society and History* 38, no. 2 (1998): 348.

11. See e.g. "Margarete Köppke ... als Hofmarschall Lea Giba in Wedekinds 'Kaiserin von Neufundland,'" *Die Dame,* no. 9, 2nd January Issue 1926, inside cover; "Elisabeth Bergner in einem neuen Film 'Der Geiger von Florenz,'" *Die Dame,* no. 14, 1st April Issue 1926, 5; Niezky, "Unsere Bühnen- und Flimmersterne IV: Henny Porten/Asta Nielsen," *Ulk,* no. 12, 21 March 1924, 47; "Unsere Bühnen- und Flimmersterne XII: Emmy Sturm in ihrer dreifachen Rolle im 'Süßen Kavalier,'" *Ulk,* no. 35, 12 September 1924, 139; "Schokoladenhusar," *Das Magazin,* no. 20, April 1926, 362.

12. Alfred Holtmont, *Die Hosenrolle. Variationen über das Thema: Das Weib als Mann* (Munich: Meyer & Jessen, 1925), 168.

13. "Die Diva braucht..," *Das Magazin,* no. 6, February 1925, 25.

14. Martha von Zobeltitz, "Die Hosenrolle," *Sport im Bild,* no. 9, 9 May 1924, 458; Trude John, "Hosenparade: Eine Sammlung amüsanter Hosenrollen," *Das Magazin,* no. 72, August 1930, 5031ff.

15. Holtmont, *Die Hosenrolle*, 177f.
16. Vern L. Bullough and Bonnie Bullough, *Cross Dressing, Sex, and Gender* (Philadelphia: University of Pennsylvania Press, 1993), 229.
17. Holtmont, *Die Hosenrolle*, 177f.
18. Ibid., 206.
19. Holtmont argues that a reduction in male tyranny will lead to a decline in lesbianism, because the dependent, unintelligent "pure woman" who forms the object of desire of the homosexual "man-woman" will become almost nonexistent: ibid., 206, 208ff., 228f.
20. John, "Hosenparade," 5031ff.
21. "Rahna," *Das Magazin*, no. 37, September 1927, 1337.
22. Holtmont, *Die Hosenrolle*, 8f.
23. Ludwig Sternaux, "Die Hosenrolle," *Die Woche*, no. 8, 21 February 1925, 170.
24. "Nun aber genug! Gegen die Vermännlichung der Frau," *Berliner Illustrirte Zeitung*, no. 13, 29 March 1925, 389.
25. Garber, *Vested Interests*, 28; see also Berlanstein, "Breeches," 354–68; Bullough and Bullough, *Cross Dressing*, 227ff.
26. Terry Castle, "In Praise of Brigitte Fassbaender: Reflections on Diva-Worship," in Blackmer and Smith, *En travesti*, 22.
27. Ellis and Symonds, *Sexual Inversion*, 95; Krafft-Ebing, *Psychopathia sexualis*, 284.
28. Prof. Karsch-Haack, "Junggesellin und Junggeselle (8. Fortsetzung)," *Garçonne*, no. 4, 18 February 1931, 2.
29. Professor Karsch-Haack, "Historische Männinnen: Die französische Sängerin Julie Maupin," *Die Freundin*, no. 7, 18 April 1927, 3ff.; Prof. Karsch-Haack, "Junggesellin und Junggeselle (3. Fortstetzung)," *Garçonne*, no. 4, 1 December 1930, 5.
30. Dr. Eugen Gürster, "Hosenrolle und Frauenemanzipation," *Frauen Liebe und Leben*, no. 2, 1928, 18.
31. Ellen, "Unsere Leser haben das Wort," *Die Freundin*, no. 5, 29 January 1930, 6.
32. Zobeltitz, "Die Hosenrolle," 459.
33. Holtmont, *Die Hosenrolle*, 7, 9.
34. See e.g. Raven (Leipzig), "Die Welt der Transvestiten: Das Empfindungsleben der Transvestiten," *Die Freundin*, no. 50, 14 December 1932, 6; Hilde Baronin Rotenburg, "Die Welt der Transvestiten: Die Not der Transvestiten," *Die Freundin*, no. 9, 28 August 1929, 5f.; Maria Weis, "Transvestitismus und Gesellschaft," *Frauenliebe*, no. 12, n.d. 1930, 2.
35. Garber, *Vested Interests*, 182ff.
36. André, *Voicing Gender*, 103. On the history of casting women in the roles of adolescent boys see also Dietz-Rüdiger Moser, "Hosenrollen: Zum Kleider- und Geschlechtertausch, besonders im Leben, im Volksbrauch und auf der Bühne," *Literatur in Bayern* 21 (2006): 3, 5; Blackmer and Smith, *En travesti*, 5, 10; Martin Essinger, "Die Hosenrolle in der Oper," in *Frauenstimmen, Frauenrollen in der Oper und Frauen-Selbstzeugnisse*, ed. Eva Rieger and Gabriele Busch-Salmen (Herbolzheim: Centaurus, 2000), 300ff.; Berlanstein, "Breeches," 353f.
37. Zobeltitz, "Die Hosenrolle," 459; Sternaux, "Die Hosenrolle," 170.
38. Holtmont, *Die Hosenrolle*, 162.
39. Berlanstein, "Breeches," 351, 353, 368; see also Thomas Walter Laqueur, *Making Sex: Body and Gender from the Greeks to Freud* (Cambridge, MA: Harvard University Press, 1990).
40. Petro, *Joyless Streets*, 105, 110.
41. Richard Dyer, "Less and More than Women and Men: Lesbian and Gay Cinema in Weimar Germany," *New German Critique*, no. 51 (1990): 8.
42. Gleber, *Art of Taking a Walk*, 179f.; see also Petro, *Joyless Streets*.
43. For a survey of the cinematic trouser role that encompasses the Weimar period see Madeleine

Bernstoff and Stefanie Hetze, eds., *Frauen in Hosen: Hosenrollen im Film* (Munich: Münchner Filmzentrum e.V., 1989).

44. Barbara Creed, *Pandora's Box: Essays in Film Theory* (Melbourne: Australian Centre for the Moving Image and University of Melbourne, 2004), 126.

45. For a comparison of the two versions, see Lehnert, *Wenn Frauen,* 100–110. For analyses of the US version, see Rebecca Louise Bell-Metereau, *Hollywood Androgyny* (New York: Columbia University Press, 1985), 224ff.; Vito Russo, *The Celluloid Closet: Homosexuality in the Movies* (New York: Harper & Row, 1987), 280ff.; Straayer, *Deviant Eyes,* 64ff.

46. Straayer, *Deviant Eyes,* 54. For formulations of the "queer gaze" and "queer spectatorship" see Halberstam, *Female Masculinity,* 175ff.; Creed, *Pandora's Box,* 132ff.; Judith Mayne, *Cinema and Spectatorship* (London: Routledge, 1993).

47. Dyer, "Less and More," 34.

48. Andrea Weiss, "'A Queer Feeling When I Look at You': Hollywood Stars and Lesbian Spectatorship in the 1930s," in *Multiple Voices in Feminist Film Criticism,* ed. Diane Carson et al. (Minneapolis: University of Minnesota Press, 1994), 332.

49. Creed, *Pandora's Box,* 19; see also Rebecca Kennison, "Clothes Make the (Wo)man: Marlene Dietrich and 'Double Drag,'" *Journal of Lesbian Studies* 6, no. 2 (2002): 147–56.

50. Mulvey, "Visual Pleasure," 746–57; Doane, "Film and the Masquerade," 758–72.

51. Garber, *Vested Interests.*

52. E.g. "Frauen machen Frauen-Filme," *Berliner Illustrirte Zeitung,* no. 50, 13 December 1931, 1944; Eduard Oskar Püttmann, "Mädchen in Uniform," *Die Freundin,* no. 3, 20 January 1932, 4f.

53. B. Ruby Rich, "From Repressive Tolerance to Erotic Liberation: *Mädchen in Uniform,*" in *Chick Flicks: Theories and Memories of the Feminist Film Movement,* ed. B. Ruby Rich (Durham: Duke University Press, 1998), 182.

54. Ibid., 181. Dyer points to two classic studies of Weimar film that read the film as a protest against authoritarianism, Siegfried Kracauer's *From Caligari to Hitler* and Lotte Eisner's *The Haunted Screen:* "Less and More," 27ff. McCormick analyzes the film's reception and depiction of sexuality and late-Weimar politics in *Gender and Sexuality,* 146–62.

55. Wolfgang Weber, "Junge Mädchen im Kaiserin-Augusta-Stift in Potsdam," *Die Dame,* no. 25, 1st September Issue 1932, 7; Püttmann, "Mädchen in Uniform," 4f.; for an example of a review that denied the film's lesbian eroticism see Schacht, "Ein Film setzt sich durch," 6–8, 52.

56. Dyer, "Less and More," 37ff.; see also McCormick, *Gender and Sexuality,* 152, 158. This interview can be found in Karola Gramann and Heide Schlüpmann, "Unnatürliche Akte: Die Inszenierung des Lesbischen im Film," in *Lust und Elend: Das erotische Kino,* ed. Karola Gramann et al. (Munich: Bucher, 1981), 28ff.

57. Straayer, *Deviant Eyes,* 124; Silke von der Emde, "'Mädchen in Uniform': Erotic Self-Liberation of Women in the Context of the Film Discussion in the Weimar-Republic," *Kodikas Code-Ars Semiotica* 14, no. 1–2 (1991): 35–48; Nina Zimnik, "No Man, No Cry? The Film *Girls in Uniform* and Its Discourses of Political Regime," *Women in German Yearbook* 15 (2000): 161–83.

58. Rich, "From Repressive Tolerance," 189; Dyer, "Less and More," 8, 29, 34; Straayer, *Deviant Eyes,* 125.

59. Rich, "From Repressive Tolerance," 188f.

60. Bakhtin, *Rabelais,* 34, also 10.

61. McCormick, *Gender and Sexuality,* 161.

Chapter 5

BEYOND BERLIN

Female Masculinities in Weimar Fiction

"Clubs—you say that there are clubs. Then the women who belong to these clubs are happy?" asked [Fräulein von Raitzold]. Lania shrugged her shoulders.

"I never thought about it much. It's not a problem for me."

"Perhaps it isn't a problem—there—where you live. Here it is a problem," said the Fräulein, stood there for another moment, then suddenly blushed deeply, which looked quite strange on her brown, weathered skin. "I'm sorry for this outburst," she added and quickly withdrew.

Vicki Baum, *Zwischenfall in Lohwinckel*

*I*n this excerpt from popular novelist Vicki Baum's 1930 novel *Zwischenfall in Lohwinckel* (Results of an Accident), we see the minor character Fräulein von Raitzold, a financially troubled member of the landed gentry in an isolated country town, enter into a tentative conversation about Berlin's lesbian clubs with the exotic Lania, a would-be film star from the city who has found herself in Raitzold's care following an automobile accident. The decidedly masculine Fräulein von Raitzold, who is elsewhere characterized as a pipe-smoking Amazon with a fondness for high riding boots, is having her first glimpse of a nonheterosexual community of likeminded "inverts," who, unlike members of her own rural community of Lohwinckel, would presumably not dismiss her as a "crazy old spinster."[1] Although the narcissistic Lania is herself staunchly heterosexual and presumably only visits these clubs because they add a cosmopolitan "edge"

Notes for this section begin on page 177.

to her social image, for Raitzold this conversation serves as a glimmer of hope that somewhere ("there—where you live")—specifically, in the Berlin metropolis—there is a community of women like herself: masculine women who desire other women. This conversation illustrates the stark divide between urban and rural experience in the Weimar period, a divide frequently commented upon by contemporaries at a period when German modernity and culture were increasingly associated with the nation's metropolis. Moreover, although Baum can certainly not be characterized as a "lesbian" author, in this scene there is a particular focus on how issues of place and space impact upon what might now be termed "queer" experience, a question that has emerged repeatedly in recent scholarship. Shifting the focus outward from Berlin, this chapter uses literary texts to examine how the cultural divide between the city and the provinces shaped Weimar-era representations of sex-gender otherness, and of "queer" female masculinities in particular.

On several fronts, then, this final chapter marks a departure from the media-based analyses of the previous chapters. Moving away from the Berlin-based press that has been the focus so far, the following analysis draws on novels by renowned Weimar authors including Irmgard Keun, Alfred Döblin, and Erich Kästner, as well as the best selling Vicki Baum. These authors explicitly used their fiction to comment on the masculine woman of post–World War I Germany in more detailed, complex, and creative ways than was possible for mass media journalists. Their depictions of masculine and/or homosexual women are informed by contemporary sexological ideas about homosexuality and sex-gender inversion, by categories of race and class, and by stereotypes of metropolitan perversion—or, alternatively, the "naturalness" of rural settings. Yet these authors were also writing from a largely heteronormative perspective; consequently, their writings are contrasted here with fictional representations of female masculinities by authors writing from within and for the Weimar homosexual subculture, including short fiction published within the subcultural magazines and Anna Elisabet Weirauch's popular trilogy *Der Skorpion* (1919/1921/1931).

Feminist literary scholars have clearly established the importance of popular literature for women at this period. Although Vibeke Petersen points to the relative lack of studies of Weimar popular fiction in comparison to other cultural forms such as the cinema, she insists that "(p)opular culture, especially fiction, has, more than any other form of 'high' culture, created texts where life is mediated through a woman's story."[2] Barndt's work on "New Woman" novels of the Weimar era is likewise exemplary of attempts to reevaluate women's roles in cultural production and consumption at this period. Barndt uses the concept of the "*gutgemacht Mittleren*" or "middlebrow" culture to describe the realm of women's popular fiction, locating the New Woman novel in a literary space between "educated middle-class ambitions" and "market-oriented entertainment culture."[3] My analysis is indebted to such scholars' refusal to be constrained by hierarchically gendered distinctions between "high" and "low" culture in relation to women's cultural production, and draws on a range of magazine fiction, "highbrow" and proudly "middlebrow" literature: Vicki Baum famously characterized herself as a "first-class second-rate author." At the same time, it extends upon existing research into 1920s German literature through a specific focus on "queer" female masculinities: I argue that Weimar authors—male and female, heterosexual and homosexual—used the visual and behavioral codes associated with the masculine woman as a primary means of representing female homosexuality, to the extent that masculinity in a female character could generally be read as synonymous with nonheterosexual desire.

This chapter draws together many of the themes discussed throughout this volume. The identification of female homosexual characters in Weimar literary texts relies on a familiarity with the masculine hairstyles and fashions popular within the female homosexual subculture at this period, as discussed in chapter 1. Stereotypes of the masculine female artist, intellectual, and emancipist, examined in chapter 3, likewise reappeared in literary contexts, where they sometimes received a more differentiated treatment than in the popular media, as did sexological theories of the masculine homosexual woman. Notions of the theatrical and carnivalesque, discussed in relation to the *Hosenrolle*, also helped to shape boundaries of "acceptable" and "unacceptable" female masculinity within fictional contexts. The following analysis begins with an examination of how the subcultural magazines negotiated issues of sexuality in relation to the rural-urban divide, goes on to trace depictions of the masculine female homosexual in novels by Baum, Kästner, Döblin, and Keun, and ends with an extended analysis of *Der Skorpion*, one of the most popular novels among homosexual German women during the Weimar era.

Provincial Voices in the Subcultural Media

Halberstam notes that studies of sexuality have largely ignored the specificities of rural queer lives, and that even recent work on sexuality, community, and gender demonstrates "an active disinterest in the productive potential of non-metropolitan sexualities, genders, and identities." Yet she demonstrates that the rural-urban divide has been a central factor in conceptualizing queer community and identity, with regional areas frequently perceived as places of hostility and isolation, whereas the cities are imagined as places of freedom and tolerance, and as such a "natural habitat" for queers.[4] Although Halberstam's work focuses largely on the United States, her claims about the current state of queer studies can be usefully applied to the majority of sexuality-oriented research on 1920s and 1930s Germany, which in focusing on the subcultures of cosmopolitan Berlin has largely neglected issues of place. By taking rural-urban difference as a central analytical focus, this chapter seeks to challenge the privileging of urban experience within Weimar queer studies.

For the Weimar period, what queer studies describes as the rural-urban divide is best understood in terms of the split, both geographical and imagined, between the metropolis of Berlin on the one hand, and the so-called *Provinz* or provinces on the other, which were broadly understood to include everywhere outside of Berlin and also encompassed smaller cities such as Cologne. The lack of scholarly research into nonmetropolitan queer lives at this period is partly due to the scarcity of historical source materials, an issue discussed at some length by Plötz, whose research demonstrates the value of subcultural magazines such as *Die Freundin* and *Garçonne* as sources for the study of regional homosexual existence in 1920s Germany.[5] For women who lived in places without a homosexual subculture, such magazines represented one of the only possibilities to come into contact with other nonheterosexual women, even though their location meant that women in the provinces often had to rely on more expensive and thus less accessible subscription access.[6] Accordingly, one letter to *Garçonne* declared in 1931: "This paper means just about everything to me, for Görlitz is too small and without a single club"; another, this time to *Die Freundin,* directly addressed members of the Berlin scene with the lament: "Believe me, you Berliners, it may be beautiful here in the Rhineland, but we have to struggle very, very hard."[7] Although the content of these magazines was predominantly focused on the Berlin scene, such letters show that the magazines fulfilled an important function in breaking down a sense of rural isolation.

The fact that these magazines were distributed throughout Germany and even across national borders meant that they enabled the creation—to borrow Benedict Anderson's terminology—of an "imagined community" among German-speaking homosexual women.[8] Although in almost all cases Berlin was the focal point of this homosexual imaginary, Plötz notes that at least one letter also pointed to Hamburg as a lesbian utopia.[9] Furthermore, there is evidence that some readers located outside of the metropolis used these publications as a direct medium for community formation. In a series of letters to *Garçonne* during 1931, reader F. Thoma bemoaned the isolation of Swiss lesbians, and called upon urban homosexuals to help their provincial brothers and sisters through wide distribution of their magazines. Thoma underlines the importance of the homosexual periodicals in relation to her own biography, as she tells of how, after experiencing marriage, divorce, and a near breakdown, she met a German woman with a copy of *Frauenliebe* that "opened up before me a whole new world." A letter from the following year shows that her efforts at creating a lesbian community in and around Zurich had been successful, as she reports on the founding of the Swiss ladies' club "Amiticia," and notes the importance of *Garçonne* in facilitating this development.[10] In other examples of provincial community building, both *Die Freundin* and *Garçonne* regularly advertised meetings for "like-minded" women

in smaller cities as far away as Hamburg, Düsseldorf, and Königsberg, and published personal advertisements from across the German-speaking realm.[11]

While the homosexual magazines thus functioned as a direct medium of non-
metropolitan community formation, some of the short fiction published in these
periodicals was also intended to break down the isolation of women in the provinces. In romantic and often melodramatic short stories, authors included self-
reflexive moments whereby a copy of *Die Freundin* or *Garçonne* poking out of a
handbag becomes a secret sign between women in public spaces such as trains or
regional cafes, or even a catalyst for nonheterosexual identity formation. A short
story by Anny Dolder-Uhl in *Garçonne* tells of a female chicken farmer named
Loni who has an awakening when a woman traveler leaves her with a magazine
that includes a review of Radclyffe Hall's 1928 novel *The Well of Loneliness*. "It
was the first time that Loni had had the opportunity to read such a newspaper,"
the narrator observes, and when Loni proceeds to order Hall's novel, she is "in-
describably happy" to receive with it a free copy of *Garçonne*. After reading *The
Well* Loni fantasizes about having a female lover, and with the help of a personal
advertisement, again in *Garçonne*, she gets one and they live happily ever after
on the farm.[12]

Although it would be easy to interpret this romantic tale as a blatant plug
for *Garçonne*'s classifieds column, it is more productive to read such stories as a
conscious reflection on the role of the subcultural magazines in breaking down
the very real isolation of nonheterosexual provincial women. Dolder-Uhl's short
story is only one of many similar narratives of happy queer meetings and relationships in the provinces, although there were also stories that thematized
depression, isolation, and suicide. Such stories could play an important role in
developing and reaffirming individual readers' subjectivities in the absence of an
obvious subculture, and reassure them of the possibility of nonheterosexual happiness even outside of the cities. They contributed to the creation of a sense of
community that crossed geographical boundaries and connected readers of the
subcultural magazines, if only at the level of the imagination.

Provincial Female Masculinities in Vicki Baum's Best Sellers

The fictional thematization of rural isolation in the subcultural magazines functioned as a self-conscious strategy for confronting the very real geographical divide between nonheterosexual women in rural and metropolitan locations during
the Weimar period. Within the broader realm of mainstream women's fiction,
Vicki Baum likewise decided to locate two of her female homosexual characters
in the provinces. In the best selling *stud. chem. Helene Willfüer* (Helene, 1928,
hereafter *Helene*) and the lesser-known *Zwischenfall in Lohwinckel* (hereafter *Zwischenfall*), the second of which has been largely overlooked in scholarship to date,

geographical location has important consequences for the portrayal of nonheteronormative genders and sexualities.

Helene and *Zwischenfall* were each published as serialized novels in the *BIZ* with enormous success before being printed in book form—*Helene* in particular is said to have attracted 200,000 new readers to the paper during its run.[13] Because they were first published in this mass culture format, both of these novels reached a potential audience of millions of readers, according to the *BIZ*'s own circulation figures. Baum, an employee of the Ullstein publishing house that published both the *BIZ* and her interwar novels, came to enjoy immense popularity as an author of "middlebrow" fiction during the second half of the Weimar period.[14] Responding to the Zeitgeist with narratives of single mothers who were also doctoral students in chemistry (*Helene*), or of the disruption wrought upon a quiet country town following a dramatic car crash involving wealthy socialites, film, and sport stars from Berlin (*Zwischenfall*), Baum's novels brought issues of rural isolation, class, race, and sexuality to the attention of a mass reading public. In each of these works, a decidedly unfeminine and homosexual woman plays a minor but telling role in the narrative.

As indicated above, in *Zwischenfall* the exotic film star "Lania" is assigned after her accident to the aristocratic but financially stricken Raitzold siblings, who run a property outside of the village of Lohwinckel. By having fate bring characters from Berlin to a provincial town for an extended period, the narrative reverses the "arrival in the city" motif that, as Ankum observes, was frequently employed in 1920s cultural texts to establish urban spaces as a place of opportunity for women. This literary trope of movement toward urban centers also has parallels with Halberstam's observation that stories of spatial migration from country to city have played a major role within queer contexts, and have often been conflated with temporal narratives of "coming out."[15] By reversing this narrative trope, Baum creates a moment of contact between the countryside and the metropolis that is firmly located within the provinces, opening up possibilities for nonheteronormative desire outside of metropolitan spaces, and for reflection on the "naturalness" and biological inevitability of sex-gender otherness.

Baum's depiction of Fräulein von Raitzold draws on contemporary sexological theories about the gender inversion of homosexual women espoused by the likes of Krafft-Ebing, Ellis, and Hirschfeld. As noted in the introduction, these scholars categorized various states of female inversion, ranging from the thoroughly masculinized, congenital invert through to feminine, "social" inverts who were open to the attention of masculine inverts but also to the possibility of heterosexuality. Raitzold can also be usefully compared with the character of Stephen in Hall's almost contemporary *Well of Loneliness,* for as with Stephen, Raitzold's sexuality is depicted as inborn and closely related to her masculine gender expression.[16] Indeed, the fact that Raitzold has developed a masculine homosexual identity in the complete absence of a homosexual subculture can be interpreted as supporting Hirschfeld's writings on the congenital nature of homosexuality, while her wholesome country heritage distances her from contemporary theories of racial and moral degeneration that focused overwhelmingly on urban centers, and were closely connected with discourses of sexual pathology. Her masculine gender presentation is further protected by her aristocratic class privilege, which enables her to dress, work, and smoke like a man with a minimum of censure in the community, as long as she remains single. Raitzold shares this situation of being tolerated yet isolated with the local Jewish shopkeeper Markus, an intellectual who yearns for the vibrant surroundings of Berlin. In Baum's novel, religious/ethnic otherness thus constitutes a comparable "affliction" to nonnormative gender and sexuality, and for both characters the metropolis serves as a symbolic utopian space that seems destined to remain out of reach.[17]

That Fräulein von Raitzold yearns for a community of likeminded women becomes pointedly evident from her conversations with her glamorous patient Lania. Lania is well aware of Raitzold's erotic attraction to her, and she encourages it by bragging about a Berlin flatmate who has had a lesbian affair. In the conversation cited earlier, she also boasts about the lesbian clubs she herself sometimes frequents in the city—although with the quick reassurance that "I'm not going in heavily for this new fashion."[18] While it seems unlikely that this conversation will inspire Raitzold to actually leave her brother and their failing estate in search of personal happiness in the city, her contact with the cosmopolitan Lania provides her with a moment of escapist insight, allowing her entry into an imagined homosexual community that might at least soothe her sense of isolation.

Baum's characterization of the masculine female homosexual in *Zwischenfall* reaffirms a range of stereotypes about the rural-urban divide: the tolerant cosmopolitanism of the cities versus the narrow-mindedness of the provinces, and the sexual perversion of the metropolis versus the naturalized biological variation found in the countryside. Yet it is important to recognize the real and potentially positive implications that even stereotyped characters such as Fräulein von Raitzold could have when included within a piece of popular fiction, with its broad reach and easy accessibility. Petersen's research emphasizes the central role that popular literature can play in how individuals constitute their subjectivities, forming part of a cultural system of meaning that constitutes our "real" lives.[19] Baum's acknowledgement of masculine homosexual women via the character of Raitzold may well have served as a lifeline for some readers in the provinces who did not have access to the affirming narratives available in the subcultural magazines, as they sought to understand and actively constitute their own gender and sexual identities.

Whereas *Zwischenfall* contains a generally sympathetic portrayal of rural sex-gender otherness that is protected by class privilege, the best seller *stud. chem. Helene Willfüer* combines stereotypes of the intellectual Jew and the homosexual woman in a less flattering way in the minor character of Gudula Rapp. The narrative, which centers around the bright young chemistry student Helene Willfüer, is set in a university town that closely resembles Heidelberg, indicating a location less isolated than Raitzold's home of Lohwinckel, but still a long way from the urban subculture of Berlin. Gudula is a shy and bookish Jewish doctoral student with a weak constitution—the polar opposite of her healthy, Germanic and heterosexual roommate Helene. Even her neuter nickname "das Gulrapp" points to an asexual gender identification, and Gudula herself encourages this perception: "When they talk about love or graceful femininity they don't mean me."[20] I agree with Barndt's assessment of Gulrapp's relationship to Helene as one based on difference and intended to distract sexual suspicions away from Helene.[21] However, Gulrapp is not quite the "sexologically classified man-woman" that Barndt suggests: although clearly a repressed homosexual, her sex-gender orientation is represented above all in terms of lack: as sexual neutrality rather than masculinity.

At the expense of both her physical and mental health, Gudula displaces her passions for other women, including Helene, onto her doctoral thesis. Accordingly, when Helene asks her, "Do you never experience longing, Gulrapp?" the latter replies that there is a series of bronze monks in China that she longs to see (*H* 23). Her stifled passions surface only once in the narrative, when she anxiously inquires after Helene's health following a botched abortion attempt. As the narrator observes: "in this one question something suddenly wells up in her, a tenderness, a fear, a secret, lost, confused, concealed, deviant love" (*H* 63). Petersen reads this account of Gudula's feelings for Helene as an "unveiled homophobic utterance" on Helene's behalf, however I interpret it rather as a narrative insight into how Gudula sees herself.[22] Although both Helene and the omniscient narrator elsewhere express sympathy for Gudula, this euphemistic passage serves to effectively link Gudula's fragile mental and physical condition to notions of perversion and pathology.

The sex-gender inversion embodied by Gudula presents a stark contrast to the congenital, naturalized homosexuality represented by the physically hardy Fräulein von Raitzold in *Zwischenfall*. Whereas Raitzold fits neatly into Krafft-Ebing's taxonomy of the masculine lesbian, Gudula reflects other sexological theories that associated homosexuality with nervousness and hysteria. In particular, Frame has shown that her character demonstrates the "modern" affliction of neurasthenia, which was associated with biological degeneration and the stresses of urban life.[23] The sexual invert, according to Ellis, "is specially liable to suffer from a high degree of neurasthenia, often involving much nervous weakness and irritability, loss of self-control and genital hyperaesthesia."[24] Although Ellis came to these conclusions in the late nineteenth century, the links between mental illness and homosexuality were still of concern to Weimar-era sexologists: in 1921 one Arthur Kronfeld, a leading doctor at Hirschfeld's Institute for Sexual Science, published an article on homosexual neuroses, which he argued were the product of social factors such as isolation and ostracization.[25]

Frame makes the important observation that neurasthenia was also associated with racial otherness: "Race works to reinforce Gudula's image as aberration, as

Other, but simultaneously provides a 'scientific apology' for her sexual deviance and a basis for her sympathetic portrayal."[26] Such an implicitly racialized representation of sexual deviance may seem implausible given Baum's own status as an assimilated Jew; however, Frame points to Sander Gilman's research on Jewish doctors at this period who adopted anti-Semitic discourses in an effort to distance themselves professionally from "aberrations" among their own race, and suggests that Gudula's apparent Jewishness may have served a similar function for Baum.[27] Furthermore, Barndt notes the influence on Baum of Weininger's philosophical treatise *Sex and Character*, which equated Jewishness with femininity and with physical and mental degeneracy, while Atina Grossmann has highlighted how stereotypes of the prostitute, the Jewess, and the lesbian often converged at this period in more malicious stereotypes of the New Woman.[28] In short, Gudula's sex-gender transgressions become all the more sinister against the dual backdrop of university life and suspected Jewishness, as she is situated as a physically degenerate intellectual who is doubly "othered" by her ethnic difference. This characterization differs sharply from Raitzold's naturalized gender and sexual identifications, which are protected by her upper-class Germanic heritage and rural location.

Zwischenfall and *Helene* provide insights into how a liberal, Berlin-based, heterosexual author such as Baum interpreted contemporary ideas about race, class, gender, and sexuality, and combined these with ideas about the modern but degenerate metropolis and the healthy yet backward provinces. In many ways, these are uncritical, stereotypical representations of sex-gender "others" that follow the dominant mythology of "metronormativity" identified by Halberstam, which labels rural queer life as sad and lonely and privileges urban spaces.[29] Yet despite their failings, these representations are significant not least because of their potential to reach millions of readers, many of whom were living outside of Berlin. Within this mainstream context, Baum's characterizations can be considered surprisingly sympathetic toward sex-gender otherness, unlike some of the works examined below. Deliberately thematizing rural lives and experiences at a time when so much German cultural attention was centered on the metropolis, Baum included important nods to both her nonheterosexual and nonmetropolitan readers, and at least in the case of *Zwischenfall*, this included reflecting on the possibility of nonheterosexual community and existence outside of the metropolis.

Metropolitan Perversion in Novels by Erich Kästner, Alfred Döblin, and Irmgard Keun

Whereas the novels cited above broke the mold by representing sex-gender otherness within provincial settings, other Weimar-era authors chose to engage with a much more pervasive stereotype of female inversion: that of the masculinized

Berlin lesbian, whose metropolitan location only underlined her associations with sexual perversion and urban degeneracy. Novels by Erich Kästner, Alfred Döblin, and Irmgard Keun reaffirm stereotypes of the provinces as sites of isolation and the cities as the location of a thriving but perverse homosexual subculture. In doing so, they align with broader Weimar cultural critiques of modernity that had been circulating since the turn of the century and viewed the cities as hubs of sexual immorality and degeneracy: it is not by coincidence that Döblin's *Berlin Alexanderplatz* (1929) famously imagined Berlin in terms of a sexually devouring woman; the so-called "whore of Babylon."

Dorothy Rowe has demonstrated how the sexualization of metropolitan space formed the basis of various late-nineteenth-century and fin-de-siècle texts, including Krafft-Ebing's *Psychopathia Sexualis* and the popular series of *Großstadt-Dokumente* (Metropolitan Documents), edited by social critic Hans Ostwald between 1905 and 1908. She observes that many of the sexual concerns of the modern city covered by Ostwald's series, including homosexuality, dance houses, prostitution, gamblers, illegitimacy, the women's movement, and the white slave trade, resurfaced in representations of Berlin during the Weimar period.[30] This alliance within the popular German imagination between the metropolis and decadent, dangerous sexuality, and female sexuality in particular, provides the backdrop for the following literary representations of the metropolitan masculine female homosexual.

Erich Kästner's novel *Fabian: Die Geschichte eines Moralisten* (Fabian: The Story of a Moralist, 1931), a late-Weimar example of the sober, critical style of New Objectivity, is a self-proclaimed satire of the decline of post–World War I German society. Its protagonist Jakob Fabian, a disillusioned intellectual who works writing advertising copy before he joins the ranks of the unemployed, moves as a critical but passive *flâneur* through the spaces of Berlin. Fabian visits various seedy sex clubs, where he participates in the action whilst maintaining a rather hypocritical sense of moral superiority. As McCormick observes, Kästner's critique of the chaos and instability of modernity centers on the sexual immorality and perversity of the metropolis, which is most clearly evidenced when Fabian and his friend Labude visit a lesbian bar, the "Cousine."[31] This bar is frequented by women who assume male nicknames such as "the baron," dress in tuxedos, smoke cigars, drink hard liquor, and most importantly, take on the "male" role in their sexual relationships:

> The "Cousine" was a club frequented mostly by women. They danced together. They sat arm in arm on little green sofas. They looked deeply into each other's eyes. They drank schnapps, and some wore tuxedo jackets and high-necked blouses, in an attempt to look very similar to men. The proprietress bore the same name as her club, smoked black cigars, and acquainted people with one another. She went from table to table, greeted the guests, told robust jokes, and drank like a fish.[32]

As far as Fabian is concerned, these drinking, smoking, cross-dressing women represent the extremes of sexual abandonment and symbolize a lack of bourgeois morality and profound disrespect for patriarchal relationship structures that is firmly located within the metropolis.

The negative connotations of female masculinity in Kästner's novel are made repeatedly evident during Fabian's contact with Berlin's lesbian subculture. In the studio of artist Ruth Reiter, who is busy creating a sculpture of her naked girlfriend Selow, Fabian asks his new (heterosexual) friend Cornelia Battemberg how many "female creatures" are present, to which she answers with a laugh: "I'm the only one" (*F* 88–89). In this instance, homosexuality and female masculinity are construed as one and the same, and femininity is the sole preserve of heterosexual women. Feminine homosexual men are viewed as similarly suspicious and morally degenerate: when Reiter's friend Kulp, a lesbian and prostitute, has a nervous breakdown in the "Cousine," she is rescued by the "Doctor," a male-to-female transvestite who makes a living from prescribing morphium to fellow addicts. In contrast, heterosexual men are posited as relative upholders of morality, even as they engage in gratuitous sex and voyeurism: "Labude indicated that he had moral reservations"; "Fabian politely said that he was no friend of games of chance" (*F* 88). Heterosexual women sit somewhere in the middle of this moral scale: even though bourgeois double standards of sexual behavior are directly thematized and critiqued in a conversation between Fabian and Cornelia, they are hard at work in the characterization of the sexually voracious Irene Moll, who appears at various pivotal points in the narrative. While it is important to acknowledge Kästner's satirical agenda in examining the misogynistic representation of women and female sexuality in the narrative, it is equally important, as McCormick insists, to factor in the claims of both Kästner and his protagonist to be "moralists," for "the basically conservative moral thrust of [the novel's] satire cannot be denied."[33]

Masculine female homosexuals represent not only the least moral sexual possibility offered within Kästner's narrative, but also the least authentic. Thus Fabian explains to Cornelia that most of the women in the club are not "real" lesbians, but have simply had bad experiences with men:

> The first can't find a man, the second finds too many, the third is terrified of the consequences. There are many women sitting here who are just cross with men. Selow, who's squatting over there with my friend, belongs to this sort. She's only a lesbian because she's in a huff with the other sex. (*F* 94)

Selow soon proves Fabian right, denouncing her girlfriend as a "randy goat" and publicly dumping her in favor of Labude, declaring: "I want a man! ... Long live the small difference!" (*F* 95). In this way, the nonheteronormative desires of masculine female homosexuals are constructed as temporary sexual positionings that can be abandoned at a whim, and as having resulted from disappointment with the men of the city. Yet while efforts are thus made to reappropriate lesbian characters into heteronormative structures and undermine their sex-gender identifications, the masculine homosexual woman continues to represent the depths of urban degeneracy within the framework of Kästner's novel.

Whereas Kästner negotiates the stereotype of the masculinized metropolitan lesbian in a clearly fictionalized, moralistic manner, Alfred Döblin chooses a documentary, journalistic style for his narrative *Die beiden Freundinnen und ihr Giftmord* (Two Girlfriends and How They Murdered with Poison, 1924), which appeared as the first volume of the series *Außenseiter der Gesellschaft: Die Verbrechen der Gegenwart* (Outsiders of Society: The Crimes of the Present). This "ambitious but short-lived series" of sensational criminal case studies was narrated by a range of prominent contemporary authors that also included Egon Erwin Kisch, Ernst Weiß, Iwan Goll, and Theodor Lessing, and was published in 1924/25 by the left-wing publishing house Die Schmiede. As Todd Herzog observes, the fourteen volumes in this series document "some of the innovative ways in which criminality was understood in Weimar Germany" and combined reportage, fictional techniques, and scientific analysis to comment on an area that was otherwise the domain of legal and medical specialists.[34]

Based on a widely publicized Berlin court case from 1923, much of which he had witnessed firsthand, Döblin's novella describes the development of a homosexual affair between two Berlin housewives, "Elli Link" and "Grete Bende," and how they conspire to murder Link's brutally abusive and emotionally manipulative husband with rat poison. Pseudonyms are used for the "real-life" perpetrators Ella Klein and Margarete Nebbe, although scholars have observed that their identities would have been obvious to any informed contemporary reader; at several points in the text the actual names are used uncorrected, even in recent editions. For a long time Döblin's narrative was neglected by scholars, but recent research has done much to clarify the book's modernist narrative approaches, its negotiations with issues of fact and fiction, guilt and causality, and its engagement with contemporary criminological, sexological, and pathological discourses.[35]

From the novella's self-reflexive epilogue, it is apparent that Döblin was attempting to provide a more measured, complex account of this already notorious sexual crime than was available within sensationalized media accounts, without seeking to justify or defend the behavior of the women in question: "I wanted to show the difficulties of the case, to blur the impression that one understood everything or even most of such a massive slice of life."[36] Döblin thus assumes a position that is infused with "objective" sociological authority, while at the same time questioning the ability of the observer to ever understand all of the factors that contribute to such a case. Yet his narrativization of the relationship between Link/Klein and Bende/Nebbe and its criminal outcome is ultimately far more judgmental than this epilogue suggests. In particular, Döblin's account draws upon sexological associations between female inversion and criminality, with ominous consequences for the depiction of the masculine female homosexual.

Döblin's text associates masculine women not only with the kind of metropolitan sexual perversion spurned by Kästner's Fabian, but with a moral and mental degeneracy that crosses over into the pathological and criminal—a connection that sexologists such as Ellis had also made in relation to working-class women. Whereas the excessive sexuality of Kästner's masculine homosexual women is restricted to the safely voyeuristic setting of Berlin's homosexual clubs, the sexual pathology of Döblin's working-class subjects causes them to blatantly disregard patriarchal legal and relationship structures, and become a menace to the metropolis on a much larger scale. Link's affair with Bende is portrayed as bringing out in her a masculine confidence and manner critical in shaping their relationship to one another: "It was especially this passion that caused Elli to rise up in heroic fashion, that drove her to masculinity and heroism; over and over the words 'I'll prove my love to you'" (*DbF* 39). Moreover, the simultaneous emergence of Elli's masculinity and homosexuality are constructed as the factors that enable her to access a "male" form of criminal agency: "Now Elli was her [Grete's] husband. ... Her activity, her masculine determination gained a sexual foundation and thereby a dangerous dimension" (*DbF* 25). Petersen has shown that it is the moment of genital contact between the two women that provides the point of both gender and criminal transgression: Elli is transformed from a childlike figure who is disgusted by marital sex into a sexually confident masculine lesbian, and this transformation provides the necessary prerequisite for her murderous act.[37] In the context of Döblin's narrative, then, Elli's female masculinity is simultaneously the source of her empowerment and her criminality. This in turn negates any possibility of a justificatory depiction of what could, in another context, have been read as an act of self-defense.

Elli's development of a pathological masculine sex-gender identity is firmly linked to her metropolitan surroundings. Although Döblin refrains throughout the narrative from explicitly attributing causality to specific biographical events, it is no accident that the opening lines of the narrative announce the importance of place in Elli's narrative: "The pretty blonde Elli Link came to Berlin in 1918. She was 19 years old. Before that she had begun to work as a hairdresser in Braunschweig, where her parents were cabinetmakers" (*DbF* 5). This concise introduction prioritizes "Elli's" provincial, working-class upbringing, her "girl next door" Germanic physical appearance, and her move to the metropolis at an impressionable age. It is only here that she develops the masculine sex-gender identification that Döblin constructs as the enabling factor for her murderous act. Rowe observes that for commentators and sexologists such as Krafft-Ebing, "the city induces far more serious consequences of deviant sexual behaviour including, at the worst extreme, acts of random sexual murder."[38] While Link's crime is not a sexual murder or *Lustmord* in the sense indicated by Rowe or thematized in the contemporary art of Otto Dix and George Grosz—crimes that consistently featured *male* perpetrators and *female* victims of rape and mutilation—it is nonetheless clearly linked to both her metropolitan location and newfound masculine agency.[39]

Although Elli's masculine sex-gender identification provides the enabling prerequisite for her act of murder, it is no surprise that the women choose *Giftmord*, murder by poison, as their method. This methodical, subtle form of killing was explicitly gendered female within both media and expert commentary at this time, as Hania Siebenpfeiffer has demonstrated. Criminological, sexological, and psychological discourses all associated *Giftmord* with various female sexual pathologies, including sadism, infantilization, and female homosexuality.[40] The successful 1920s *Bilder-Lexicon der Sexualwissenschaften* (Illustrated Encyclopedia of Sexology) declared: "Murderesses who use poison generally tend toward sexual pathologies. Poison is the method of sexual murder chosen by women because of the low expenditure of physical strength involved."[41] Taking up these links between sexual pathology and crime, scholars have examined how contemporary descriptions of the Klein/Nebbe case—media accounts as well as Döblin's novel—combined stereotypes from nineteenth-century criminal anthropology and the sexual sciences to pathologize and criminalize the figure of the masculine lesbian. Hacker, for example, analyzes how the figures of the born invert and the born criminal interacted in late nineteenth- and early twentieth-century discourse to constitute the boundaries of cultural femininity. "Desire and crime, both coded as masculine, confirm the masculinity of those who acted aggressively," she argues, so that both the lesbian and the criminal woman were seen to negate femininity.[42] The Klein/Nebbe case thus represents something of a paradox—on the one hand their crime is specifically gendered female, according to contemporary expert discourses, but on the other hand its execution requires Elli to assert a "masculine" independence and thereby deny her femininity.

The paradoxes inherent in Döblin's construction of the pathological homosexual murderer continue as he recounts the expert witness statement of "Sanitätsrat (medical consultant) Dr. H." a thinly veiled reference to the prominent Berlin sexologist Magnus Hirschfeld:

> He is a matter-of-fact, precise person, a scientist, also a fighter. He is the man with the greatest practical experience in cases of this particular nature, namely, same-sex relationships. He arrived at the conclusion that this slow murder by poison was the result of a deep hatred. In the accused Link a physical and psychological developmental disorder was identified, in Bende a lack of intellectual capacity resulting from a hereditary condition. … The cause of the deep hatred he sees above all in the homosexual tendencies of the women. (*DbF* 68)

Hirschfeld's status as sexological researcher lends weight to his assessment of the two women's stunted physical, mental, and emotional development, which he sees as intricately linked to their homosexuality and the root cause of their crime.

While this account of inborn homosexual degeneracy in one sense aligns with Hirschfeld's theories that sexual intermediary forms are congenital and therefore natural, they are used here to condemn the legal rights and status of the homosexual, in stark contrast to Hirschfeld's efforts in other contexts as a homosexual rights campaigner. The contradictions inherent in this witness account are typical of the novella as a whole, for as Herzog argues, Döblin employs a "multiperspectival narrative" that at times seems to agree with those experts who saw the crime as a result of physical or psychological abnormalities, and at others with those who argued that social conditions were at the root of the murder.[43] The result is that an act that in another account might have been constructed as a show of strength and independence against a viciously violent husband becomes merely further evidence for the extent of Elli Link/Klein's sex-gender perversion and moral degeneracy, a form of sexual pathology that is firmly located within the metropolis.

Irmgard Keun's successful 1932 novel *Das kunstseidene Mädchen* (The Artificial Silk Girl) provides a further example of the literary representation of metropolitan masculine lesbians within mainstream Weimar literature. Keun is far less interested than Döblin in pathologizing the figure of the masculine female homosexual, although her characterizations of Berlin's lesbian subculture do bear parallels to Kästner's portrayal of homosexual excess and depravity. At the same time, the representation of female homosexuality in Keun's novel is more complex than in Kästner's moralistic narrative, for while her protagonist Doris condemns what she sees as "perverse" masculine lesbians, she shows a marked sympathy for other, more gender-normative portrayals of female homosexuality, including the character of Manuela in the contemporary film *Mädchen in Uniform* (1931).

Das kunstseidene Mädchen is a New Woman novel that, like Kästner's *Fabian*, is written in the pragmatic Weimar style of New Objectivity. It traces the adventures, impressions, and desires of its upwardly desiring heterosexual protagonist Doris, a stenotypist who moves to Berlin from the provinces in search of glamour and fame—and also to avoid a theft charge in her hometown. The novel does not engage with homosexual themes until late in the narrative, after Doris has been rescued from near destitution and life as a street prostitute by a loner named Ernst. Ernst, who pines after his former wife, surprises Doris by not demanding any sexual favors from her; each day he goes off to work while Doris cleans the house and makes dinner. One day, she takes a look at a pile of books on his night table. Alongside an exotic mix of publications in Japanese and French, Doris spots a work by Baudelaire in German translation that grabs her attention. Although she does not give a title (presumably she is referring to the poem "Lesbos" from the poetry collection *Les fleurs du mal,* 1857), she describes her initial impressions: "Lesbos, you island of hot withering nights ... I know exactly what's going on, I get it—it's downright indecent. Withering nights! Lesbos! One knows enough about men and about Berlin as well."[44] Doris immediately associates female homosexuality with both indecency and perversion, but also with the sexual enlightenment that she considers an inevitable consequence of living as a woman in the German metropolis. This discovery prompts her to reflect on her own contact with Berlin's female homosexuals, whom she identifies primarily via visual signifiers of female masculinity:

> There are bars where women sit wearing stiff collars and ties and are so frightfully proud of being perverse, as if it wasn't something that no one can do anything about. I've always said to Therese: I'm glad I have such well-formed large eyes, but they were given to me, I'm not stuck up about them. But the perverts fancy themselves. There's a similar place in the Marburger Strasse. Some men like it. Is he one of them? I'm not. And I didn't even really want to read Van de Velde when Therese gave me the book. Those things are downright filthy in writing. Lesbos, you island—thank God there are no pictures. (*KM* 171–72).

What Doris finds most difficult to stomach about such urban club lesbians is not so much their "perverse" sexuality, but rather what she sees as their need to flaunt it via performances of female masculinity. Masculine formal wear, including stiff collars and ties, serves to unabashedly advertise these women's erotic desires for other women, leading Doris to question why they pride themselves on their perversion as if it were a talent. Her mention of a club in the Marburger Strasse is significant in this context, for Café Domino, located at number 13, was reportedly a favored hangout of wealthy, tuxedo-clad masculine homosexual women and their feminine partners or "Mädis." In her guide to the Berlin lesbian club scene, Ruth Roellig adds that Domino was a popular venue for masculine female homosexuals and voyeuristic tourists alike, which helps to explain Doris's familiarity with this place.[45]

Doris's discomfort with such overt expressions of sexuality also extends in this instance to heterosexual practices, as evidenced by the rather scathing reference to Th. H. van de Velde's popular marital sex handbook *Die vollkommene Ehe* (Ideal Marriage, 1926). This is somewhat surprising, given that elsewhere in the novel she employs a pragmatic cost-benefit approach to her relationships with men—as McCormick observes, "Doris's story is that of a woman who consciously uses her sexuality in a bid to achieve both autonomy and upward mobility."[46] She is further discomforted by the thought of heterosexual men being titillated by the kind of lesbian material she finds near Ernst's bed. In contrast, it becomes evident at several points later in the narrative that Doris is able to cope quite well with the idea of homosexuality as long as this is not associated with blatant forms of sexual expression or gender transgression. Homosexuality is no barrier to sympathy when, for example, Doris encounters an effeminate gay man named Gustav in the waiting room of Bahnhof Zoo, where the common experience of hunger and exhaustion overpowers her sense of his perversion: "And he's so tired that he completely forgets to be gay, because that much hunger and tiredness makes you normal again" (*KM* 151). This experience is repeated following a visit to the cinema, when Doris sympathizes with, rather than rejects, the lovesick character of Manuela in *Mädchen in Uniform.*

As described in the previous chapter, *Mädchen* depicts the schoolgirl crushes of new girl Manuela von Meinhardis and her fellow students for their young teacher Fräulein von Bernburg at a strict Prussian boarding school. Bernburg, in turn, encourages these affections with her caring nature and goodnight kisses. In one of the most important instances of cultural intertextuality in Keun's novel, Doris reports her experiences of watching the film, which she goes to see with Ernst.[47] She finds that she can relate quite well to the girls' passions and heartbreak, despite the fact that their affections are directed toward a woman: "They were girls of a better class, but they felt the same way I do. You love someone, and sometimes that gives you tears and a red nose. You love someone—and that's beyond understanding, it doesn't matter if it's a man or a woman or God" (*KM* 191–92).

According to Barndt, Doris interprets Manuela's love for her teacher less in terms of lesbian love than as an adolescent fantasy, thus neutralizing any explicit connections with sexuality. This interpretation allows Doris to be drawn into the film at an emotional level, even though elsewhere in the novel she rejects lesbians and their lifestyle.[48] In contrast, Lensing suggests that Doris's sympathetic approach to this particular depiction of homosexuality is evidence of the emancipatory potential of the new medium of film, and he reads Doris's trip to the cinema as an indication of film's ability to change the social and political behavior of its audience in progressive ways.[49] Both of these positions have merit, but a third factor is also in play here. Certainly, as Lensing suggests, Doris may well have undergone a cinematically driven character development that enables her to take a more tolerant approach toward homosexuality by the end of the novel. Secondly, and in line with Barndt's reading, the relative absence of overt sexual expressions in Sagan's film distances this representation of female homosexuality from the more sordid sexual scenes depicted in Ernst's bedtime reading. Thirdly, however, it is the relative lack of gender "inversion" in *Mädchen* that enables Doris to engage emotionally with this film. As discussed earlier, the film's characters are all unambiguously "feminine," and the only example of female masculinity occurs within the sanctioned and culturally unthreatening space—at least initially—of a theatrical performance. In contrast, the overt sexuality and masculine gender performances that Doris associates with Berlin's lesbian scene are clearly too much for her, and she rejects them with disgust.

This separation between good/feminine and morally questionable/masculine female homosexuals likewise structures one of the most significant lesbian-themed novels from this era, Anna Elisabet Weirauch's trilogy *Der Skorpion.* As with the texts cited so far, the multiple, often ambivalent incarnations of the masculine homosexual woman in Weirauch's novel are crucially shaped by ideas about place, race, and class. *Der Skorpion* differs significantly from these more mainstream texts, however, in that masculine homosexual women provide an essential point of departure in the protagonist Mette's journey toward a spiritually and emotionally satisfying homosexual identity.

Female Masculinities and Homosexual Identities in *Der Skorpion*

Published in three volumes that spanned the course of the Weimar era (1919/1921/1931) and rediscovered by feminists in the 1970s when it also reappeared in English translation, *Der Skorpion* (The Scorpion) was enormously popular among German homosexual women in the 1920s and early 1930s. Widely advertised in contemporary subcultural magazines such as *Die Freundin*, there was also a Berlin women's club of the same name, as well as plans for the book to be filmed.[50] Weirauch's novel provides glimpses into the breadth of 1920s female homosexual subcultures in Germany, as imagined by a member of that culture. Although a number of scholars have emphasized the importance of *Der Skorpion* for feminist and queer literary studies, none of these analyses have identified the notion of female masculinity as central to Mette's identity development. Indeed, Nancy Nenno argues quite the opposite, suggesting that Weirauch focuses on women's romantic friendships and feminine lesbian identification in order to counter more prevalent, voyeuristic accounts of lesbian sexuality of the Weimar period.[51] While I agree that Weirauch's protagonist is best described as "feminine" and acknowledge the ambivalent role that masculine homosexual women play in this novel, I argue that Mette's feminine homosexual identification develops only through her contacts with overtly masculine members of the homosexual subculture, who proudly differentiate themselves and their gender performances from the heterosexual mainstream. At times Mette aligns herself with their highly visible embodiments of queerness; at other times she seeks to distance herself from what she perceives as a degenerate urban subculture of "drugs, drink and illicit love," as Weirauch describes in the foreword.[52] Weirauch's trilogy provides a further example of how scientific and popular discourses about gender, sexuality, and female masculinities could be interpreted and reproduced within fictional contexts. It does so, however, from a subcultural perspective, and with a concerted view to supporting the development of nonheteronormative identificatory possibilities.

In a long and unashamedly melodramatic fashion Weirauch's trilogy follows the emotional, sexual, and spiritual development of its protagonist Mette Rudolph. Petersen describes this style of "melodramatic excess" as a characteristic strategy of 1920s German lesbian fiction, whereby intense emotionalism functioned to shield lesbian bodies from the patriarchal gaze.[53] Starting with her wealthy but troubled childhood, the novel traces Mette's brief but intense relationship with an older woman named Olga, her encounters with the urban homosexual subculture, including a brief relationship with the fashionable young flapper Gisela, and her eventual decision to move to the countryside and tend to her house and garden. Through its depiction of a range of nonheteronormative lives, *Der Skorpion* variously confirms and counters stereotypes of the city as a homosexual utopia, providing a more complex account of the relationships between sexual identity, gender performance, and geographical space than the other texts discussed in this chapter.

Mette's first homoerotic experience occurs when, as a child, she falls in love with her governess, a rite of passage later echoed by Stephen in Hall's *Well of Loneliness*.[54] Unlike her British counterpart, however, Mette does not grow up to become a stereotypical masculine lesbian; instead, as a young woman, she finds herself falling for one. Fascination and admiration characterize Mette's initial attraction to the compelling older woman Olga Radó, who is described as very tall and slender with a "beautiful and boldly chiseled" face, a deep "cello-like" voice and "downright masculine behavior" (*S1* 32). Although the narrator has already predicted Olga's "seduction" of Mette, the older woman's same-sex tendencies are also signaled at the beginning of the novel via her masculine manner: she smokes cigarettes while sitting at her large diplomat's desk and is constantly engrossed in her books. Further hints of Olga's "inversion" include her request that Mette read to her from Walt Whitman and her address in the Motzstrasse near Nollendorfplatz, a hub of Weimar Berlin's homosexual subculture.

In order to comprehend the significance of Olga's masculine appearance and behavior in Mette's as yet unarticulated process of homosexual identity formation, it is necessary to situate her character within a larger subcultural context and history that frequently drew on masculine tropes to find its expression. As noted previously, such intellectual signifiers were typical of stereotypes of the masculine homosexual woman, and here they subtly influence the narrator's description of the effect that Olga has on the young and still-naïve Mette: "There was something in her manner of dress that Mette liked, without being able to put her finger on just what it was. A word like 'tasteful' or even 'elegant' or 'smart' wasn't enough. Mette vaguely felt that: this is how I would like to dress" (*S1* 32). Although the narrator explains that Mette's desire to dress like Olga is due to the latter's penchant for expensive clothing, her unmistakably masculine clothing and manner clearly suggest a further, if unarticulated, subtext to this desire.

Der Skorpion directly thematizes the role of sexological knowledges in Mette's development. A pivotal scene depicts Mette meeting with a psychiatrist under duress from her family, who are suspicious of her relationship with Olga and the fact that she has pawned the family silver in order to help her friend. This meeting with the "Professor" is telling, for although he does not explicitly name Mette's "condition," his belief in her "abnormal" sexuality is evident from his interest in her smoking and studies, and his description of Olga as a morally corrupt and even criminal influence (*S1* 135–36). The meeting also reveals the fear held by

Mette's family that her homosexuality is congenital. Aunt Emily, who had earlier accused Mette of being one of those degenerate women "who feel themselves drawn by a pathological lapse of taste to all that is repulsive and unhealthy" (*S1* 83), angrily reprimands the Professor for not undertaking a physical examination: "You told me, Professor, that you wanted to perform an examination in order to assess any potential physical anomalies" (*S1* 139).

Her family's belief in Mette's bodily abnormality highlights a gap between the "scientific" research of the likes of Ellis or Krafft-Ebing and popular understandings of homosexuality. According to contemporary sexology, Mette's femininity should have classed her as physically "normal" and her inversion as curable; in contrast, the family's insistence that her condition is physical as well as psychological reflects a less differentiated fear of what has been described as "the modern 'plague' of female intersexuality."[55] Like the masculine female characters in Vicki Baum's novels, this depiction of contact with the medical establishment opens a literary window onto some of the ways in which sexological theories on female homosexuality were interpreted by and for a lay audience. Yet unlike the sexological outsider, who, as Halberstam observes, "does not have access to the structures of social, sexual, and casual interaction that organize any sexual subculture," Weirauch has the advantage of an "insider" perspective.[56] Consequently, her fictional representations of the masculine homosexual woman offer a more differentiated picture than either the sexological texts or more mainstream novels from this period.

The failure of sexological writings to adequately reflect the lives and experiences of nonheterosexual-identifying women is further illustrated in a scene that takes place after the death of Mette's father, at a time when Mette spends long hours studying in her father's office. Paralleling Stephen's discovery of her father's scientific texts in *The Well*, Mette uncovers a multitude of pamphlets, novels, medical works, and daily papers, "all treating of one theme":

> There were strange and uncanny stories of countesses who hang out in dives wearing men's clothing before being lured into an ambush and brutally murdered. Or reports of revolting orgies in large clubs where hundreds of women dressed and acted like men, or of men who ran around in makeup, curly wigs, and openwork silk stockings, and with naked powdered arms and shoulders. There were statistical claims about all of the unfortunate victims who had been ruined by softening of the brain or consumption or similar as a result of unnatural sexual acts, or who had gone insane. Or accounts of the inner life of inverts which led one to suppose that these thousands of people together constituted a large community that was united ... by nothing other than a sexual drive toward the same kind of excess. (*S1* 207)

Through these texts, Mette becomes aware of the existence of sex-gender "inverts," although at this point in the narrative she refuses to identify herself with these objects of study. Indeed, her strong disavowal of these sexual "others" is expressed through feelings of physical repulsion, hinting at a psychosomatic reaction against her own repressed sexual abnormality: "She became physically ill just from touching the books" (*S1* 207). For Mette, these texts reveal more than just the existence of an unfamiliar community of urban homosexuals: for the first time, she is confronted with explicit, scientific references to masculine women who are characterized, among other things, by their superior intellect, luxurious tastes, and thirst for knowledge. Mette is somewhat bewildered as she recognizes a certain resemblance to her beloved Olga, and she is seized by "the tormented need to pack up these works and take them to Olga Radó and say: Explain it to me. Do such people exist? Are you like this? Am I? What do you know about it, and what do you think about it?" (*S1* 208). Unlike Fräulein von Raitzold's first hopeful glimpse of a homosexual community in the stories of her patient Lania in *Zwischenfall*, Mette's first insight into the urban subculture is delivered in an over-whelmingly negative and distorted fashion in the form of these sexological texts.

Scholars agree that this scene is pivotal in situating Weirauch's narrative in re-lation to contemporary sexological discourses. Petersen suggests that the contrast between the good and proper Mette and the "litany of sexual perverts" represented in the books in her father's study situates Weirauch as a "vigorous critic of such popular depictions"; similarly, Sabine Puhlfürst reads this scene as an indication that many lesbians at this period did not identify at all with sexological repre-sentations of homosexual women.[57] Yet these critiques underestimate the impor-tance of this scientific evidence of homosexuality for Mette's own development of a homosexual identity. Although Mette feels repulsed by these books, they nonetheless enable her to recognize both female masculinity and homosexuality as categories that can help her to make sense of her own relationships with other women. This pattern recurs repeatedly throughout the novel: while Mette rejects masculine women as direct role models, she consistently finds herself attracted, fascinated, and influenced by women who exhibit decidedly masculine character-istics, and who thus help to structure her search for identity and community.

Although Mette has relationships with various women during her youth and early twenties, it is only when she moves to the city following Olga's suicide—a result of homophobic persecution and tragic misunderstanding—that she comes into contact with a thriving homosexual subculture. The members of this met-ropolitan scene are clearly marked by signs of gender inversion, from effeminate gay men in silk stockings to women with mannish haircuts dressed in severely cut suits. It is here, in an anonymous urban hotel, that Mette meets the fashion-able Gisela Werkenthin. She finds herself immediately attracted to this drinking, smoking, in many ways stereotypical representative of the 1920s New Woman, who sports a slim, boyish build and a dark pageboy haircut (*S2* 40–41). Before she knows it, Mette is thrust into Gisela's circle of decadent, artistic types, from the corset-wearing "pretty Giesbert" (*S2* 56) to the boyish John with his "girlishly soft" gestures (*S2* 91). Here she finds herself repeatedly caught between disgust at such openly displayed inversion and a strong desire to belong.

In deciphering Mette's ambivalent reactions to this urban subculture, ideas about cross-dressing, sex-gender inversion, and class all play a central role. As with the theatrical *Hosenrolle*, cross-dressing functions in *Der Skorpion* as a liminal space that helps Mette to differentiate between acceptable and unacceptable forms of gender inversion or homosexuality. Often she makes this distinction only at the level of gut feeling, as an unarticulated yet clearly felt attraction or repulsion, and these physical reactions stand in direct relation to the transgressiveness of the gender performance. Thus on the one hand, Olga represents for Mette an acceptable level of female masculinity that is characterized by bourgeois values of strength and independence and does not threaten to descend into perversion or degeneracy. On the other hand, Mette finds the overtly effeminate and crossdressing John intolerable, and thinks to herself: "It's a good thing he's not my son" (*S2* 147). The limits of acceptable gender inversion are delineated in a scene in which Mette attends an artists' ball hosted by her friends Nora and Sophie, a prominent artistic couple in the local scene. At the ball, Mette finds herself desiring a woman masquerading as a pageboy, a typical *Hosenrolle* costume, in black silken knee breeches, white stockings, tails worn with lace cuffs, and dark curly hair tied at the neck with a large black bow (*S2* 69). Mette allows herself to desire this woman in spite of the latter's obvious gender transgression because, like *Hosenrolle* actors, the "page" is dressed in men's clothing only within the spatial and temporal constraints of the ball. It is the carnivalesque nature of the page's gender performance that allows the easily confused Mette to distinguish between this woman, whom she admires and desires, and the inverts who had so repulsed her in her father's study.

This psychological process of distinguishing between acceptable and unacceptable forms of sex-gender identification reaches a crisis point in the second volume of the trilogy, when Mette visits a queer club accompanied by her current girlfriend Gisela and several friends. Like the "Cousine" in Kästner's *Fabian*, everything about this club signifies urban perversion and decadence, including its dim lighting, black and purple walls and carpet, heavy silk curtains, and antique furniture and ornaments. The club's décor reflects Elaine Showalter's definition of "decadence" as "the pejorative label applied by the bourgeoisie to everything that seemed unnatural, artificial, and perverse, from Art Nouveau to homosexuality, a sickness with symptoms associated with cultural degeneration and decay."[58] Mette is particularly fascinated by the masculine women inhabiting this liminal space, whose homoerotic desires are signified by their appearance: they wear "male" formal attire of stiff collars, dark jackets, and men's hats, and their faces betray "intelligence" and "character":

> There was a whole hierarchy of visual styles. Some wore stiff collars with their dark dresses, jackets with lapels and breast pockets, and covered their short hair with a small gentleman's hat—others only gave themselves away by a faint nuance—the sharp features of others

spoke of intelligence and character, while others again were purely of the cocotte type. (*S2* 313–14)

The reference here to a "whole hierarchy of visual styles" serves to further position the novel in relation to contemporary sexological theories that categorized both gender and sexuality as a continuum of natural biological possibilities or types. In spite of her longing for bourgeois acceptance and normality, which have increased steadily with the progression of the narrative, Mette finds herself attracted to a tall woman with "short, golden brown curls and the build and profile of a Greek boy" (*S2* 314). Yet she is also losing her bearings: along with a snort of cocaine, a kiss from the beautiful "Greek boy" proves to be the final straw:

> She got so dizzy that she had to hold tightly to her seat with both hands. She had the feeling that the stool was leaning to one side, that the room was swaying, that she was on a swing that was flying through the air as if torn from its bearings, or on a ship where the broken planks were being devoured by a swirling chasm. (*S2* 321–22)

It is significant that Mette has this nervous breakdown in such a morbidly colored and decidedly queer cosmopolitan space, filled with homosexuals drinking and doing cocaine. Immediately prior to her collapse, Mette had had a *völkisch* vision of herself sitting by the Rhine and listening to folk songs while drinking from a fragrant champagne punch. This comforting Germanic pastoral vision, with its implicit rejection of her immediate "perverse" surroundings, presages her later plan to build a house in an area in which she knows no one and will remain alone and without temptation.

Mette's retreat into an imagined rural idyll that she believes to be free of the sex-gender inversion that surrounds her in the metropolis represents an attempt to resolve her own identity crisis, whereby her desire for other women conflicts with her increasingly bourgeois worldview. Thus Mette is overcome by joy and relief when her uncle Jürgen, who had earlier looked after her as a wayward youth, now entrusts his troublesome daughter into her care: "I was so filled by the knowledge of my strength and purity and incontestability. And that is the best feeling that one can have. Particularly when one is as filled with longing for bourgeois conformity as I am" (*S3* 331). Even though Mette's contact with the urban subculture has been crucial in enabling her to acknowledge and accept her own homosexuality following Olga's suicide, this self-acceptance increasingly entails a disavowal of less gender-normative members of the community. From the moment of her nervous breakdown, Mette superimposes her rejection of queer gender inversion onto the rural-urban divide, seeing the countryside as a pure and simple place characterized by a clear gender order and untainted by perversion and degeneracy. Significantly, Mette's worldview is not shared by most other characters in the novel; nor does Weirauch allow Mette's actual move to the country to fulfill her sanitized bourgeois expectations. Mette's disavowal of the city lifestyle can be read as a form of denial, particularly when one considers that other characters refuse to accept her rather simplistic moralizing based on binary structures of country/city and purity/perversion.

When she first moves to the country, Mette's visions of a rural idyll appear to be fulfilled, as she spends her days doing simple, hard work in her house and fertile garden. We learn that the region is so healthy that the local pharmacy even has to stock all sorts of nonmedical wares in order to stay in business (*S3* 219). But when Mette denounces the cities as centers of vice and perversion, her good friend Eccarius chastises her for making statements that he does not think she actually believes, and points to various examples of sexual "perversity," including pedophilia and transvestism, within the local rural community (*S3* 260–62). In reply, Mette somewhat desperately tries to replace her geographical illusion of natural purity with a temporal one: "It's something about our time ... our whole time is sick and rotten and reeks of disease and degeneracy and decomposition" (*S3* 262). Through such exchanges, Weirauch highlights her protagonist's investment in oversimplified, anti-modern, bourgeois ideas about sexual morality that link the countryside to notions of purity and fertility, while at the same time showcasing the denial and hypocrisy inherent in such attitudes.

In a further illustration of such denial and ambivalence, Mette hopes that her Berlin-based but decidedly feminine lover Corona/Fiamma[59] will join her in the countryside, but rejects gender-deviant visitors from the urban subculture, specifying that her visitors will be restricted to "nice harmless people with lots of children" (*S3* 272–73). Mette's adoption of a puppy, as Nenno notes, can also be read as evidence of her attempt to reintroduce heteronormative/maternal structures into her life.[60] Earlier in this final volume, Mette had been no less than outraged upon being introduced to Corona's friend, the masculine "Countess," "a tall, strong-boned woman with short grey hair" who smokes an "enormous cigar" (*S3* 98). Although frightened by her own prejudice, Mette finds herself asking: "[W]hy must she have her hair cut like that? Why must she wear such collars? She can't have any sense of shame if it means nothing to her that street urchins laugh at her behind her back and point their fingers at her." (*S3* 98–99) Mette is thus far from pleased when Corona invites the Countess to Mette's housewarming in the country:

> She imagined the stir that the figure of the countess would provoke in the small town, with her skirt and vest, stand-up collar and gentleman's hat. It didn't suit her at all to show herself among people who were dressed in this way, and for whom she had not even the slightest friendly feelings. (*S3* 114)

In Mette's eyes, this overtly masculine homosexual woman is not only "outrageously dressed" but also lacks an appropriate sense of shame regarding her appearance. The Countess represents a final test of Mette's tolerance of sex-gender "others," which has decreased steadily throughout the course of the novel, at first following the trauma of Olga's persecution and suicide, and later in reaction to Mette's own experiences in the metropolitan scene. Within her new rural setting, Mette attempts to draw clear conservative moral boundaries that legitimate her own feminine gender performance and (homo-)sexuality. These boundaries leave no room for the flamboyant female masculinity and homosexuality embodied by the Countess, whose appearance might well have been celebrated in other contexts as an erotically and politically powerful performance in defiance of stifling gender norms. Despite evidence to the contrary, Mette continues to link such obvious embodiments of queerness to the metropolis, and she cannot cope with the thought that they pervade the countryside as well.

Notably, Mette experiences this, her strongest reaction against a masculine woman, in the third and final volume of *Der Skorpion*. Published a good ten years after the preceding volumes, in 1931, this installment faced an increasingly conservative cultural atmosphere and a society in which the mainstream media was seeking to reimpose a clear, patriarchal sex-gender order in the face of increasing economic and political chaos. Particularly the pastoral setting and gender normativity of the novel's conclusion point to the type of conservative Christian/Aryan values that were increasingly gaining strength toward the end of the Weimar era. Scholars have consequently described Mette's move to the countryside as "an alignment with anti-urban and anti-modern values," or as a withdrawal that "mirrors the withdrawal into the home space that characterizes many of the narratives by women from the early 1930s."[61] Yet such conclusions overlook the fact that Mette's moralistic bourgeois attitudes toward the rural-urban divide are not endorsed by the novel's larger narrative structure. Even though Mette views the Countess' proud exhibition of sex-gender "inversion" as an inappropriate and even despicable form of attention-seeking, Weirauch is careful to frame Mette's rejection of the metropolitan subculture as the product of a rather narrow minded brand of middle-class morality. Supporting this argument is the inclusion of several critical discussions among Mette's city-based friends on topics such as homophobic persecution, blackmail, and sexology, including a clear condemnation of Weiningerian misogyny (*S3* 131). Also telling a tale different from Mette's are the numerous happy characters who themselves embody less normative forms of homosexual happiness and kinship, including the matriarchal couple Sophie and Nora who form a pillar of warmth and stability for their urban queer circle.

Mette's rejection of the Countess also highlights the significance of class in her assessment of nonheteronormative genders and sexualities. Mette relies heavily on her bourgeois identification and upbringing to determine which members of the homosexual subculture fit her self-imposed boundaries of moral propriety. The Countess fails Mette's test on several counts: her gender transgression aligns not only with her metropolitan location, but also with Mette's bourgeois prejudices against aristocratic decadence, a prejudice familiar from contemporary media critiques of the male dandy. The Countess exemplifies Halberstam's obser-vation that in the early twentieth century, "[m]asculine identification with social impunity required money and social status."[62] Like Baum's—admittedly poorer—aristocratic character Fräulein von Raitzold, the Countess's independent wealth and upper-class status mean that she can sport an overtly masculine appearance more easily than other characters such as Olga, an unmarried lower middle–class woman who relies on her teaching income, and for whom relative gender con-formity may well be a choice but is also a financial necessity. At the other end of the spectrum, Mette also rejects working-class versions of homosexuality, most notably in the form of her girlfriend Gisela, who at one point explicitly attacks Mette's class prejudice: "you find some things improper because you come from a different social sphere. You're just a spheroid" (*S2* 255). In contrast, the fact that Mette allows herself to enter into more serious relationships with Olga and Co-rona is due not least to their shared socioeconomic backgrounds, value systems, and ideas about gender conformity.

The end of the trilogy leaves Mette content in her rural location, surrounded by friendly neighbors. By reappropriating the countryside as a haven for its hero-ine, Weirauch counters dominant narratives from this period that locate homo-sexual happiness only in the urban centers. Yet can this be considered a successful "queer" ending, given that the still-young Mette's story ends when she is without a girlfriend and likely to remain so? There are several points to consider here. Firstly, Mette has not relinquished her homosexual identity by moving to the country, as some scholars have suggested, but had rather hoped that her lover Corona would join her there. It is only because Corona feels so strongly drawn to her socialite urban lifestyle and Mette to her country abode that they finally and wistfully part ways.[63] This refusal to emulate heteronormative relationship structures could itself be termed a "queer" lifestyle choice, as Mette sacrifices normative coupledom in favor of a single but satisfying lifestyle. Secondly, just as Butler describes how members of the New York drag ball scene reappropriate the heteronormative terms of kinship to sustain their own queer community, Mette establishes a network of alternative kinship structures within her new rural loca-tion by encouraging queer-friendly contacts from her urban existence to join her as neighbors.[64] Thus it is only on the surface that the final volume of *Der Skor-pion* cedes to the anti-industrial, anti-urban Germanic pastoral values that were being increasingly propagated by conservative and right-wing forces in the late Weimar era. Beneath this surface, Weirauch's novel counters dominant narratives that associate queerness exclusively with the metropolis, through a reevaluation of hegemonic structures of gender, sexuality, class, and space. Demonstrating the potential for a satisfying homosexual existence in both urban and regional set-tings, *Der Skorpion* reappropriates the masculine homosexual woman as central to ideas of female homosexual identity and community within 1920s German sexual subcultures.

The novels examined in this chapter demonstrate how the rural-urban divide ran like a fault line through the Weimar cultural imagination, interacting with ideas about gender and sexuality to create complex constellations of identity, opportunity, and prejudice at this critical historical moment. The city-country binary provided some authors with a means of distinguishing between "natural" and "perverse" forms of sexual and gender expression, as they sought ways to reimpose a clear gender order, bourgeois sexual values and double standards, and perhaps most importantly, a sense of control onto a society that had undergone massive changes since the beginning of the century and was becoming increasingly polarized in the late Weimar period. Authors such as Erich Kästner and Alfred Döblin drew selectively on sexological and criminological discourses about female sex-gender inversion to align female homosexuality with masculine forms of gender expression, metropolitan spaces, and criminality, at a time when the cities were increasingly viewed as centers of vice and perversion. Yet other novels from this period highlight the superficiality of restricting homosexual characters to metropolitan locations and reflect a more differentiated and tolerant appreciation of contemporary sexual subcultures than was available within scientific texts.

In all of the texts examined here, female masculinities play a central role in signaling homosexual identification and desire, not only among members of the subculture but also for outsiders. So, too, does the Berlin homosexual scene, which—despite being out of reach for many contemporaries—played a central and mostly positive role in the Weimar homosexual imaginary and provided a backdrop against which characters and readers alike could begin to come to terms with their own, nonheteronormative gender and sexual identities. This is evident not only from letters to the homosexual magazines, but also from the novels of authors such as Baum or Weirauch. Despite their flaws, both literary and political—which of course can only ever really be judged with the benefit of hindsight—the novels examined here had the potential to affect how nonheterosexual women in 1920s Germany imagined and lived their lives. At least some of these texts did so in emancipatory and unexpected ways, combating issues of rural isolation, showing possibilities for nonheterosexual life trajectories, and positing masculine women as figures of identification and desire.

Notes

1. Vicki Baum, *Zwischenfall in Lohwinckel* [1930] (Munich: Droemer Knaur, 1973), 157.
2. Petersen cites Lynda King's research on Vicki Baum and the collection *Women in the Metropolis,* edited by Katharina von Ankum, as notable exceptions: *Women and Modernity,* 9.
3. Barndt, *Sentiment und Sachlichkeit,* 22 and passim.

4. Judith Halberstam, *In a Queer Time and Place: Transgender Bodies, Subcultural Lives* (New York: New York University Press, 2005), 15, 34ff.

5. Apart from Plötz's study of German provincial lesbian experience (*Einsame Freundinnen*), studies of "third sex" communities at this period that *do* thematize issues of place include Hacker's research into women's relationships in Austria (*Frauen und Freundinnen*), and Lybeck's analyses of women civil servants in Hamburg and Frankfurt and the avant-garde homosexual community in pre–World War I Munich ("Female Homosexuality," chaps. 3 and 8).

6. Plötz, *Einsame Freundinnen*, 30, 32, 40ff.

7. K. L., "Zuschriften aus dem Leserkreis," *Garçonne*, no. 8, 15 April 1931, 12; Ein Rheinlandmädel, "Achtung!! Rheinland!!" *Die Freundin*, no. 19, 6 November 1929, 6. Other examples of letters from readers thematizing rural isolation and hostility include "Briefe, die uns erreichen," *Garçonne*, no. 24, 25 November 1931, 4; Hans Irmgard Markus, "Briefe, die man der 'Freundin' schreibt: Und wir Frauen in der Provinz?" *Die Freundin*, no. 11, 28 May 1928, 5; Ingeborg Wilhelm and Johanna D., "Und wir Frauen in der Provinz?" *Die Freundin*, no. 13, 25 June 1928, 6.

8. Anderson develops this concept in relation to ideas about national identity: Benedict Anderson, *Imagined Communities: Reflections on the Origin and Spread of Nationalism* (London: Verso, 1983). Kath Weston's concept of "sexual imaginaries" also informs my use of this term, whereby the "gay imaginary is not just a dream of a freedom to be gay that requires an urban location, but a symbolic space that configures gayness itself by elaborating an opposition between urban and rural life": "Get Thee to a Big City: Sexual Imaginary and the Great Gay Migration," *GLQ* 2, no. 3 (1995): 274. Since writing this chapter, Marti Lybeck's analysis of the role of the Weimar homosexual magazines in creating an "imaginary sphere of belonging" appeared, in which she comes to similar conclusions. I refer readers to this discussion and forthcoming book publication: "Female Homosexuality," 342ff.

9. Plötz, *Einsame Freundinnen*, 44.

10. F. Thoma, "Eine Stimme aus der Schweiz," *Garçonne*, no. 8, 15 April 1931, 1f.; "Leidensgenossinnen der Schweiz vereinigt Euch!" *Garçonne*, no. 11, 27 May 1931, 1; Fredy Thoma, "Schwestern Lesbos, brechet Bahn," *Garçonne*, 6 January 1932, 3f.

11. The significance of personal advertisements in the homosexual magazines as a means of establishing sexual contacts, networks, and identities is examined further in Plötz, *Einsame Freundinnen*, 47ff.; and Lybeck, "Female Homosexuality," 291ff.

12. Anny Dolder-Uhl, "Skizze," *Garçonne*, no. 25, 9 December 1931, 3f.

13. This figure comes from a 1948 study by Ilse-Lore Worch, cited in Marckwardt, *Illustrierten*, 107.

14. A 1929 advertisement for the novel cited circulation figures of up to two million, noting that the published book had already surpassed twenty-five thousand copies: *Berliner Illustrirte Zeitung*, no. 8, 24 February 1929. On Baum's commercial success see Lynda J. King, *Best-sellers by Design: Vicki Baum and the House of Ullstein* (Detroit: Wayne State University Press, 1988).

15. Ankum, "Introduction," 1ff.; Halberstam, *In a Queer Time*, 35.

16. Cf. Radclyffe Hall, *The Well of Loneliness* [1928] (New York: Anchor Books, 1990); see also Esther Newton, "The Mythic Mannish Lesbian: Radclyffe Hall and the New Woman," *Signs: Journal of Women in Culture and Society* 9, no. 4 (1984): 557–75.

17. Weston emphasizes that the distinction between the urban and the rural that props up the gay imaginary is a symbolic one, and thus constitutes a dream of an elsewhere that promises a freedom it can never provide. See discussion in Halberstam, *In a Queer Time*, 30.

18. Baum, *Zwischenfall*, 175.

19. Petersen, *Women and Modernity*, 2, 12.

20. Vicki Baum, *stud. chem. Helene Willfüer* [1928] (Munich: Wilhelm Heyne, 1956), 23. Subsequent references to this novel will be cited in-text with the abbreviation *H*.

21. Barndt, *Sentiment und Sachlichkeit,* 99–101.
22. Cf. Petersen, *Women and Modernity,* 100.
23. Frame, "Gretchen, Girl, Garçonne," 27.
24. Ellis and Symonds, *Sexual Inversion,* 144.
25. Arthur Kronfeld, MD, PhD [Leitender Arzt am Institut für Sexualwissenschaft], "Nervöse Folgeerscheinungen der Homosexualität," *Jahrbuch für sexuelle Zwischenstufen* 20, no. 3–4 (1920): 101ff.
26. Frame, "Gretchen, Girl, Garçonne," 28.
27. Sander L. Gilman, *Difference and Pathology: Stereotypes of Sexuality, Race, and Madness* (Ithaca: Cornell University Press, 1985), 156–62, discussed in Frame, "Gretchen, Girl, Garçonne," 27f.
28. Barndt clarifies, however, that Weininger's text was only one of numerous influences on Baum's writings on Jewish topics: *Sentiment und Sachlichkeit,* 93f.; Grossmann, "The New Woman," 167.
29. Halberstam emphasizes that it is necessary to complicate this mythology by acknowledging that rural environments "nurture elaborate sexual cultures even while sustaining surface social and political conformity": *In a Queer Time,* 35.
30. Dorothy Rowe, *Representing Berlin: Sexuality and the City in Imperial and Weimar Germany* (Aldershot: Ashgate, 2003), 89ff.; on how the decadence of the city was fictionalized in terms of unchecked female sexuality see also Petersen, *Women and Modernity,* 6.
31. McCormick, *Gender and Sexuality,* 111. Similarly, Petersen observes that it is the sexual excesses of the lesbians that most clearly represent the decline or degeneration of the city: *Women and Modernity,* 104f.
32. Erich Kästner, *Fabian: Die Geschichte eines Moralisten,* 19th ed. [1931] (Munich: dtv, 2003), 93f. Subsequent references to this novel will be cited in-text with the abbreviation *F.*
33. McCormick, *Gender and Sexuality,* 111.
34. Todd Herzog, "Crime Stories: Criminal, Society, and the Modernist Case History," *Representations* 80 (2002): 35f.
35. See e.g. Hanna Hacker, "Zonen des Verbotenen: Die lesbische Codierung von Kriminalität und Feminismus um 1900," in *Que(e)rdenken: weibliche, männliche Homosexualität und Wissenschaft,* ed. Barbara Hey et al. (Innsbruck: Studien Verlag, 1997); Herzog, "Crime Stories"; Hania Siebenpfeiffer, *Böse Lust: Gewaltverbrechen in Diskursen der Weimarer Republik* (Cologne: Böhlau, 2005), 95–149.
36. Alfred Döblin, *Die beiden Freundinnen und ihr Giftmord* [1924] (Düsseldorf: Artemis & Winkler, 2001), 79. Subsequent references to this novel will be cited in-text with the abbreviation *DbF.*
37. Petersen, *Women and Modernity,* 102.
38. Rowe, *Representing Berlin,* 89.
39. On the gendered implications of *Lustmord* and its artistic treatment in the Weimar era, see Tatar, *Lustmord;* Siebenpfeiffer, *Böse Lust,* 185–248; Beth Irwin Lewis, "*Lustmord:* Inside the Windows of the Metropolis," in Ankum, *Women in the Metropolis,* 202–32.
40. Siebenpfeiffer, *Böse Lust,* 98.
41. Cited in ibid., 95f.
42. Hacker, "Zonen," 54, see also 49–55; see also Lynda Hart, *Fatal Women: Lesbian Sexuality and the Mark of Aggression* (Princeton: Princeton University Press, 1994).
43. Herzog, "Crime Stories," 52, 56.
44. Irmgard Keun, *Das kunstseidene Mädchen* [1932] (Munich: List, 2001), 171. Subsequent references to this novel will be cited in-text with the abbreviation *KM.*
45. Roellig, "Café Domino," in Meyer, *Lila Nächte,* 40.
46. McCormick, *Gender and Sexuality,* 132.

47. Keun's novel contains numerous references to contemporary film stars, songs, and other cultural products; however, as Barndt points out, this particular instance of intertextuality is different because it directly influences the narrative: *Sentiment und Sachlichkeit*, 205.

48. Ibid., 207.

49. Leo Lensing, "Cinema, Society and Literature in Irmgard Keun's *Das kunstseidene Mädchen*," *Germanic Review* 60 (1985): 133.

50. On the novel's popularity see Meyer, *Lila Nächte*, 37; Nenno, "*Bildung* and Desire," 208; Claudia Schoppmann, '*Der Skorpion*': *Frauenliebe in der Weimarer Republik* (Hamburg: Libertäre Assoziation, 1985), 10.

51. Cf. Nenno, "*Bildung* and Desire," 207–21.

52. Author's foreword to the English translation of *The Outcast*, the sequel to *The Scorpion* (which was published in English in only two volumes): Anna Elisabet Weirauch, *The Outcast* [1933], trans. Guy Endore (New York: Arno Press, 1975), vii. Subsequent references to this novel will be cited in-text and refer to the following German editions, whereby the three volumes of the trilogy are distinguished using the abbreviations *S1, S2*, and *S3*: Anna Elisabet Weirauch, *Der Skorpion* [1919], 3 vols., vol. 1 (Frankfurt/Main: Ullstein, 1993); Anna Elisabet Weirauch, *Der Skorpion* [1921], 3 vols., vol. 2 (Maroldsweisach: Feministischer Buchverlag, 1993); Anna Elisabet Weirauch, *Der Skorpion* [1931], 3 vols., vol. 3 (Maroldsweisach: Feministischer Buchverlag, 1993).

53. Petersen, *Women and Modernity*, 92–101. Lybeck adds that the repetition inherent to melodramatic homosexual plots of this period "reflects the on-going necessity of remaking the boundaries between acceptable and unacceptable": "Female Homosexuality," 426ff.

54. Further parallels between these two almost contemporary novels are examined in Nenno, "*Bildung* and Desire," 207–21.

55. Frame, "Gretchen, Girl, Garçonne," 22.

56. Halberstam, *Female Masculinity*, 77; on the treatment of sexological ideas by early lesbian writers see also 75–110, and Doan, *Fashioning Sapphism*, 126–63.

57. Petersen, *Women and Modernity*, 95; Sabine Puhlfürst, '*Mehr als blosse Schwärmerei*': *die Darstellung von Liebesbeziehungen zwischen Mädchen/jungen Frauen im Spiegel der deutschsprachigen Frauenliteratur des 20. Jahrhunderts* (Essen: Die blaue Eule, 2002), 92n333.

58. Elaine Showalter, *Sexual Anarchy: Gender and Culture at the fin de siècle* (New York: Viking, 1990).

59. Variations on both of these names, including "Cora" and "Fiammetta," are used throughout the narrative to designate Mette's lover, who is also Olga's former lover.

60. Nenno, "*Bildung* and Desire," 218.

61. Petersen, *Women and Modernity*, 96f.; Nenno, "*Bildung* and Desire," 218.

62. Halberstam, *Female Masculinity*, 87.

63. Cf. Petersen, who argues that "the novel seems to advocate a lesbian identity that … must eschew sexuality if it cannot be controlled," and Nenno, who argues that Corona comes to symbolize the Berlin that Mette ultimately rejects: Petersen, *Women and Modernity*, 96f.; Nenno, "*Bildung* and Desire," 219.

64. Butler, *Bodies that Matter*, 137; this discussion of queer kinship is continued in *Undoing Gender*, 102–30.

CONCLUSION

Oh woman!
You learn to fly a plane,
to hire able seamen,
to steer a four-horse carriage
like a man.

Men are getting ever smaller,
nothing is unachievable now—:
But dear woman! There is always someone
flying there behind you.

You can calculate salary charts,
conduct a band,
because a woman can do everything
like a man.

Do it all. But someone small
is following you over land and sea.
And there is always someone
flying there behind you.

....
Theobald Tiger, "Oh Frau!" *Uhu*, April 1927

*I*n April 1927 *Uhu* published a cartoon by Georg Robbe of a woman flying a light plane over the countryside, looking nervously over her shoulder at a large stork following close behind with a swaddled baby dangling from its beak, with the caption "There is always one flying behind her!" The accompanying verses by Theobald Tiger, one of the numerous pseudonyms of prominent satirist Kurt

---

Notes for this section begin on page 185.

Tucholsky, lament the modern woman's neglect of her maternal instincts and responsibilities. This image was reprinted in the same magazine in October 1933, nine months after the National Socialist seizure of power and at a time when those mass media outlets that had not been banned or burned were being increasingly subjected to the censorship of Nazi cultural coordination. An additional editorial comment in this later version clarifies that this was an image specifically intended to poke fun at the "masculinization of woman." Such an obvious undermining of the achievements of the modern woman undoubtedly resonated just as strongly in a newly Nazified society as it had in 1927, when concerns about women's masculinization had been at the forefront of popular discourse. Both image and verse illustrate two central themes of this study: the widespread anxieties in 1920s Germany about women's mobility, political emancipation, and increasing equality with men, expressed so frequently in terms of the "masculinization" of the nation's womanhood; and the increasing trend toward more conservative, domesticated, and maternal ideals of womanhood as the end of the Weimar era approached.

Several scholars have argued that the demise of the 1920s New Woman in Germany was as prompt and complete as her rise, and coincided neatly with the end of the Weimar era— that "this modernist female persona was as short-lived and ambiguous as it was generational."[1] Yet such assertions brush too lightly over not only the historical links between the masculinized woman of the Weimar period and her pre–World War I suffragette predecessors, but also the ways in which this cultural phenomenon helped to fundamentally transform ideas about how women and men should look, act, and interact with one another even beyond 1933. Even though the popular media increasingly sought to limit women to the traditional roles of wife and mother toward the end of the 1920s, paving the way for the Nazi gender propaganda of *Kinder, Küche, Kirche,* the female ideal had by this stage been irrevocably modernized—and masculinized. Images of "mothers" by the early 1930s were far more likely to incorporate the short haircuts, slim and boyish fashion lines, and even athletic pursuits of the 1920s New Woman than the corsets and braids of her Wilhelmine predecessor.

This transformation also extended to sexual relations between men and women, so that even while commentators increasingly advocated women's return to the domestic sphere, they often did so with the awareness that women who had learned to drive cars, lift weights, fly planes, and work in offices would no longer be content with the patriarchal back seat, and would expect to relate to their husbands in the spirit of friendly rivalry and companionship well practiced in the mixed sporting clubs that boomed throughout the 1920s. Although the flamboyant performance of masculinity by the monocled, tuxedoed, mid-1920s Garçonne had by the end of the Weimar period become an easy target for popular ridicule, other aspects of women's "masculinization" had successfully entered the mainstream and become part of a larger, modernized ideal of German womanhood—albeit one still strongly defined by parameters of (middle) class, (white) race, (Christian) religion, and (hetero)sexuality.

This book has argued that the masculine woman provided a central and familiar locus for discourses of change in the Weimar period. Although her apparent desire to become like men was one of her most controversial aspects, the symbolic power of this cultural stereotype extended far beyond the ongoing evolution of gender relations, as the masculine woman came to embody an increasingly urbanized, rationalized German workforce and society, a cynical, objective approach to love and morality, and a democratized, consumerist culture—in short, the "crisis" of German modernity itself. Consequently, critiques of women's "masculine" fashions, their competition with men on the sporting field, or the audacity of female actors taking trouser roles off the stage were always more than just that— they were implicated in wider, often reactionary discourses negotiating a rapidly changing society plagued by political and economic insecurities and by a deeply destabilized masculinity following the nation's defeat in World War I.

Given her significance as a symbol of rapid and often daunting social change, it is no surprise that Weimar critics sought to defuse the threat of the masculine woman, and in several chapters I have pointed to strategies of containment that appeared repeatedly in popular media coverage of this phenomenon. These included a ridiculing of masculine and implicitly "perverse" excesses, a corresponding overemphasis on the femininity and heterosexuality of the modern woman, "narratives of transformation" that illustrated her morphing from edgy Garçonne to overtly feminine lady, discourses of theatricality and performance that permitted masculine transgressions only within strict spatial and temporal boundaries, and representations that attempted to reconcile the various roles of comrade, wife, athlete, worker, modern woman, and mother. Yet I have also drawn attention to instances of resistance to these strategies, particularly from within the female homosexual community, which continued—albeit not uncritically—to celebrate masculine visual signifiers, behaviors, identities, and desires well after the Garçonne had all but faded from mainstream media commentary. The film *Mädchen in Uniform* provides another important example of such resistance to the increasingly conservative and heteronormative female ideal of the late Weimar period, reappropriating the masculine space and privilege of the trouser role as a space from which to challenge traditional gender hierarchies and articulate nonheteronormative desires.

The identification of "queer" female masculinities in the Weimar media has been an important thread running throughout this volume. In chapter 3 I argued that whereas associations with sex-gender inversion were often used to deliberately taint representations of the masculine woman in the mainstream media, the subcultural periodicals from this era constitute a rich source for the study of early queer genders. Contributors to these magazines differentiated carefully between various forms of masculine female embodiment, including passing women (who were sometimes coopted into narratives of homosexual desire), female-to-male transvestites, and "virile" homosexual women. These subcultural commentators drew critically and selectively on available sexological knowledges, using scientific discourse in order to help defend the naturalness of a range of sex-gender embodiments, but also going beyond the clinical coldness of the case studies to actively incorporate masculine and feminine homosexual women into narratives of homoerotic desire. Often, these narratives were structured by the gendered binary of virile/feminine, and it is important to recognize the extent to which such models remained implicated in dominant, patriarchal definitions of gender and privilege. This issue was debated in remarkable depth by members of the Weimar subculture themselves, who questioned the right of masculine-identifying homosexual women to sleep around, or to see themselves as in any way superior to their feminine partners. Yet as recent analyses of lesbian butch-femme clarify, it is also important to acknowledge the potential of such queer relationship forms to destabilize heteronormative structures, undoing the latter's claim to be "natural" or "original" forms of social organization by demonstrating "how the so-called originals, men and women within the heterosexual frame, are similarly constructed, performatively established."[2]

Much work remains to be done in the history of sexuality and queer genders in pre-Nazi Germany. One could, for example, productively compare the women's subcultural magazines with homosexual men's publications from this period, asking whether male homosexual, "third sex," and "transvestite" relationships on the one hand, and their "female" counterparts on the other were structured along similarly gendered lines; whether the "feminine" partners in such relationships were necessarily disadvantaged; and why such heteronormative structures provided an attractive model for homosexual men and women at this period. Comparative research could also interrogate the degree to which male effeminacy was caricatured within the mainstream media, and the extent to which male stereotypes such as the dandy were read as symptomatic of male homosexuality. Such research would provide a valuable counterpoint to this examination of female masculinities, and highlight the increasing impact of "queer" genders on the German cultural consciousness in the early twentieth century.

Emphasizing the influence of location and rural-urban differences in the representation of female masculinities, the final chapter of this study likewise points to an area of Weimar studies that has often been neglected, as scholars have—perhaps understandably—focused on the hub of the new and the modern that was metropolitan Berlin in the 1920s. Yet the provinces and provincial identity constituted crucial reference points within Weimar culture, and not only as the supposed antithesis of modernity and focus of subsequent Nazi idealizations of Germanic pastoralism. Ideas about place were instrumental in shaping ideas about gender and sexuality in 1920s and early 1930s Germany, as the "reconstruction of traditional femininity was paralleled by a political reorientation toward the provinces and away from the city."[3] This study has shown that representations of nonheterosexual subjects within Weimar cultural texts did not always conform to "metronormative" narratives that would position the cities as the only "true" or "natural" home for homosexual subjects—texts such as Weirauch's *Der Skorpion* reveal resistances to the idea that "queer" lives and kinship forms were confined to the metropolis at this time. Despite the pioneering efforts of a few scholars, work remains to be done on gender and sexuality in the context of rural life in this period, and on the continuities and ruptures of these experiences into the Nazi era.

It has been argued that the best forms of history "transcend ... the antiquarian impulse, seeking, of course, to understand the past in its proper contexts but seeking also to play with the ways in which the past illuminates the present and the present illuminates the past."[4] This study, with its focus on the still emergent theoretical field of female masculinities and other "queer" genders, is very much grounded in present academic interests. Consequently, as well as seeking to extend existing research on this pivotal period between World War I and National Socialism, it has sought to shed light on early discussions of gender categories, identities, and performances that still have meaning for people today. Just as ideas about women's "emancipation" have come to the forefront of public discourse at various junctures of German history, including the late nineteenth century, the 1920s, and the 1960s—its forms, goals, and self-definitions evolving over time—female masculinities constitute a series of gender "performances" that have resonated throughout twentieth-century German history, albeit with wildly varying connotations: from the female concentration camp officers of the Nazi era to muscular East German athletes, from the drag kings, butch dykes, and transmen of contemporary queer subcultures to the masculinity still frequently attributed to prominent feminists or female politicians. As a historical fixture the masculine woman has, as Halberstam observes, informed and challenged cultural discourse for at least the last two centuries.[5] The masculine woman neither made her first appearance nor disappeared with the *Bubikopf,* but in the Weimar period she attracted a level of mainstream media commentary unsurpassed either beforehand or since. Her prominence in cultural discourse at this period points to the extreme anxiety in 1920s Germany about gender roles in "crisis" and a society in transition, and underlines the ongoing relevance of gender as a category of historical analysis.

Notes

1. Ankum, "Introduction," 4; see also Bock, "Zwischen den Zeiten," 36.
2. Butler, *Undoing Gender,* 209.
3. Ankum, "Introduction," 3.
4. Bennett, "'Lesbian-Like,'" 4.
5. Halberstam, *Female Masculinity,* 45.

BIBLIOGRAPHY

Newspapers and Periodicals

Berliner Illustrirte Zeitung
Die Dame: ill. Mode-Zeitschrift
Frauenliebe: Wochenschrift für Freundschaft, Liebe und sexuelle Aufklärung [later:
  Garçonne]
Frauen Liebe und Leben
Frau und Gegenwart: Zeitschrift für die gesamten Traueninteressen
Die Freundin: Wochenschrift für ideale Frauenfreundschaft
Garçonne (*Die Junggesellin*)
Das Magazin
Der Querschnitt
Simplicissimus
Sport im Bild: Kultur, Gesellschaft, Mode
Uhu: das neue Ullsteinmagazin
Ulk: illustriertes Wochenblatt für Humor und Satire
Die Woche: moderne illustrierte Zeitschrift

Published Sources

Adams, Rachel. "Masculinity without Men." *GLQ: A Journal of Lesbian and Gay Studies*
  6, no. 3 (2000): 467–78.
Aldrich, Robert, and Garry Wotherspoon. *Who's Who in Contemporary Gay and Lesbian
  History.* London: Routledge, 2001.
Anderson, Benedict. *Imagined Communities: Reflections on the Origin and Spread of
  Nationalism.* London: Verso, 1983.

André, Naomi Adele. *Voicing Gender: Castrati, Travesti, and the Second Woman in Early-Nineteenth-Century Italian Opera.* Bloomington: Indiana University Press, 2006.

Ankum, Katharina von. "Introduction." In *Women in the Metropolis: Gender and Modernity in Weimar Culture,* edited by Ankum, 1–11.

———, ed. *Women in the Metropolis: Gender and Modernity in Weimar Culture.* Berkeley: University of California Press, 1997.

Bakhtin, Mikhail. *Rabelais and His World.* Translated by Helene Iswolsky. Bloomington: Indiana University Press, 1984.

Barndt, Kerstin. *Sentiment und Sachlichkeit: Der Roman der Neuen Frau in der Weimarer Republik.* Cologne: Böhlau, 2003.

Barnes, Ruth, and Joanne B. Eicher, eds. *Dress and Gender: Making and Meaning in Cultural Contexts.* Providence: Berg, 1992.

Baum, Vicki. *stud. chem. Helene Willfüer.* [1928]. Munich: Wilhelm Heyne, 1956.

———. *Zwischenfall in Lohwinckel.* [1930]. Munich: Droemer Knaur, 1973.

Behling, Laura L. *The Masculine Woman in America, 1890–1935.* Urbana: University of Illinois Press, 2001.

Bell-Metereau, Rebecca Louise. *Hollywood Androgyny.* New York: Columbia University Press, 1985.

Benedek, Susanne, and Adolphe Binde. *Von tanzenden Kleidern und sprechenden Leibern: Crossdressing als Auflösung der Geschlechterpolarität?* Dortmund: Edition Ebersbach, 1996.

Bennett, Judith M. "'Lesbian-Like' and the Social History of Lesbianisms." *Journal of the History of Sexuality* 9, no. 1–2 (2000): 1–24.

Berg, Jan. "Asta Nielsen: Darstellung von Weiblichkeit und Weiblichkeit als Darstellung." In *Idole des Deutschen Films: Eine Galerie von Schlüsselfiguren,* edited by Thomas Koebner, 54–74. Munich: Edition Text und Kritik, 1997.

Bergmann, Dr. W. *Die Frau und der Sport.* Oldenburg i.O.: Gerhard Stalling, 1925.

Berlanstein, Lenard R. "Breeches and Breaches: Cross-Dress Theater and the Culture of Gender Ambiguity in Modern France." *Comparative Studies in Society and History* 38, no. 2 (1998): 338–69.

Bernstoff, Madeleine, and Stefanie Hetze, eds. *Frauen in Hosen: Hosenrollen im Film.* Munich: Münchner Filmzentrum e.V., 1989.

Bertschik, Julia. *Mode und Moderne: Kleidung als Spiegel des Zeitgeistes in der deutschsprachigen Literatur (1770–1945).* Cologne: Böhlau, 2005.

Birrell, Susan, and Cheryl L. Cole. "Double Fault: Renee Richards and the Construction and Naturalization of Difference." In *Women, Sport, and Culture,* edited by Susan Birrell and Cheryl L. Cole, 373–93. Champaign: Human Kinetics, 1994.

Blackmer, Corinne E., and Patricia Juliana Smith, eds. *En travesti: Women, Gender Subversion, Opera.* New York: Columbia University Press, 1995.

Bland, Lucy, and Laura Doan. *Sexology Uncensored: The Documents of Sexual Science.* Cambridge: Polity Press, 1998.

Block, Sigrid. *Frauen und Mädchen in der Arbeitersportbewegung.* Münster: Lit, 1987.

Bock, Petra. "Zwischen den Zeiten: Neue Frauen und die Weimarer Republik." In *Neue Frauen zwischen den Zeiten,* edited by Petra Bock and Katja Koblitz, 14–37. Berlin: Edition Heinrich, 1995.

Bollé, Michael, ed. *Eldorado: Homosexuelle Frauen und Männer in Berlin 1850–1950. Geschichte, Alltag und Kultur.* Berlin: Rosa Winkel, 1984.

Boyd, Nan Alamilla. "The Materiality of Gender: Looking for Lesbian Bodies in Transgender History." *Journal of Lesbian Studies* 3 (1999): 73–81.

Breger, Claudia. "Feminine Masculinities: Scientific and Literary Representations of 'Female Inversion' at the Turn of the Twentieth Century." *Journal of the History of Sexuality* 14, no. 1–2 (2005): 76–106.

Bridenthal, Renate, and Claudia Koonz. "Beyond *Kinder, Küche, Kirche:* Weimar Women in Politics and Work." In *When Biology Became Destiny: Women in Weimar and Nazi Germany,* edited by Renate Bridenthal, Atina Grossmann, and Marion Kaplan, 33–65. New York: Monthly Review Press, 1984.

Browne, Kath. "Genderism and the Bathroom Problem: (Re)materialising Sexed Sites, (Re)creating Sexed Bodies." *Gender, Place and Culture* 11, no. 3 (2004): 331–46.

Bullough, Vern L., and Bonnie Bullough. *Cross Dressing, Sex, and Gender.* Philadelphia: University of Pennsylvania Press, 1993.

Butler, Judith. *Bodies that Matter: On the Discursive Limits of "Sex."* New York: Routledge, 1993.

———. *Gender Trouble: Feminism and the Subversion of Identity.* New York: Routledge, 1999.

———. *Undoing Gender.* London: Routledge, 2004.

Cahn, Susan K. *Coming on Strong: Gender and Sexuality in Twentieth-Century Women's Sport.* New York: Free Press, 1994.

Canning, Kathleen. "Claiming Citizenship: Suffrage and Subjectivity in Germany after the First World War." In *Gender History in Practice: Historical Perspectives on Bodies, Class and Citizenship,* 212–37. Ithaca: Cornell University Press, 2006.

Castle, Terry. "In Praise of Brigitte Fassbaender: Reflections on Diva-Worship." In *En travesti: Women, Gender Subversion, Opera,* edited by Blackmer and Smith, 20–58.

Chauncey, Jr., George. "From Sexual Inversion to Homosexuality: The Changing Medical Conceptualization of Female 'Deviance.'" In *Passion and Power: Sexuality in History,* edited by Kathy Peiss, Christina Simmons, and Robert A. Padgug, 87–117. Philadelphia: Temple University Press, 1989.

Conor, Liz. *The Spectacular Modern Woman: Feminine Visibility in the 1920s.* Bloomington: Indiana University Press, 2004.

Creed, Barbara. *Pandora's Box: Essays in Film Theory.* Melbourne: Australian Centre for the Moving Image and University of Melbourne, 2004.

Davis, Natalie Zemon. *Society and Culture in Early Modern France: Eight Essays.* Cambridge: Polity, 1987.

Dekker, Rudolf, and Lotte van de Pol. *Frauen in Männerkleidern: Weibliche Transvestiten und ihre Geschichte.* Berlin: Verlag Klaus Wagenbach, 1989.

De Ras, Marion E. *Körper, Eros und weibliche Kultur: Mädchen im Wandervogel und in der Bündischen Jugend 1900–1933.* Pfaffenweiler: Centaurus, 1988.

Doan, Laura. *Fashioning Sapphism: The Origins of a Modern English Lesbian Culture.* New York: Columbia University Press, 2001.

———. "Topsy-Turvydom. Gender Inversion, Sapphism, and the Great War." *GLQ: A Journal of Lesbian and Gay Studies* 12, no. 4 (2006): 517–42.

Doane, Mary Ann. "Film and the Masquerade." In *Film Theory and Criticism: Introductory Readings,* edited by Gerald Mast, Marshall Cohen, and Leo Braudy, 758–72. New York: Oxford University Press, 1999.

Döblin, Alfred. *Die beiden Freundinnen und ihr Giftmord.* [1924]. Düsseldorf: Artemis & Winkler, 2001.

Dworkin, Shari, and Michael Messner. "Just do ... what? Sport, Bodies, Gender." In *Gender and Sport: A Reader,* edited by Scraton and Flintoff, 17–29.

Dyer, Richard. "Less and More than Women and Men: Lesbian and Gay Cinema in Weimar Germany." *New German Critique,* no. 51 (1990): 5–60.

Eisenberg, Christiane. "Massensport in der Weimarer Republik: Ein statistischer Überblick." *Archiv für Sozialgeschichte* 33 (1993): 137–77.

Ellis, Havelock, and John Addington Symonds. *Sexual Inversion.* [1897]. New York: Arno, 1975.

Emde, Silke von der. "'Mädchen in Uniform': Erotic Self-Liberation of Women in the Context of the Film Discussion in the Weimar-Republic." *Kodikas Code-Ars Semiotica* 14, no. 1–2 (1991): 35–48.

Essinger, Martin W. "Die Hosenrolle in der Oper." In *Frauenstimmen, Frauenrollen in der Oper und Frauen-Selbstzeugnisse,* edited by Eva Rieger and Gabriele Busch-Salmen, 299–317. Herbolzheim: Centaurus, 2000.

Evans, Richard. *The Feminist Movement in Germany, 1894–1933.* London: Sage, 1976.

Fausto-Sterling, Anne. *Sexing the Body: Gender Politics and the Construction of Sexuality.* New York: Basic Books, 2000.

Felski, Rita. *The Gender of Modernity.* Cambridge, MA: Harvard University Press, 1995.

Foucault, Michel. *The History of Sexuality.* [1976]. 3 vols. Vol. 1: The Will to Knowledge. London: Penguin, 1998.

Frame, Lynne. "Gretchen, Girl, Garçonne? Weimar Science and Popular Culture in Search of the Ideal New Woman." In *Women in the Metropolis: Gender and Modernity in Weimar Culture,* edited by Ankum, 12–40.

Freud, Sigmund. "The Libido Theory and Narcissism." In *Introductory Lectures on Psychoanalysis,* edited by James Strachey and Angela Richards, 461–81. London: Penguin, 1973.

———. "The Psychogenesis of a Case of Homosexuality in a Woman." In Sigmund Freud, *Sexuality and the Psychology of Love,* edited by Philip Rieff, 133–59. New York: Collier, 1963.

Gaines, Jane, and Charlotte Herzog. *Fabrications: Costume and the Female Body.* New York: Routledge, 1990.

Garber, Marjorie. *Vested Interests: Cross-dressing and Cultural Anxiety.* London: Routledge, 1992.

Garelick, Rhonda K. *Rising Star: Dandyism, Gender, and Performance in the fin de siècle.* Princeton: Princeton University Press, 1998.

Garvey, Ellen Gruber. "Reframing the Bicycle: Advertising-Supported Magazines and Scorching Women." *American Quarterly* 47, no. 1 (1995): 66–101.

Giese, Fritz. *Girlkultur: Vergleiche zwischen amerikanischem und europäischem Rhythmus und Lebensgefühl.* Munich: Delphin-Verlag, 1925.

Gilman, Sander L. *Difference and Pathology: Stereotypes of Sexuality, Race, and Madness.* Ithaca: Cornell University Press, 1985.

Gleber, Anke. *The Art of Taking a Walk: Flanerie, Literature, and Film in Weimar Culture.* Princeton: Princeton University Press, 1999.

Gramann, Karola, and Heide Schlüpmann. "Unnatürliche Akte: Die Inszenierung des Lesbischen im Film." In *Lust und Elend: Das erotische Kino,* edited by Karola Gramann et al., 28–31. Munich: Bucher, 1981.

Griffin, Pat. "Changing the Game: Homophobia, Sexism and Lesbians in Sport." In *Gender and Sport: A Reader,* edited by Scraton and Flintoff, 193–208.

Grossmann, Atina. "*Girlkultur* or Thoroughly Rationalized Female: A New Woman in Weimar Germany?" In *Women in Culture and Politics: A Century of Change,* edited by Judith Friedlander, Blanche Wiesen Cook, Alice Kessler-Harris, and Carroll Smith-Rosenberg, 62–80. Bloomington: Indiana University Press, 1986.

———. "The New Woman and the Rationalization of Sexuality in Weimar Germany." In *Powers of Desire: The Politics of Sexuality,* edited by Ann Snitow, Christine Stansell, and Sharon Thompson, 153–71. New York: Monthly Review Press, 1983.

———. *Reforming Sex: The German Movement for Birth Control and Abortion Reform, 1920–1950.* New York: Oxford University Press, 1995.

Guenther, Irene. *Nazi chic? Fashioning Women in the Third Reich.* Oxford: Berg, 2004.

Hacker, Hanna. *Frauen und Freundinnen: Studien zur "weiblichen Homosexualität" am Beispiel Österreich 1870–1938.* Weinheim and Basel: Beltz Verlag, 1987.

———. "Zonen des Verbotenen: Die lesbische Codierung von Kriminalität und Feminismus um 1900." In *Que(e)rdenken: weibliche, männliche Homosexualität und Wissenschaft,* edited by Barbara Hey et al., 40–57. Innsbruck: Studien Verlag, 1997.

Hake, Sabine. "In the Mirror of Fashion." In *Women in the Metropolis: Gender and Modernity in Weimar Culture,* edited by Ankum, 185–201.

Halberstam, Judith. *Female Masculinity.* Durham, NC: Duke University Press, 1998.

———. *In a Queer Time and Place: Transgender Bodies, Subcultural Lives.* New York: New York University Press, 2005.

Hall, Radclyffe. *The Well of Loneliness.* [1928]. New York: Anchor Books, 1990.

Handke, H. *Der Bubikopf von Agamemnon bis Stresemann.* Berlin: Verlag für Kulturpolitik, 1926.

Harrowitz, Nancy A., and Barbara Hyams, eds. *Jews and Gender: Responses to Otto Weininger.* Philadelphia: Temple University Press, 1995.

Hart, Lynda. *Fatal Women: Lesbian Sexuality and the Mark of Aggression.* Princeton: Princeton University Press, 1994.

Hartmann-Tews, Ilse, and Sascha Alexandra Luetkens. "The Inclusion of Women into the German Sport System." In *Sport and Women: Social Issues in International Perspective,* edited by Ilse Hartmann-Tews and Gertrud Pfister, 53–69. London: Routledge, 2003.

Harvey, Elizabeth. "The Failure of Feminism? Young Women and the Bourgeois Feminist Movement in Weimar Germany 1918–1933." *Central European History* 28, no. 1 (1995): 1–28.

Hausman, Bernice. *Changing Sex: Transsexualism, Technology, and the Idea of Gender.* Durham, NC: Duke University Press, 1995.

Heilmann, Ann, and Margaret Beetham, eds. *New Woman Hybridities*. New York: Routledge, 2004.

Hermand, Jost, and Frank Trommler. *Die Kultur der Weimarer Republik*. Frankfurt/Main: Fischer, 1988.

Hermes, Joke. *Reading Women's Magazines: An Analysis of Everyday Media Use*. Cambridge: Polity Press, 1995.

Herzog, Todd. "Crime Stories: Criminal, Society, and the Modernist Case History." *Representations* 80 (2002): 34–61.

Hetze, Stefanie. "Die Hosenrolle im Theater." In *Frauen in Hosen: Hosenrollen im Film. Texte und Materialien,* edited by Madeleine Bernstoff and Stefanie Hetze, 5–8. Munich: Münchner Filmzentrum e.V., 1989.

Hill, Darryl. "Sexuality and Gender in Hirschfeld's *Die Transvestiten*: A Case of the 'Elusive Evidence of the Ordinary.'" *Journal of the History of Sexuality* 14, no. 3 (2005): 316–32.

Hirschfeld, Magnus. *Berlins drittes Geschlecht*. [1904]. Berlin: Rosa Winkel, 1991.

———. *Die Transvestiten: Eine Untersuchung über den erotischen Verkleidungstrieb*. Berlin: Med. Verlag Alfred Pulvermacher, 1910.

———. *Sexuelle Zwischenstufen: Das männliche Weib und der weibliche Mann*. 2nd ed. Vol. 2, *Sexualpathologie: Ein Lehrbuch für Ärzte und Studierende*. Bonn: A. Marcus & E. Webers, 1922.

Hollander, Anne. *Sex and Suits*. New York: Alfred A. Knopf, 1994.

Holtmont, Alfred. *Die Hosenrolle. Variationen über das Thema: Das Weib als Mann*. Munich: Meyer & Jessen, 1925.

Jensen, Erik N. "Images of the Ideal: Sports, Gender, and the Emergence of the Modern Body in Weimar Germany." PhD diss., University of Wisconsin, 2003.

Kaes, Anton, Martin Jay, and Edward Dimendberg. *The Weimar Republic Sourcebook*. Berkeley: University of California Press, 1994.

Kästner, Erich. *Fabian: Die Geschichte eines Moralisten*. [1931]. 19th ed. Munich: dtv, 2003.

Kennedy, Elizabeth Lapovsky, and Madeline Davis. *Boots of Leather, Slippers of Gold: The History of a Lesbian Community*. New York: Routledge, 1993.

Kennison, Rebecca. "Clothes Make the (Wo)man: Marlene Dietrich and 'Double Drag.'" *Journal of Lesbian Studies* 6, no. 2 (2002): 147–56.

Kessemeier, Gesa. *Sportlich, sachlich, männlich: Das Bild der 'Neuen Frau' in den Zwanziger Jahren. Zur Konstruktion geschlechtsspezifischer Körperbilder in der Mode der Jahre 1920 bis 1929*. Dortmund: Ed. Ebersbach, 2000.

Keun, Irmgard. *Das kunstseidene Mädchen*. [1932]. Munich: List, 2001.

King, Lynda J. *Best-sellers by Design: Vicki Baum and the House of Ullstein*. Detroit: Wayne State University Press, 1988.

Kokula, Ilse. "Lesbisch leben von Weimar bis zur Nachkriegszeit." In *Eldorado: Homosexuelle Frauen und Männer in Berlin 1850–1950. Geschichte, Alltag und Kultur,* edited by Bollé, 149–61.

Kracauer, Siegfried. *Die Angestellten: Aus dem neuesten Deutschland*. [1929]. Frankfurt/Main: Suhrkamp, 1971.

Krafft-Ebing, R. von. *Psychopathia sexualis: Mit besonderer Berücksichtigung der konträren*

Sexualempfindung. Eine medizinisch-gerichtliche Studie für Ärzte und Juristen. 15th ed. Stuttgart: F. Enke, 1918.

Krafka, Elke. "Die Hosenrolle am Theater—Kostümierung oder Grenzüberschreitung?" In *Sakkorausch und Rollentausch: männliche Leitbilder als Freiheitsentwürfe von Frauen,* edited by Andrea Stoll and Verena Wodtke-Werner, 35–54. Dortmund: Edition Ebersbach, 1997.

Kronfeld, MD, PhD, Arthur. "Nervöse Folgeerscheinungen der Homosexualität." *Jahrbuch für sexuelle Zwischenstufen* 20, no. 3–4 (1920): 101–3.

Kuzniar, Alice. *The Queer German Cinema.* Stanford: Stanford University Press, 2000.

Landschoof, Regina. "Frauensport im Faschismus." In *Frauensport im Faschismus,* edited by Regina Landschoof and Karin Hüls, 8–88. Hamburg: Ergebnisse, 1985.

Laqueur, Thomas Walter. *Making Sex: Body and Gender from the Greeks to Freud.* Cambridge, MA: Harvard University Press, 1990.

Lehnert, Gertrud. *Wenn Frauen Männerkleider tragen: Geschlecht und Maskerade in Literatur und Geschichte.* Munich: dtv, 1997.

Lengerke, Wolfgang von. *Die Amazone Gloria.* Berlin: Weltbücher Verlag, 1928.

Lensing, Leo. "Cinema, Society and Literature in Irmgard Keun's *Das kunstseidene Mädchen.*" *Germanic Review* 60 (1985): 129–34.

Lewis, Beth Irwin. "*Lustmord:* Inside the Windows of the Metropolis." In *Women in the Metropolis: Gender and Modernity in Weimar Culture,* edited by Ankum, 202–32.

Lybeck, Marti M. "Gender, Sexuality, and Belonging: Female Homosexuality in Germany 1890–1933." PhD diss., University of Michigan, 2007.

Mak, Geertje. "'Passing Women' im Sprechzimmer von Magnus Hirschfeld: Warum der Begriff 'Transvestit' nicht für Frauen in Männerkleidern eingeführt wurde (transl. Mirjam Hausmann)." *Österreichische Zeitschrift für Geschichtswissenschaften* 9, no. 3 (1998): 384–99.

Marckwardt, Wilhelm. *Die Illustrierten der Weimarer Zeit: Publizistische Funktion, ökonomische Entwicklung und inhaltliche Tendenzen (unter Einschluß einer Bibliographie dieses Pressetyps 1918–1932).* Munich: Minerva, 1982.

Martin, Biddy. *Femininity Played Straight: The Significance of Being Lesbian.* New York: Routledge, 1996.

Mason, Tim. "Women in Germany, 1925–1940: Family, Welfare and Work. Part I." *History Workshop* 1 (1976): 74–113.

Mayne, Judith. *Cinema and Spectatorship.* London: Routledge, 1993.

McCormick, Richard W. *Gender and Sexuality in Weimar Modernity: Film, Literature, and 'New Objectivity.'* New York: Palgrave, 2001.

Meskimmon, Marsha. *We Weren't Modern Enough: Women Artists and the Limits of German Modernism.* Berkeley: University of California Press, 1999.

Meyer, Adele, ed. *Lila Nächte: Die Damenklubs im Berlin der zwanziger Jahre.* Berlin: Edition Lit.Europe, 1994.

Meyer-Büser, Susanne, ed. *Bubikopf und Gretchenzopf: die Frau der zwanziger Jahre.* Heidelberg: Edition Braus, 1995.

Moore, F. Michael. *Drag! Male and Female Impersonators on Stage, Screen, and Television: An Illustrated World History.* Jefferson, NC: McFarland, 1994.

Moser, Dietz-Rüdiger. "Hosenrollen: Zum Kleider- und Geschlechtertausch, besonders im Leben, im Volksbrauch und auf der Bühne." *Literatur in Bayern* 21 (2006): 2–15.

Müller, Martin L. "Turnen und Sport im sozialen Wandel: Körperkultur in Frankfurt am Main während des Kaiserreichs und der Weimarer Republik." *Archiv für Sozialgeschichte* 33 (1993): 107–36.

Mulvey, Laura. "Visual Pleasure and Narrative Cinema." In *Film Theory and Criticism: Introductory Readings,* edited by Gerald Mast, Marshall Cohen, and Leo Braudy, 746–57. New York: Oxford University Press, 1999.

Nenno, Nancy. "*Bildung* and Desire: Anna Elisabet Weirauch's *Der Skorpion.*" In *Queering the Canon,* edited by Christoph Lorey and John Plews, 207–21. Columbia: Camden House, 1998.

Newton, Esther. "The Mythic Mannish Lesbian: Radclyffe Hall and the New Woman." *Signs: Journal of Women in Culture and Society* 9, no. 4 (1984): 557–75.

Noble, Jean Bobby. *Masculinities without Men? Female Masculinity in Twentieth-Century Fictions.* Vancouver: UBC Press, 2004.

Nordau, Max. "Muskeljudentum." *Die Jüdische Turnzeitung,* no. 2 (1900): 10–11.

Olivier, Antje, and Sevgi Braun. *Anpassung oder Verbot: Künstlerinnen und die 30er Jahre.* Düsseldorf: Droste, 1998.

Parr, Leslie, ed. *Lesbianism and Feminism in Germany, 1895–1910.* New York: Arno, 1975.

Petersen, Vibeke Rützou. *Women and Modernity in Weimar Germany: Reality and Representation in Popular Fiction.* New York: Berghahn Books, 2001.

Petro, Patrice. *Joyless Streets: Women and Melodramatic Representation in Weimar Germany.* Princeton: Princeton University Press, 1989.

Peukert, Detlev. *The Weimar Republic: The Crisis of Classical Modernity.* Translated by Richard Deveson. London: Penguin, 1991.

Pfister, Gertrud. "Demands, Realities and Ambivalences: Women in the Proletarian Sports Movement in Germany (1893–1933)." *Women in Sport and Physical Activity Journal* 3, no. 2 (1994): n.p. (electronic version).

———, ed. *Frau und Sport.* Frankfurt/Main: Fischer, 1980.

———. "Körperkultur und Weiblichkeit: Ein historischer Beitrag zur Entwicklung des modernen Sports in Deutschland bis zur Zeit der Weimarer Republik." In *Sport und Geschlecht,* edited by Michael Klein, 35–59. Reinbeck bei Hamburg: Rowohlt, 1983.

———. "Sport for Women." In *Sport and Physical Education in Germany,* edited by Roland Naul and Ken Hardman, 165–90. London: Routledge, 2002.

Pfister, Gertrud et al. "Women and Football—A Contradiction? The Beginnings of Women's Football in Four European Countries." In *Gender and Sport: A Reader,* edited by Scraton and Flintoff, 66–77.

Pfister, Gertrud, and Toni Niewerth. "Jewish Women in Gymnastics and Sport in Germany." *Journal of Sport History* 26, no. 2 (1999): 287–325.

Pieper, Mecki. "Die Frauenbewegung und ihre Bedeutung für lesbische Frauen (1850–1920)." In *Eldorado: Homosexuelle Frauen und Männer in Berlin 1850–1950,* edited by Bollé, 116–24.

Plötz, Kirsten. *Einsame Freundinnen: Lesbisches Leben während der zwanziger Jahre in der Provinz.* Hamburg: MännerschwarmSkript-Verl., 1999.

Presner, Todd Samuel. "'Clear Heads, Solid Stomachs, and Hard Muscles': Max Nordau and the Aesthetics of Jewish Regeneration." *Modernism / modernity* 10, no. 2 (2003): 269–96.

Prosser, Jay. "Transsexuals and the Transsexologists: Inversion and the Emergence of Transsexual Subjectivity." In *Sexology in Culture: Labelling Bodies and Desires,* edited by Lucy Bland and Laura Doan, 116–31. Cambridge: Polity, 1998.

Puhlfürst, Sabine. *'Mehr als blosse Schwärmerei': die Darstellung von Liebesbeziehungen zwischen Mädchen/jungen Frauen im Spiegel der deutschsprachigen Frauenliteratur des 20. Jahrhunderts.* Essen: Die blaue Eule, 2002.

Rich, B. Ruby. "From Repressive Tolerance to Erotic Liberation: *Mädchen in Uniform.*" In *Chick Flicks: Theories and Memories of the Feminist Film Movement,* edited by B. Ruby Rich, 179–206. Durham, NC: Duke University Press, 1998.

Rippey, Theodore F. "Athletics, Aesthetics, and Politics in the Weimar Press." *German Studies Review* 28, no. 1 (2005): 85–106.

Roberts, Mary Louise. *Civilization without Sexes: Reconstructing Gender in Postwar France, 1917–1927.* Chicago: University of Chicago Press, 1994.

Rowe, Dorothy. *Representing Berlin: Sexuality and the City in Imperial and Weimar Germany.* Aldershot: Ashgate, 2003.

Rüle-Gerstel, Dr. Alice. *Das Frauenproblem der Gegenwart: Eine psychologische Bilanz.* Leipzig: S. Hirzel, 1932.

Russo, Vito. *The Celluloid Closet: Homosexuality in the Movies.* New York: Harper & Row, 1987.

Scanlon, Jennifer. *Inarticulate Longings: The Ladies' Home Journal, Gender, and the Promises of Consumer Culture.* New York: Routledge, 1995.

Schader, Heike. "Virile homosexuelle Frauen im Spiegel ihrer Zeitschriften im Berlin der zwanziger Jahre." In *Verqueere Wissenschaft?* edited by Ursula Ferdinand, Andreas Pretzel, and Andreas Seeck, 137–46. Munich: LIT, 1998.

———. *Virile, Vamps und wilde Veilchen: Sexualität, Begehren und Erotik in den Zeitschriften homosexueller Frauen im Berlin der 1920er Jahre.* Königstein/Taunus: Ulrike Helmer, 2004.

Schlierkamp, Petra. "Die Garconne." In *Eldorado: Homosexuelle Frauen und Männer in Berlin 1850–1950,* edited by Bollé, 169–79.

Schoppmann, Claudia. *Days of Masquerade: Life Stories of Lesbians during the Third Reich.* New York: Columbia University Press, 1996.

———. *'Der Skorpion': Frauenliebe in der Weimarer Republik.* Hamburg: Libertäre Assoziation, 1985.

Schwarz, Gudrun. "'Mannweiber' in Männertheorien." In *Frauen suchen ihre Geschichte: Historische Studien zum 19. und 20. Jahrhundert,* edited by Karin Hausen, 62–80. Munich: C. H. Beck, 1983.

Scraton, Sheila, and Anne Flintoff, eds. *Gender and Sport: A Reader.* London: Routledge, 2002.

Sharp, Ingrid. "Riding the Tiger: Ambivalent Images of the New Woman in the Popular Press of the Weimar Republic." In *New Woman Hybridities,* edited by Heilmann and Beetham, 118–41.

Showalter, Elaine. *Sexual Anarchy: Gender and Culture at the fin de siècle.* New York: Viking, 1990.

Siebenpfeiffer, Hania. *Böse Lust: Gewaltverbrechen in Diskursen der Weimarer Republik.* Cologne: Böhlau, 2005.

Smith-Rosenberg, Carroll. "The New Woman as Androgyne: Social Disorder and Gender Crisis, 1870–1936." In Carroll Smith-Rosenberg, *Disorderly Conduct: Visions of Gender in Victorian America*, 245–96. New York: Oxford University Press, 1985.

Sperlings Zeitschriften- u. Zeitungs-Adreßbuch. Handbuch der deutschen Presse. Vol. 54. Leipzig: Verlag des Börsenvereins der Deutschen Buchhändler, 1928.

Stallybrass, Peter, and Allon White. *The Politics and Poetics of Transgression*. London: Methuen, 1986.

Steinach, Eugen, and Josef Loebel. *Sex and Life: Forty Years of Biological and Medical Experiments*. London: Faber, 1940.

Stephan, Inge. "'Da werden Weiber zu Hyänen...' Amazonen und Amazonenmythen bei Schiller und Kleist." In *Aus dem Verborgenen zur Avantgarde: Ausgewählte Beiträge zur feministischen Literaturwissenschaft der 80er Jahre*, edited by Hiltrud Bontrup and Jan Christian Metzler, 96–117. Hamburg: Argument, 2000.

Straayer, Chris. *Deviant Eyes, Deviant Bodies: Sexual Re-orientations in Film and Video*. New York: Columbia University Press, 1996.

Tatar, Maria. *Lustmord: Sexual Murder in Weimar Germany*. Princeton: Princeton University Press, 1995.

Tripp, Anna, ed. *Gender*. Houndmills, Basingstoke: Palgrave, 2000.

Usborne, Cornelie. *The Politics of the Body in Weimar Germany: Women's Reproductive Rights and Duties*. Basingstoke: Macmillan, 1992.

Vicinus, Martha. *Intimate Friends: Women Who Loved Women, 1778–1928*. Chicago: University of Chicago Press, 2004.

———. "'They Wonder to Which Sex I Belong': The Historical Roots of the Modern Lesbian Identity." *Feminist Studies* 18, no. 3 (1992): 467–97.

Vinken, Barbara. *Mode nach der Mode: Kleid und Geist am Ende des 20. Jahrhunderts*. Frankfurt/Main: Fischer, 1993.

Vogel, Katharina. "Zum Selbstverständnis lesbischer Frauen in der Weimarer Republik: Eine Analyse der Zeitschrift 'Die Freundin' 1924–1933." In *Eldorado: Homosexuelle Frauen und Männer in Berlin 1850–1950*, edited by Bollé, 162–68.

Wedemeyer-Kolwe, Bernd. *'Der neue Mensch': Körperkultur im Kaiserreich und in der Weimarer Republik*. Würzburg: Königshausen & Neumann, 2004.

Weininger, Otto. *Geschlecht und Charakter: Eine prinzipielle Untersuchung*. [1903]. Munich: Matthes & Seitz, 1997.

Weirauch, Anna Elisabet. *Der Skorpion*. [1919]. 3 vols. Vol. 1. Frankfurt/Main: Ullstein, 1993.

———. *Der Skorpion*. [1921]. 3 vols. Vol. 2. Maroldsweisach: Feministischer Buchverlag, 1993.

———. *Der Skorpion*. [1931]. 3 vols. Vol. 3. Maroldsweisach: Feministischer Buchverlag, 1993.

———. *The Outcast*. [1933]. Translated by Guy Endore. New York: Arno Press, 1975.

Weiss, Andrea. "'A Queer Feeling When I Look At You': Hollywood Stars and Lesbian Spectatorship in the 1930s." In *Multiple Voices in Feminist Film Criticism*, edited by Diane Carson et al., 330–42. Minneapolis: University of Minnesota Press, 1994.

Wesp, Gabriela. *Frisch, fromm, fröhlich, Frau: Frauen und Sport zur Zeit der Weimarer Republik*. Königstein/Taunus: Ulrike Helmer, 1998.

Weston, Kath. "Get Thee to a Big City: Sexual Imaginary and the Great Gay Migration." *GLQ: A Journal of Lesbian and Gay Studies* 2, no. 3 (1995): 253–78.

Wheelwright, Julie. *Amazons and Military Maids: Women Who Dressed as Men in the Pursuit of Life, Liberty, and Happiness.* London: Pandora, 1989.

Wolter, Gundula. *Hosen, weiblich.* Marburg: Jonas, 1994.

Zimnik, Nina. "No Man, No Cry? The Film *Girls in Uniform* and Its Discourses of Political Regime." *Women in German Yearbook* 15 (2000): 161–83.

INDEX

Page numbers in bold are references to figures.

www.ingramcontent.com/pod-product-compliance
Lightning Source LLC
Chambersburg PA
CBHW060038030426
42334CB00019B/2389